CHANGING THE GAME

CHANGING THE GAME

*Organizational Transformations
of the First, Second, and Third Kinds*

Eric G. Flamholtz
Yvonne Randle

With a Foreword by
Howard Schultz
Founder and Chair, Starbucks Coffee

New York   Oxford
Oxford University Press
1998

Oxford University Press

Oxford   New York
Athens   Auckland   Bangkok   Bogotá   Bombay
Buenos Aires   Calcutta   Cape Town   Dar es Salaam
Delhi   Florence   Hong Kong   Istanbul   Karachi
Kuala Lumpur   Madras   Madrid   Melbourne
Mexico City   Nairobi   Paris   Singapore
Taipei   Tokyo   Toronto   Warsaw

and associated companies in
Berlin   Ibadan

Copyright © 1998 by Eric G. Flamholtz and Yvonne Randle

Published by Oxford University Press
198 Madison Avenue, New York, New York 10016

Oxford is a registered trademark of Oxford University Press

Library of Congress Cataloging-in-Publication Data
Flamholtz, Eric.
Changing the game : organizational transformations
of the first, second, and third kinds /
Eric G. Flamholtz and Yvonne Randle.
p. cm.   Includes bibliographical references and index.
ISBN 0–19–511764–6
1. Organizational change.
2. Organizational change—United States—Case studies.
3. Organizational effectiveness.
4. Corporate culture—United States.
I. Randle, Yvonne.   II. Title.
HD58.8.F545 1998   658.4'06—dc21   98–4074

1 3 5 7 9 8 6 4 2
Printed in the United States of America
on acid-free paper

CONTENTS

PREFACE

Why do some organizations succeed while others fail? Some entrepreneurial organizations like Microsoft, Starbucks, Nike, Compaq Computers, Wal★Mart, and Southwest Airlines have grown to become dominant forces in their industries. Others, such as Osborne Computers, People Express, and LA Gear, "burn out" like a meteor after a promising start.

Why do once powerful organizations go into decline and some never return? Giants like IBM, K-Mart, Sears, and Chrysler have lost their dominance and are now attempting to remake themselves in the face of significant competition. Still other organizations, like AT&T and Disney have reconceptualized their businesses in the face of a changing environment. And still others that were household names, such as PanAm, did not survive to see the next millennium.

Based on our study of organizations conducted over more than twenty years, we believe that the answer to these questions lies in the extent to which organizations recognize and are able to change the "game" they are playing to better meet organizational and/or environmental demands.

In technical terms, "changing the game" refers to making a major organizational transformation or metamorphosis. This might involve changing how a business is managed (a managerial transformation) or becoming a very different type of business (a business vision transformation). Stated differently, changing the way a business is managed involves changing the *way* the game is being played; becoming a different type of business involves changing *what* game is being played. These aspects of changing the game are the focus of this book.

The "game" metaphor as well as the notion of "changing the game" are powerful concepts to help senior managers and the organizations they lead understand and cope with the most complex challenge they face in the new millennium.

Successfully completing a transformation requires a very different set of skills and ways of operating (i.e., a new game) than those an organization has relied on in the past. Organizations that recognize the need to change the game and take steps to do so increase the probability of survival into the future; those that do not will experience significant problems and, perhaps, complete failure.

This book introduces and explains the concept of organizational transformations, and identifies three different "games" or types of transformations. It also presents a comprehensive framework to help managers understand the rules of the new games and what they need to do to manage the organizational transformation process. The framework for managing transformations that we describe is broader in scope and more practical to implement than any previously offered in management literature.

The book includes a number of examples and case studies of organizations that have been successful or unsuccessful in managing the three major kinds of organizational transformations. Many of these examples are from high-profile companies, such as IBM, AT&T, Sears, Kodak, Disney, Nike, Compaq, and Starbucks, and we identify the lessons to be derived from each company's experience. All examples used are for learning and not for criticism.

All the companies cited are real, but in some instances we have used pseudonyms to protect their privacy; in a few cases we have gone a step further by altering our description of their business. We have also, in a few instances, created "composite" companies, based on two or more actual organizations.

This book has been a major undertaking for several years and has gone through a number of its own "transformations." Throughout this process, several people played significant roles and made a variety of contributions.

We would first like to thank Denise Marcil, our literary agent, who not only helped in shaping the proposal of the book but believed in it from the outset and helped us find exactly the right publisher. Denise was supportive the whole way and we appreciate her efforts very much.

We must also acknowledge the efforts of Herbert J. Addison, our editor. Herb was a true partner with us throughout the entire writing process and the book is significantly better because of his insight, experience, wide knowledge, and overall concern. Being an author is difficult at best and Herb understood exactly how to balance constructive criticism with support. He was demanding in the best sense of that word, which led to our rewriting (and as a result, improving) the overall book.

Although we have done consulting work with a number of the companies cited throughout, in most instances when they were publicly held companies, we drew primarily on public information rather than our firsthand knowledge of the organization. In other cases, however, we relied on our own consulting experiences. We would like to thank all those firms who consented to have us use them as examples. Special acknowledgment is due to Howard Schultz, Chairman and CEO of Starbucks Coffee. Howard not only permitted us to prepare an example dealing with Starbucks, but also participated in an in-depth discussion with Eric Flamholtz to deepen our insights into the nature of the transformations at Starbucks. Orin Smith, President and COO at Starbucks, and Howard Behar, President of the International Division, also read the portion of the manuscript dealing with Starbucks.

For several years we have joked with some of the firms we worked with that we were writing two books: one dealing with examples of great companies and one with companies that have experienced difficulty and cannot, by any stretch of the imagination, be described as effectively managed. When we approached Tim and Jud Carter, the co-owners of Bell Carter Olive Company, about the possibility of serving as an example, they both agreed. Then Jud asked, "Which book will we be in?" That comment captures the essence of working with Bell Carter Olive Company. We had a great deal of fun working with the Carters and their colleagues and appreciate their willingness to let us share their story. Tim Carter, in particular, took time out of his busy schedule to be interviewed for the initial draft of his company's story. He, Jud Carter, and the other members of Bell Carter's Executive Team then reviewed the example and provided comments that helped enrich it. Clearly they belong in the book about successful transformations and, in fact, serve as a capstone example of such transformations.

We also appreciate the willingness of Jim Stowers and his colleagues at American Century Investors who permitted us to prepare an example about them and their transformation from an entrepreneurship to a professionally managed firm. We had the opportunity to work with American Century Investors (formerly known as Twentieth Century Investors) for a number of years and not only want to thank Jim Stowers, Jr., who is the founder of the company but also Jim Stowers, III, who is currently CEO, and all the other members of the executive committee. We would also like to thank Paris Couturiaux, who was then the VP of Human Resources and introduced us to American Century Investors. Paris is currently Senior VP of Human Resources at Cendant Mortgage.

We also want to thank Norma Sutcliffe, currently Assistant Professor in Business Administration at Marquette University, who served as Eric Flamholtz's research assistant for many years while she was earning her Ph.D. at UCLA. Norma assisted with research and a draft of the examples of Compaq, Chrysler, and Sears. In addition, Patricia Anderson, who was then a Senior Consultant at *ManagementSystems*, assisted with the preparation of an early draft of the example of Miller Brothers. Paul Wetmore, Account Executive with Merrill Lynch, who for years has been our financial advisor, graciously provided information about the market evaluation on a variety of companies cited throughout. We also appreciate the work involved with the preparation of the manuscript by Stacy Miller and Nahir V. Jiminian, who both served as assistants to Eric Flamholtz at *ManagementSystems* Consulting Corporation. Diana Troik, co-owner and EVP of *ManagementSystems* Consulting Corporation, read the manuscript at various points of its development and provided constructive critical comments.

We have worked with a number of companies and managers over the last twenty years. Our "laboratory" for the development and testing of ideas presented in this book has been actual organizations. Although it is not possible to cite each organization and each manager individually, we are indebted for their willingness to invite us in and allow us to learn about the utility of our ideas. We hope we made a contribution to those organizations as well as the organizations who represent the readers of this book. Despite all the contributions of others, we remain responsible for any remaining imperfections.

January 1998   E.G.F.
Los Angeles   Y.R.

FOREWORD

Every entrepreneur and CEO knows how much of a challenge it is to build a company. For many of us, it is something we have not done before and it is something that we get an opportunity to do only once or twice in a lifetime. I am personally aware of this because of my experience in growing Starbucks Coffee Company from a local (Seattle) business with five stores to a company with more than 1,300 stores and 25,000 employees operating throughout North America as well as in Japan and Singapore.

Faced with the challenge of growing a company, entrepreneurs, CEOs and other senior managers would like some kind of help to facilitate the process of growing a business successfully. It is helpful to have some kind of "picture" of what needs to be done as a guide. It also helps to know what others (both individuals and companies) have done so we can learn from their lessons.

Changing the Game by Eric Flamholtz and Yvonne Randle provides the kind of resource that is valuable to people facing the challenge of building a business. The book provides a framework for thinking about the issues involved in building successful organizations and in making major organizational transformations over time as the organization grows and the environment changes.

In building Starbucks Coffee, we experienced firsthand one of the transformations described in this book: the transformation from an entrepreneurship to a professionally-managed company. In the early 1990s, we worked hard to make the transition from an entrepreneurship to a professionally-managed company while retaining our entrepreneurial spirit, our *esprit de corp,* and our ability to innovate and renew ourselves. As part of this process, we invited Eric Flamholtz to advise us on making this transformation. At Starbucks, Flamholtz worked with us to develop planning and management systems, based upon some of the concepts and ideas presented in this book.

I personally believe that corporate leaders must be open to new ideas and new approaches, regardless of our own personal propensities. Ultimately I realized the kinds of changes required to make the transformation to professional management, were essential to the continued success of Starbucks. We have now put into place at Starbucks planning and management systems which are essential for an entrepreneurially-oriented professionally managed business.

No single book or set of ideas can solve all of the problems of a business. However, a thought provoking book such as *Changing the Game* can add real value as business leaders face the kinds of issues described by Flamholtz and Randle. It gets us to think differently, and, hopefully, better about a crucial issue that all business leaders face: building a company successfully and managing transformations which are required as it grows.

Howard Schultz
Founder and Chair
Starbucks
Seattle, Washington

Part I

WHAT IT MEANS TO CHANGE THE GAME

1

CHANGING THE GAME

Every so often, such a profound change occurs in the way a competitive game (such as chess or basketball or football) is played that it constitutes not just an innovation but a fundamental transformation of the game.

For example, John Wooden, the legendary UCLA basketball coach, whose teams won ten NCAA titles, transformed the game of basketball by introducing a concept called "the zone press." The zone press was not just a tactic, but also a strategic vision of how the game ought to be played. Specifically, it consisted of an attacking defense. Instead of the offense having the initiative and momentum, the defense took the initiative and, at least psychologically, if not literally, put the offense on the "defensive." The offense had to fear that the ball would be stolen, and, accordingly, tended to play more cautiously and less aggressively. When mistakes were made and turnovers occurred, the offense became increasingly frustrated and more cautious. As a result, the tone of the game was actually changed.

This strategic innovation accomplished three things: (1) it helped UCLA win its first NCAA basketball championship in 1964 with a relatively short team (i.e., the center was only 6 feet, 4 inches tall), (2) it set in motion the events that led to Wooden's widespread recognition as perhaps the greatest coach in college basketball (he became known as "the Wizard of Westwood"), and, most important, (3) it also changed basketball itself. Other coaches had to understand the "new game" devised by Wooden and develop moves to counter the zone press. In effect, Wooden had made a strategic transformation of basketball. Although college teams were still nominally playing the game of basketball, they no longer could play it the same way against Wooden's teams.

As we will discuss throughout this book, the process of strategic transformation can be seen not only in sports but also in business enterprises. Indeed, we believe that the ability to understand and master this process of strategic transformation or "changing the game" is critical to sustaining successful organizations over the long term.

In this book, we ask you to think somewhat differently—and, perhaps, a little conceptually at first—about the nature of successful organizations. We will also demonstrate that there is a real economic payoff for this type of analysis and thinking. This book provides a perspective for understanding and dealing with the issues involved in building and maintaining successful organizations over long periods of time—which is different from classical management. More specifically, our perspective is based on the concept of viewing business as a "game" that must be changed over time to support successful organizational growth and development. The idea of changing the game will ultimately give us a simple but powerful way to examine and, ultimately, increase our effectiveness in managing one of the most significant organizational issues of the New Millennium: the transformations of organizations at different stages in their life cycles.

Throughout this chapter and the remainder of this book, we will provide examples of organizations that have been successful and/or are currently in the process of managing these kinds of transformations, as well as those that have been unsuccessful. In each example, we will attempt to identify the lessons that are relevant to other organizations faced with similar challenges.

The "Game" of Business

In its broadest sense, a game involves "procedures or strategies for gaining certain ends."[1] The game of business is to use resources (people, money, ideas, equipment, and tools) to gain certain ends desired by the organization. For a corporation, the objectives of the game are to increase profitability and shareholder value.

Whether it is recognized or not, all organizations operate under a "game plan." The "organizational game plan" consists of the basic concept of the game being played (or the business an organization is in) as well as the fundamental strategy for playing the game (i.e., the way the organization does business).

Economic Impact of the Concept of the Game

The basic concept of the game being played defines how the organization thinks about itself; it has both profound strategic significance and bottom line impact. For example, Coca-Cola has defined itself as a "beverage business," while PepsiCo (until 1997) was in the business of beverages, snack foods, and restaurants (Taco Bell, Pizza Hut). Although on the surface, both Coca-Cola and PepsiCo appear to be playing the same overall game (i.e., they are both in the beverage business), they have actually adopted significantly different business concepts that guide their efforts as organizations. In effect, they are really playing different games.

The bottom-line significance or payoff from this difference in business concept between Coca-Cola and PepsiCo can be seen very clearly in their stock prices and, in turn, their respective returns to shareholders. In January 1994, the stock prices of Coca-Cola and PepsiCo (adjusted for splits) were the same: $20 per share. However, three years later, on Wednesday, January 22, 1997, Coca-Cola's stock share was $59.75, while PepsiCo's was $32.00, a difference of $27.75. This means that PepsiCo's stock price increased by 60% during this period, while Coca Cola's stock price grew by 199%, a difference of 139%.

On Thursday, January 23, 1997, PepsiCo's Chairman and CEO, Roger Enrico, announced that the company would spin off its Taco-Bell, KFC, and Pizza Hut chains as a separate, publicly held company. The announcement came after the New York Stock Exchange closed, but rumors of the event sparked intense trading, and PepsiCo was the most actively traded stock on the exchange that day. Its share price climbed $3.50, just below its record high of $35.07. Clearly, the stock market placed a different value on the different business concepts—both in terms of Pepsi versus Coca-Cola before the proposed divestiture, and in terms of the value it placed on PepsiCo with and without the restaurant business.

It is not usually as easy to make a direct comparison of the value of different business concepts as in the example of Coca-Cola and PepsiCo, but it is just as real in other instances. Clearly, PepsiCo, which is a highly successful enterprise, had a business concept that caused it to incur an opportunity cost in terms of a relatively lower share price appreciation than Coca-Cola during the period from 1994 to 1997. Since Coca-Cola's share price increased by $27.75 more than PepsiCo's share price, this means that PepsiCo's shareholders incurred an opportunity cost of 139%, the difference between the percentage increase between Coca-Cola's and PepsiCo's share price. In brief, this is *real* economic significance, not just a conceptual distinction. Accordingly, it demonstrates why the kind of thinking and analysis provided throughout this book, especially in the framework chapters, can yield significant economic returns for the investment in time and effort that the reader is required to make in mastering the materials presented.

These different games or "business concepts" being played by Coca-Cola and PepsiCo have led each of them, in turn, to alternative strategies for maximizing success.

The Underlying Game Plan or Business Model

Taken together, these two dimensions—the underlying business concept and the resulting strategy—constitute the organization's foundational "game plan." Coke, for example, focuses primarily on the beverage business and building its brand. Pepsi, on the other hand, has worked to leverage its beverage business through the acquisition and management of restaurant chains in which Pepsi is served, along with working to sell its beverages

<table>
<tr><td>

Business Strategy

("How We'll Play the Game")

</td></tr>
<tr><td>

The Underlying Business Concept

("The Game We're Playing")

</td></tr>
</table>

Figure 1–1. The Two Components of Changing the Game.

directly to the consumer. The two components of changing the game are illustrated in Figure 1–1.

When an organization does not understand the game it is playing (or what business it is in) or has been unable to develop strategies consistent with this game, problems may result. For example, in the mid-1980s, Eastman-Kodak changed its business and its strategy, but it never really clarified what business it was in and, ultimately, it reversed itself in the early 1990s. Specifically, it divested itself of many acquisitions that it made to "diversify." This example is examined more fully in Chapter 6.

Sometimes, the game a company chooses to play is not the "right" one (given the environment in which it is operating and/or its internal capabilities). This, too, can result in problems.

Changing the Game

No matter what game an organization chooses to play or how it chooses to play it, there are certain periods in an organization's life when "the game" (either the game itself or how it is played) needs to be changed. At these times, merely fine-tuning or making incremental changes is not sufficient to enable a company to continue to operate successfully. This occurs when there have been major changes in the economic environment, or some kind of revolution in technology or the nature of competition. It can also happen simply as the result of significant, rapid organizational growth. These are periods that require a fundamental reconceptualization or reorientation in an organization's entire business, and way of doing business. In effect, the organization must undergo a transformation or metamorphosis—it must "change its game." Once a "winning team" begins to experience problems that cannot be resolved through incremental changes in the way the company operates, it must change: (1) the game it is playing, (2) the way it plays the game, or (3) both of these aspects simultaneously.

For example, IBM, long recognized as one of the most admired and best managed US corporation, faced the need for such a transformation beginning in the early 1980s. Historically, IBM's strength was based on its mainframe business. Mainframes were essentially a cash cow for IBM, with its dominant market share and high profit margins and low volume. However, as a result of changing technology, which began in the early 1980s and involved the growth and proliferation of PCs, IBM faced a crisis, requiring a major transformation in the way that it conducted business. To successfully face the future, IBM needed to change the game it was playing.

The Meaning of Changing the Game

As used in this book, the phrase, "changing the game" has a dual meaning. First, it refers to changes in the game being played by an organization. This involves changes in the business an organization is actually in. In addition, the phrase also refers to changes in the way the game is being played (i.e., how a firm operates). Both are major aspects of a business and both can require major transformations, either at different points or even at the same time. These transformations are the focus of this book and define what we mean by "changing the game."

Unfortunately, many organizations do not recognize that a fundamental reorientation in their business, and the way they manage their business is required until the business is in desperate shape. Business is so complex and the details of day-to-day operations so compelling that it is often difficult for managers to step back and gain perspective on what is really happening to the overall enterprise. Managers may be unable to recognize that a transformation (rather than incremental adjustments) is required. International Harvester, Pan Am, and K-Mart are all examples of organizations that experienced continuing erosion in their business franchises for many years, but continued to "play the same game" in basically the same way. Unfortunately, this strategy of continuing to do the same thing led Pan Am into bankruptcy and left both International Harvester and K-Mart as companies in great distress.

Other organizations recognize the need for transformation, but find the process exceedingly difficult to manage successfully. For example, Sears attempted to make the transformation from a manufacturer/retailer to (what was in essence) a diversified financial institution (a different game, played in different ways); it has now abandoned this strategy. Sears acquired a variety of nontraditional consumer retail businesses, such as Coldwell Banker (real estate), and Dean Witter (stock brokerage). Sears began this process with the development of All-State Insurance, and later Sears Savings. It also established a credit card business (the Discover Card). The common feature of all these businesses was that they were financial services. In effect, this transformed Sears into a "financial retailer." Indeed, Sears was the only "bank" that sold Levi's. Most of these businesses have been or are being sold as Sears returns to a more traditional retailing business concept. A more detailed explanation for the failure of Sears to complete this transformation successfully is presented in Chapter 6.

The problems and experiences of some of the organizations cited above are not idiosyncratic and unrelated. There *is* a pattern to what happened at each of these corporations. To more fully understand these patterns, however, we need a new way of thinking. We need a conceptual framework or "lens" to give us a more strategic perspective on organizational transformations and the need to "change the game." This, in turn, requires that we understand the causes, nature, and different types of organizational transformations.

The Concept of Organizational Transformation and "Changing the Game"

During the past few years, there has been increasing use of the terms "transformation" and "change" in business literature. Some people unfortunately use these terms synonymously. That is not the way we will use these terms in this book.

Not all change involves transformations. Transformations are a very specific type of change. As used in this context, a transformation refers to a major change that results in a metamorphosis of a business in some respect. A metamorphosis can occur either in the nature of the business an organization is in (the game being played) or in the way in which business is conducted (how the game is being played).

Accordingly, all change does not constitute "transformation." A transformation occurs when there has been a fundamental reconceptualization or reorientation in the entire business or in the way a firm conducts its business. When the underlying or basic concept of a business changes (such as Sears changing from a manufacturer/retailer to a set of "financial stores"), a transformation has occurred. Moreover, when an organization changes the fundamental way it does business (by re-engineering its operational systems or outsourcing), transformation results. Similarly, when an organization changes from an entrepreneurial style of management (the way it does business) to a professional management style, a transformation has occurred. Change can be incremental or major, but a transformation involves a strategic reorientation in either the concept of a business, the way of managing a business, or both.

Why is the notion of transformation significant? It is because transformations are qualitatively different from mere "changes" in what they require of people and organizations to be successful. It is also because organizations are often reluctant to engage in transformations since they are so complex and risky.

In brief, our focus in *Changing the Game* is on transformations rather than merely incremental changes. It is also upon two distinct aspects of transformations:

1) Changes in the game being played (or underlying business concept), and

2) Changes in the way the game is played (managerial practices).

We shall also see below that there are several different "pure" types of transformations, including what we have termed Transformations of the First, Second, and Third Kinds.

The Organizational Transformation Process: An Example

The need for organizational transformation does not appear to management like some vision out of the mist. It is a process that occurs day by day over a relatively long period. Ironically, the need for a transformation does not necessarily occur when an organization is experiencing difficulty. Indeed, at the very moment when an organization is at the peak of its success, the need for a transformation can be at its greatest. To illustrate this, let us examine the situation faced by IBM in the early 1980s.

Changing the Game at IBM

At the beginning of the 1980s, IBM was at the apex of its power and success; it was also the darling of Wall Street. It was a classic growth company. The company was not only successful in its historical stronghold of the mainframe computer, it had also effectively launched its IBM PC and captured approximately 35% of the market within a very short time.

During that period at IBM, there was a great deal of optimistic and self-congratulatory behavior as well as great expectations about the future. In 1986, IBM's strategic plan projected that the company would achieve $100 billion in revenue by 1990, and $200 billion by the year 2000. Some executives said that IBM was going to produce computers like "popcorn" or "peanuts," which were informal code words for IBM products under development.

IBM was by no means a poorly managed company then. As strange as it may seem, one of the main problems facing IBM was its own success. IBM was a successful, highly profitable, very proud organization. Ironically, these very features made it most difficult for the organization to reorganize and accept the need for metamorphosis; there was a need to "change the game" the company was playing. In this context, we are using the term changing the game in the dual sense of the managerial practices of IBM as well as the company's business concept or vision.

At the very moment IBM was at the peak of its success, the seed of its impending difficulties had taken root. First, the emergence of the PC represented a long-term threat to its core business, not just an add-on opportunity. As we have subsequently seen, the PC set in motion a variety of forces that led away from the need for large corporations to depend upon mainframes to the same extent they had in the past. Personal conputers are not only less costly than expensive mainframes, but they have the ability to be utilized by a wide variety of individuals, rather than just the corporate information systems group. In addition, their ability to be networked enabled them to ultimately perform many of the functions previously reserved for mainframes.

In the mid-1980s, IBM had more than 400,000 employees. There is no doubt in our minds that many people among these 400,000 plus understood the technological capabilities of the PC and what it might ultimately become. Unfortunately, their voices were not heard, or at least were not listened to by IBM's senior executives. While it is totally understandable that an organization such as IBM would not want to do anything to undermine the profitability of its most profitable product (the mainframe), it is also necessary for the senior management of an organization to understand that it may be "betting the company" by its failure to make a decision as much by any decision it actually makes. IBM essentially chose an incremental (some might say "business as usual") strategy in the face of dramatic technological and market changes set in motion by the PC. It was only as its stock price began to fall precipitously in the early 1990s that the company set in motion the internal leadership and political changes necessary to transform it from a computer equipment organization built around the mainframe toward an information solutions business.

In 1993, the board replaced John Akers as CEO with Louis Gerstner. Under Gerstner's leadership, IBM has made a variety of changes that ideally will position the company well for competition in the next century. In effect, they began the process of making a corporate transformation.

Preliminary results of the transformation being led by Gerstner are promising. IBM has not only downsized, but has initiated a variety of strategic and cultural changes. As a result, the company's stock price has climbed back from the low 40s in 1994 to more than $100 by 1997 (the equivalent of $200 after an IBM stock split). Nevertheless, the transformation remains a work in progress.

Lessons to be Learned from IBM

The purpose of this example is not to criticize IBM. This company is a national treasure and its success is ultimately significant not only to IBM shareholders and employees, but also to the nation as a whole. Nevertheless, there are some important lessons to be learned by the experiences at IBM. Specifically, the failure to recognize what is going on in the environment and prepare the organization to make a fundamental transformation (in its business concept and in the way it does business) can lead an organization to the brink of disaster. Even an organization as large and strong as IBM—which had at its peak approximately $69 billion in annual revenue and in excess of $6.1 billion in profits—cannot continue to play the same game in the face of significant environmental changes.

Three Different Types of Game Changes: A Topology of Organizational Transformations

Although companies come in various shapes and sizes, three basic kinds of "game changes" or transformations can be identified:
1. Entrepreneurial transformations to professional management, including the special case of family business transformations.
2. Revitalization transformations of established companies.
3. Business vision transformations.

We call these Transformations of the First, Second, and Third Kinds, respectively. Although we will describe each type of transformation, we must note at the outset that actual organizations sometimes engage in compound transformations, consisting of more than one type of transformation simultaneously. Each of these transformations requires an organization to play a very different game, as described below.

Entrepreneurial Transformations

Transformations of the First Kind occur when an organization has reached a stage of growth where it can no longer operate in an informal and unstructured way, and must become more "professionally managed." The need for this transformation typically begins at about $10 million in annual revenue, although it may occur when an organization has reached a much larger size. This type of transformation usually occurs without a corresponding change in an underlying business concept or vision. Instead, the changes most typically occur in the firm's business strategy (or how it plays the game).

During the early stages of growth, a company is, essentially, an extension of a single entrepreneur, or a group of entrepreneurs. As it grows and becomes more successful, the company's sheer size requires that it transform the way it does business from a relatively "pure entrepreneurship" to an "entrepreneurially oriented, professionally managed firm."[2] This transformation requires that the organization develop its infrastructure, management systems, and culture in a way that is fundamentally different from being an entrepreneurship. In essence, it needs to change its underlying business strategy, or how it is playing the game.

The transformation of Apple Computers from the way it was managed under Steven Jobs, its founder, to the way it was managed by John Sculley is one example of this type of transformation. Under Jobs, Apple was extremely entrepreneurial—not just in developing products, but also in terms of how the company operated. Most systems and processes operated fairly informally (consistent with Apple's culture). As the company grew into a billion-dollar-plus firm, however, it began to experience problems that might eventually have led to its demise. These included:
- Problems with the manufacturing and quality of the Lisa computer (the predecessor to the Macintosh).

- Culture "clashes" between Apple II and Macintosh employees that resulted in some productivity problems.
- Inadequately developed management control systems needed to support a billion dollar plus company.
- Inadequate focus on developing and supporting the management capabilities needed to effectively direct the efforts of the very large firm that Apple had become.

In part to address these problems, Apple brought in John Sculley, a professional manager from PepsiCo. Sculley began to focus on creating and implementing the more formal processes and structures needed to support a multibillion dollar firm. Although the transformation of Apple did not happen overnight, the eventual implementation and continued focus on these systems and processes helped ensure that the company would continue its success into the future—at least for a time. Eventually, however, Apple began to face new problems (brought on by a changing environment and increased competition). Sculley was eventually replaced as were two subsequent CEOs.

Failure to make this type of transformation can lead to corporate disaster. For example, Osborne computers (the first "portable" computer maker) achieved revenues of $100 million after its first two years of existence, but went into bankruptcy in its third year because the company was unable to make the appropriate transformation in the way it played the game. Once high flying companies such as People Express, Victor Technologies, L.A. Gear, AST Research, Ashton-Tate, and MaxiCare all failed to successfully make this kind of transformation, and, in turn, experienced great difficulties and in some cases failure. Other companies that have succeeded and failed in making this type of transformation are cited in Chapter 3.

A special type of entrepreneurial transformation is the "Family Business Transformation." This involves the transformation from an entrepreneur or family that founded the business to either the next generation of the same family or a group of professional managers. This process involves personal as well as emotional considerations and is typically complex. We will present an example of this special type of transformation in Chapter 3, which deals with entrepreneurial to professional management transformations.

The driving force that leads an organization to transform from an entrepreneurship to a professionally managed firm is that it has "outgrown" the organizational systems and managerial practices that served it so well when it was a smaller organization. In effect, the company must change the *way* it is playing the game.

Revitalization Transformations

Transformations of the Second Kind occur when a business has gone into decline and needs revitalization. The transformation faced by Compaq Computers in the early 1990s was essentially such a transformation. It, and other examples of revitalization transformations, are described in Chapter 4.

These types of transformations (like those of the First Kind) also involve changing the way a business is being managed (i.e., changing *how* the game is being played).

In a revitalization transformation, the organization continues in the same business it has been in, but focuses on "rebuilding" an infrastructure that will increase its ability to operate effectively and efficiently in the market(s) it competes in. In effect, it continues to play the same game, but must learn to play it differently.

Business Vision Transformations

Transformations of the Third Kind occur when an organization changes the basic concept of the business it is in. This involves altering a firm's existing business vision to a fundamentally different one; this is a "high risk, high return" strategy. There are several examples of companies that have attempted but *not* successfully accomplished this, and only a few that have done it. For example, Sears, AT&T, UAL Corp., and Kodak have all been unsuccessful with this kind of transformation; while Disney, Nike, Navistar, IBM, Edison International, and Hughes have either been successful, at least in part, or appear to be headed for ultimate success. We examine examples of successful business vision transformations in Chapter 5; unsuccessful examples are discussed in Chapter 6.

The driving force behind these types of transformations can be external factors (i.e., technological change, changes in the market from demographics or competition, and the like) or internal factors (such as changes in leadership, culture, or managerial viewpoint). Business vision transformations are perhaps the most risky types of transformations because they involve redefining the enterprise's very essence. By definition, business vision transformations are changes in the game that is being played. However, as a result of this change, the way the game is being played must change as well.

Compound Transformations

A compound transformation occurs when an organization simultaneously undergoes more than one of the three basic kinds of transformations. Clearly, a compound transformation is even more complex than a "simple" transformation of the First, Second, and Third Kinds. Nevertheless, actual organizations often face the need for the more complex compound transformations. For example, an organization can undergo an entrepreneurial transformation to professional management *and* a business vision transformation simultaneously, as at Disney in the mid-1980s. Similarly, an organization can undertake a revitalization and business vision transformation simultaneously, as AT&T did in the mid-1990s. Both examples are described in more detail in Chapters 5 and 6, respectively.

The Changing Nature of the Business Game

Changes in the game occur not only at the level of individual firms but also at the level of the business game as a whole. Specifically, the nature or tempo of modern business has changed, as we have transformed first from an economy based on agriculture to an industrial economy, and now as we are in the process of transforming from an industrial to an information-based economy.

In an agrarian era the game of business most resembled baseball. The pace was slower, and the game remained virtually unchanged over time. In this environment, business could afford to react more slowly since change was more incremental than it is today. In the industrial era, football, with its emphasis on specific roles, planned plays, and precision execution, was the new metaphor for business. Business competition had become more intense and "coaches" need to develop plans to gain their fair share of the market. As we began to transform to a post-industrial era, basketball and hockey, which are less structured than football and which involve continuous movement, were the new metaphors for the business game. The environment was ever changing, and firms needed to be prepared to respond quickly to continue their success.

Today, as we are heading into an age where computers and communications systems present us with changing information at lightning speed, the best metaphor for business is "speed chess." This game, also known as "lightning chess," is played with a time clock, where moves must be made *very* rapidly without the complete study of a situation. It is a game where planning is critical and yet must occur quickly; where decisions must also be quick, but based on a thorough understanding of the board and one's opponent. If we apply this analogy to business, it means that as we look to the future, successful firms will be those that: (1) rapidly create plans for their own development that reflect a clear understanding of their environment and the firm's own capabilities, (2) are able to make rapid changes in organizational structure and incentive systems because of new conditions, and (3) can understand and effectively manage the necessary organizational transformations. The environment is pushing firms to play a faster, more cerebral game. This game must be mastered if organizations are going to survive and progress into the millennium.

Conclusion and Overview

As we have seen, there are certain periods of corporate life when merely fine-tuning and making incremental changes are not sufficient to enable companies to continue operating successfully. Instead, the basic "game" an organization is playing or how it is playing that game need to be changed in some fundamental ways.

In the next chapter, we will continue our discussion of organizational transformations. We will present a framework that managers can use to understand what must be done to build a company successfully. Combined with the concepts introduced in this chapter, we will have a lens to help us begin to understand what to do to effectively manage transformations and change the game. Although Chapter 2 is conceptual and some readers may find it demanding, it is an essential foundation for deriving the most benefit from this book. An in-depth reading of the chapter will be useful as a frame of reference for all the remaining chapters. The reader's investment in the chapter will pay dividends later.

Chapters 3 through 6 present detailed examples of firms that have experienced or are experiencing fundamental Transformations of the First, Second, and Third Kinds. Chapters 3 through 5 describe firms that have successfully changed the games they were playing, or how they were playing the game; while Chapter 6 presents examples of firms that have been unsuccessful in making these necessary transformations. In each chapter, we identify the lessons to be learned from the unsuccessful as well as the successful companies.

The next five chapters—Chapters 7 through 11—are devoted to providing you with a set of tools and techniques for managing transformations successfully. These include:

- How to utilize planning as a tool in the transformation process (Chapter 7).
- The role that structure plays in changing the game and how to manage structure effectively (Chapters 8 and 9).
- Understanding and learning how to effectively employ tools for transforming the "behavior" of people within the organization—a key ingredient to successful transformations (Chapters 10 and 11).

Chapter 12 provides a comprehensive example of how one company— Bell Carter Olive Company—has applied all the concepts and tools presented throughout this book and has succeeded in mastering the "art" of changing the game. It also illustrates transformations throughout its development.

Chapter 13 steps back from these detailed examples and offers an integrated look at the lessons to be learned from actual companies that have experienced transformations, including the role and use of consultants in the process. In addition, it provides some final thoughts that can be useful in preparing for and implementing major transformations.

What can you expect to be able to do differently or benefit from after reading this book? When you finish you should have a thorough working knowledge of:

- What organizational transformations are.
- The different kinds of transformations.
- How to effectively manage organizational transformations (i.e., how to change the game a firm is playing).
- Some of the key tools for managing transformations, including those for planning transformations, changing organizational structure, and transforming behavior.

- How to meet the challenges and avoid the pitfalls of organizational transformations.
- How to use consultants effectively in the transformation process.
- How to apply the lens and frameworks presented in this book to any organization (including your own) to promote continued organizational success.

In addition, you should also have insights and lessons from observing several actual companies that have been engaged in the process of managing transformations.

Our intent is to provide readers with a guidebook to help "navigate" the process of managing organizational transformations. This guidebook will allow you to understand transformations in more depth, give you a lens for visualizing the terrain of transformations, provide you with a set of examples of companies that have already embarked on this journey (as well as the lessons you can derive from their experience), and outfit you with the major tools of transformation.

We will begin to develop these tools in Chapter 2. This important but conceptual chapter presents a framework for understanding how to build successful organizations. This framework is a prerequisite before we can deal with the issues involved in organizational transformations.

2

BUILDING SUCCESSFUL ORGANIZATIONS

This chapter presents a framework that we can use as a lens to understand and plan what must be done to build an organization with a high probability of long-term success. This framework provides the foundation for understanding how to manage organizational transformations successfully. We ask you to think about organizations in a different way—specifically, we view the development of organizations in terms of four critical "factors" that influence the design of a successful business enterprise:

1. The "business concept" that defines the business a company is in.
2. Six key "building blocks" of organizational success.
3. The "size" of the enterprise.
4. The "environment" (markets, competition, and trends) in which the enterprise will exist.

We will examine these critical components and the way they must interrelate to create a successful organization. The four key factors and how they influence the "design" of a business enterprise are shown schematically in Figure 2–1.

Business Concept: The Foundation of a Business

All businesses are either explicitly or implicitly based on a conceptual foundation. That business concept defines what the company is in business to do or what game the company intends to play (as discussed in Chapter 1). It addresses the question, "What business are we in?" Although this is a deceptively simple question, some firms fail or at least do not prosper because they do not really understand the nature of their business (i.e., their underlying business concept). Further, as organizations grow and their environments change, managers may need to revise the concept of their business so as to increase the "fit" (a topic we will discuss in more depth later in this chapter)

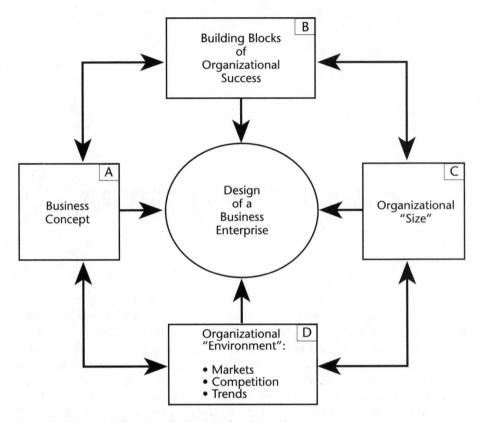

Figure 2–1. Factors Influencing the Design of an Enterprise.

between the business concept, the firm's size, and certain other key determinants of organizational success.

The business concept guides an organization's development and gives the company strategic focus. Without a clearly defined business concept, an organization has no "center." For example, many of the business conglomerates of the 1970s and early 1980s did not function effectively because there was no core concept or focus that gave the business a kind of architectural integrity. Companies such as Whittiker Corporation, ITT, and Xerox experimented with functioning as conglomerates, and each has either backed away from this concept or found it difficult to execute. For example, Whittiker, which once had $1.75 billion in revenues after several acquisitions, sold off virtually all its acquisitions and downsized to a core business of $300 million before refocusing as a single business. Xerox also sold off its acquisitions and refocused as a "document company."

It should be noted that exceptions almost always exist, and the General Electric Company (GE) is, in a sense, the "Great Exception" to the demise of conglomerates. General Electric, which is one of the most successful and admired companies in the world, is a conglomerate. However, two things about GE make it a special case. First, many of its businesses have something to do with technology, and a number of them deal with aspects of electric technology. Second, the management system developed by GE is well suited to its business, and this also differentiates it from other conglomerates, as discussed further in Chapter 8.

Problems can also arise when an organization does not fully understand what business it *really* is in. The classic illustration was the railroads, which thought they were in the "railroad" business, rather than the transportation business. Curtis Publishing is an example of a company that experienced failure, after a period of success, because it did not truly understand the business it was in. The Curtis Publishing Company was a great success during the early part of this century. Cyrus Curtis, an entrepreneur, built a publishing empire with major properties such as the *Saturday Evening Post* and the *Ladies Home Journal*. Unfortunately, the company eventually failed because it had defined its business as the "publishing business." It didn't realize that it was really in the "advertising business." In consumer media, advertising follows consumers. Therefore, one of Curtis Publishing's principal revenue streams was from advertisers. The managers of Curtis did not appreciate the implications of the new medium of television and its impact on advertising revenues. Thus, because they focused on publishing and their readers (versus their advertisers), they chose to purchase a printing plant to vertically integrate the firm's operations, turning down opportunities to acquire NBC and CBS (which siphoned off advertising dollars). This decision was disastrous.

The identification and clear articulation of a business concept is the first great challenge for building a successful organization since it affects (and should drive) the development of everything else. However, a business concept is not static. It can (and potentially *should*) change over time to support the organization's continued successful development.

Xerox, for example, was founded as a photocopying business, but today is in the document management business. Disney was founded as a motion picture company, but is now a global entertainment company. UAL was an airline, then a diversified travel company, and now is in the airline business again. PepsiCo first began in the beverage business. It then acquired snack foods and fast-food restaurants as well as beverages. Finally, it reversed direction and will focus in the future on its beverages and snack foods.

In summary, a business concept is literally the foundation of an enterprise. The nature of an enterprise's systems is derived from or determined by the underlying business concept, as explained in the next section.

Six Building Blocks of Organizational Success

Once a firm has determined the nature of the business it is in, it must develop systems and a process to effectively support this concept. Analysis of the experience of actual organizations (both successful and unsuccessful)

and research on organizational effectiveness[1] indicate that six "key building blocks" or critical factors determine organizational success over the long term. These are:
1. Identifying the market the firm wants to serve and, if possible, establishing a market niche.
2. Developing products and services appropriate to that market.
3. Acquiring and effectively managing the resources that are needed to operate the business.
4. Developing and effectively managing the day-to-day operational systems essential for the organization to function.
5. Developing the management systems necessary for long-term growth and development of the enterprise.
6. Managing the corporate culture so that it supports the enterprise's long-term goals.

We believe that if the six key building blocks are effectively managed both individually and as a system, an organization will have about a 90% chance of long-term success. In effect, these six building blocks constitute a set of critical tasks that must be performed to build a successful organization that will support the business concept the firm has established. We describe the nature of each of these critical tasks in more detail below.

Identification of a Market and Development of a Market Niche: "Markets"

The first challenge to organizational survival or success is to identify a market need (or market) for a good or service, to which the enterprise will seek to respond. A market includes the current and potential buyers of the goods and services that an enterprise intends to produce and sell. The chances of organizational success are enhanced to the extent that the enterprise identifies a need that is not being adequately met or for which there is little competition. Accordingly, the most fundamental prerequisite of a successful organization is identifying and defining an enterprise's market.

This challenge is faced by all new ventures; indeed, it is the primary challenge a new venture must overcome. Many enterprises have achieved great success merely because they were one of the first in a new market. Apple Computers, for example, grew in a few years from a small entrepreneurship in a garage to a multibillion dollar publicly held enterprise, because its founders identified the market for a personal computer.

Some enterprises have been successful because they identified and clearly defined the market (i.e., customers) they want to serve; others have floundered because they either failed to clearly define their market or mistakenly abandoned a market in which they had historically been a very strong competitor. For example, a medium-sized national enterprise that manufactured and sold specialty clothing wished to upgrade its image and products and become a high-fashion boutique. It failed to recognize that its key strengths were in understanding how to meet the needs of the "medium" market and that it didn't understand what was needed to successfully play in the high fashion marketplace. Its efforts were unsuccessful and the company almost failed.

The failure to maintain a focus on a company's market is not only a critical task for growing concerns, but it has brought many once great enterprises to near or total ruin. The American automobile manufacturers of the 1960s and early 1970s ignored the needs of customers who were looking for smaller, more fuel-efficient vehicles. Foreign automakers, recognizing the trend in customer preferences (brought about, in part, by increasing gasoline prices), came in and took away a significant portion of the market from the U.S. manufacturers.

Many enterprises survive for a long time merely because they have been able to identify a market, but organizations that achieve great success are often those that have not only identified a market need, but also captured a market niche. A "niche" is a protected place within a market where an enterprise has a relatively loyal set of customers because it has developed one or more sustainable competitive advantages. A sustainable competitive advantage is something that a firm does better than its competition and that it can hold onto for at least *two years*.

Wal★Mart, for example, first found an uncontested market for low-cost consumer products in rural geographic areas. The company grew to a point where its sheer size became a source of competitive advantage. Wal★Mart, however, also developed sophisticated distribution, logistics, and information systems that provided it with significant advantages over its major competitor—K-Mart—and helped it continue to grow at a time when K-Mart was floundering.

Intel is another example of a firm that has grown into a multibillion dollar business because it has been able to create a market niche. The advantages that Intel has over its competition include its size, the scope of its products, and its product development process. All these advantages (and no doubt others) have created a virtual monopoly for Intel in the microprocessor market.

In a completely different business, Starbucks has achieved a niche in the retail coffee "café" market by having a national distribution network and significant brand equity. Microsoft has achieved a dominant niche in computer software because its operating system is so widely adopted. As seen in the examples of Microsoft and Intel, a niche does not have to be small; a company can have a niche, a portion of the market where it possesses sustainable competitive advantages, and have the dominant market share.[2]

The determination of the market to be served goes hand-in-hand with the game the firm is trying to play or wants to play. In selecting a market, a firm is consciously or unconsciously making a decision about its playing field that includes:

• Who its customers are or will be.
• Who its competitors are or will be.

- Whether it has or can establish a significant sustainable competitive advantage that will differentiate it from others who have chosen to play the same game.

These are, in fact, key issues that must be addressed in a firm's transformational planning process. They will be further described in Chapter 7.

Development of Products or Services: "Products and Services"

Once a firm has identified the market in which it will operate (i.e., the field on which its game will be played), the second task facing the organization involves "product development." This is the process of analyzing the needs of current and potential customers in order to design the products or services that will satisfy their needs.

For example, Adam Osborne correctly perceived the need for portable personal computers and founded Osborne Computers to serve this need. Howard Schultz observed the popularity of coffee cafés in Milan, Italy, and believed that the concept would be successful in the United States. Schultz and his team created the chain of Starbucks coffee bars to meet the needs of customers in the 1990s who were looking for a place to socialize. Ted Turner recognized the demand of television viewers for greater and more varied types of programming and created a series of cable television networks to meet these diverse needs.

Although many enterprises can perceive a market need correctly, they may not be able to develop a product capable of satisfying that need. For example, Federal Express perceived the need for electronic mail and was developing a system called "Zap-Mail." However, the rise of a new and relatively inexpensive technology—fax machines—rendered the concept of "Zap-Mail" irrelevant. Federal Express was simply unable to develop the product quickly enough to establish it in the market prior to the entrenchment of fax machines.

The product development process includes not only the design of a product (defined here to include services as well), but also the ability to produce it. For a service enterprise, this involves the enterprise's service delivery system—the mechanism through which services are provided to customers.

The problem of product development faces not only relatively new or small companies, but also large, well-established enterprises. Indeed, it can even confront whole industries. The U.S. automobile industry, for example, was unsuccessful during the 1970s in creating products to meet the need for reliable, fuel-efficient, economical automobiles. Hence, they permitted powerful competitors (Japanese and German enterprises) to emerge in a market they once dominated. The result was that by the mid 1980s, the once dominant U.S. automobile companies, such as General Motors, Ford, and Chrysler, were fighting for their survival. By the late 1980s, Ford was doing well again, after the success of the Taurus in 1986; Chrysler had begun to do better (see Chapter 4); and GM continued to struggle. By the mid-1990s, however, all U.S. firms had begun to improve their performance, especially Ford and Chrysler.

The development of successful products depends, to a great extent, on understanding the field on which one has chosen to play as well as on effective strategic market planning. This type of planning involves recognizing potential customers, their needs, how they buy, and what they perceive as the value in a product. Thus, the success of product development depends on the organization's success in defining its market (i.e., the field on which it is playing). The greater the understanding of the market's needs, the more likely it is that the product development process will be effective in satisfying those needs.

Acquisition and Development of Resources: "Resources"

The third major task involved in building successful organizations is the acquisition and development of additional resources required for current and anticipated growth. An organization's success in identifying a market niche and developing products for that market will create increased demand for its products or services that, in turn, will stretch the enterprise's resources very thin. The organization suddenly finds that it requires additional physical resources (space, equipment, and so on), financial resources, and human resources. Human resources, especially management, will become particularly critical.

If a firm cannot attract or acquire enough of the "right" resources to support its growth, its ability to successfully play its chosen game can be severely undermined. Lack of space, lack of technology, lack of qualified people, and/or inadequate financing can make an organization vulnerable to its competition. Similarly, organizations that literally or figuratively "throw" money or people at problems (because they feel, for a time, that they are resource rich) can also face problems. Like an oil well, resources may dry up and the organization may be left with "too many people working on the wrong things and not enough qualified people working on the right things."

Development of Operational Systems: "Operational Systems"

To play its chosen game effectively, an organization not only must produce a product or service, but must also administer its basic day-to-day operations reasonably well. Thus, the fourth task in building a successful organization is the development of operational systems for running an organization on a day-to-day basis. These include accounting, billing, collections, advertising, personnel recruiting and training, sales, production, delivery, information/communication, and related systems.

The problems involved in the development of operational systems are varied and depend on the size of the organization involved. Entrepreneurial enterprises tend to have underdeveloped operational systems, while established companies may have bureaucratic or overly complicated systems.

Typically, entrepreneurial enterprises confronted by the tasks of developing their markets and products neglect the development of operational systems except to the extent necessary to keep functioning. For example, rudimentary accounting and information systems may be installed that provide some useful information (although not typically enough of the right types of information needed to effectively manage a large business). There may be a payroll system in place, but other human resource systems and processes (like recruiting, selection, and training procedures) may be non-existent. For many entrepreneurial organizations, the belief seems to be, "As long as we're selling our products, we must be making money. The rest of the business will just take care of itself."

As an organization grows, the strain on such basic operating systems increases. The systems no longer meet the now larger organization's more complex and sophisticated needs. For example, in one electrical components distribution enterprise with more than $200 million in annual revenues, sales personnel were continually infuriated when they found that deliveries of products they had sold could not be made because the enterprise's inventory records were hopelessly incorrect. Similarly, a small residential real estate enterprise with annual revenues of about $10 million found that it required almost a year of effort and embarrassment to correct its accounting records after its bookkeeper retired. A $100-million consumer products manufacturer had to return materials to vendors because there was simply not enough warehouse space (a fact no one noticed until the deliveries were at the door!). A $15-million industrial abrasive distributor found itself constantly unable to keep track of customer orders and inventory. The enterprise's inventory control system, which was fine when annual sales were $3 to $5 million, simply became overloaded at the higher sales volume, causing one manager to remark, "Nothing is ever stored around here where any intelligent person could reasonably expect to find it."

For larger organizations, operational systems may present problems when they have become "ends in themselves" versus "means to some other ends." In brief, some larger organizations have operational systems that create so much red tape, that they undermine the company's ability to get any real work done. In one $500-million organization, for example, the hiring process had become so mired in bureaucracy—between all the forms that had to be completed and all the people that needed to interview job candidates—that it took nearly six months to hire even an administrative assistant. Meanwhile, the company was continuing to grow at over 25% per year and desperately needed qualified people to effectively meet customer needs.

Operational systems, while not glamorous in nature, can severely help or hinder an organization's ability to play its game effectively. This organizational "plumbing" can make or break a company in a highly competitive market. As we saw previously, Wal★Mart recognized the advantages that could be created through implementing sophisticated (yet easy-to-use) information, distribution, and other operational systems. K-Mart, on the other hand, was unable to create and/or implement these systems effectively and allowed Wal★Mart to win the game of serving the needs of consumers for low-cost products in primarily rural markets.

Development of Management Systems: "Management Systems"

The fifth task required for building a successful organization is to develop the management systems that will facilitate the enterprise's long-term growth. There are four key management systems:

1. Strategic planning.
2. Organization structure.
3. Management development.
4. Control or performance management systems.

The planning system is the process of planning for the overall development of the organization as well as for scheduling and budgeting operations. It involves strategic planning, operational planning, and contingency planning. An enterprise may do planning, but lack a planning system. For example, when Compaq started, it developed a plan for its new venture, but lacked an ongoing strategic planning process. This ultimately caused the company great difficulty in the early 1990s.

The organizational structure of the enterprise includes how people are organized, who reports to whom, and how activities are coordinated. All enterprises have some organizational structure (formal or informal), but not necessarily the correct structure for their needs. Organizational structures must be designed in accordance with the company's basic business strategy.

The management development system refers to the process for developing the management capabilities needed to run an organization as it grows. The control or performance management system refers to the set of processes (budgeting, goal setting) and mechanisms (performance appraisal) used to influence the behavior of people so that they are motivated to achieve organizational objectives.

To function effectively, all organizations must have a satisfactory set of management systems. Until an enterprise reaches a certain size (which tends to differ for each organization), it can typically operate without formal management systems: planning can be done in the entrepreneur's head and is frequently performed on an *ad hoc* basis. The organizational structure tends to be informal with ill-defined responsibilities that may well overlap. Informal management development is often "on-the-job training," with managers essentially on their own. Organizations with informal systems tend to use the accounting system as a basis of organizational control rather than developing a broader approach to management control.

Larger organizations (typically those with an excess of $100 million in revenues) that ignore the development of systems can adversely affect their ability to play their chosen game effectively (especially in highly competitive markets). Lack of a well-developed plan and planning process leaves the firm vulnerable to competitors who, through more sophisticated approaches to planning, are able to better understand their markets. Better understanding of the market, along with the development and implementation of strategies for maximizing opportunities and minimizing threats, results in a more effective game.

Ignoring the impact of organization structure (which can be a source of competitive advantage) tends to result in wasted resources (due to duplication of effort) or tasks that remain undone because they were "no one's responsibility." A firm that ignores structure can help create a team on which everyone thinks that they are playing quarterback. Unfortunately, if no one is in charge of "blocking, receiving, or defense," the firm has little chance of winning its game.

Firms that underemphasize management education may have managers who are working very hard, but whose overall productivity is not what it should or needs to be. To be successful over the long term, a firm needs to have managers who understand and possess the skills to:

Clearly define the game that the firm is playing and effectively communicate the nature of this game to all players.

Clearly define *how* the game will be played.

Define a structure that will allow the firm to "win" the game it has chosen to play.

Recruit, select, and train people to fill the various roles in the structure in order to "win" the game.

Manage their own roles effectively and continue to build their skills and capabilities as the organization grows.

Firms that lack a more formal approach to management education cannot ensure that those skills or capabilities are being adequately developed. Well-designed control or performance management systems increase the probability that players (i.e., the firm's people) will behave in ways consistent with the firm's goals. When firms have vague or ill-defined control or performance management systems, it is only by chance that key plays are effectively executed and the game is won. Further, poorly designed control or performance management systems can also lead to wasted resources as players focus their energy on the "wrong" versus the "right" things.

Organizations with well-developed management systems have a significant competitive advantage. They are able to "see" the playing field more clearly and strategically execute their plays to win the game. We will return to the tools and techniques for creating and effectively managing these important systems in Chapters 7 to 11.

Managing the Corporate Culture: "Culture"

Just as all people have personalities, all organizations have cultures—shared values, beliefs, and norms that govern how people are expected to behave on a day-to-day basis. Although all enterprises have cultures that can be identified by trained observers, they may be implicit rather than explicit.

Values are what the organization believes to be important in product quality, customer service, treatment of people, and so on. Beliefs are the ideas that people in the corporation hold about themselves as individuals and about the enterprise as an entity. Norms are the unwritten rules that guide day-to-day interactions and behavior, including language, dress, and humor.

The sixth challenge in building a successful organization is to manage the corporate culture in such a way that it supports the company's goals. This means that the values, beliefs, and norms that constitute an organization's culture are explicitly identified, "designed," and influenced by management, rather than merely allowed to exist.

As with the other five variables, an organization can develop a competitive advantage based on the way it manages its culture. Southwest Airlines has developed a unique culture that, supported by operational and management systems, promotes its ability to successfully play the game of a "no frills airline that values it customers." Company personnel are friendly and encouraged to promote "fun," while at the same time efficiently loading passengers in order to keep the planes in the air (which is how airlines make money). As many passengers on the West Coast of the United States can attest, the United Airlines Shuttle system, while matching Southwest on fares, has yet to develop a culture that consistently communicates to its passengers that they are valued. (In addition, the United Shuttle system frequently experiences problems with delays and passenger loading, a symptom that its operational systems are not functioning effectively to support the game it has chosen to play).

The Pyramid of Organizational Success

Taken together, these six key building blocks of organizational success (or critical tasks of building a successful organization) constitute a "pyramid"—a series of sequential steps or tasks that must be performed in an integrated fashion in order to develop a successful organizational entity. This pyramid of organizational success is shown schematically in Figure 2–2.

The six key tasks making up the pyramid must all be developed individually, and as a system, for the organization to function effectively and increase its ability to successfully play its chosen game over the long term.

Implications of the Pyramid Framework

The pyramid of organizational success framework has a variety of implications for management. First, whether organizations are aware of it or not,

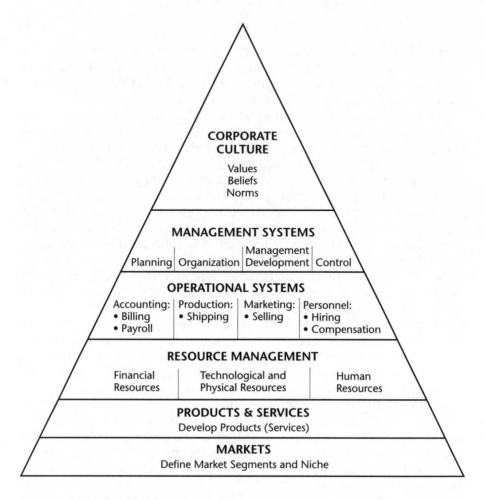

Figure 2–2. The Pyramid of Organizational Success.
Source: © Copyright *Management Systems* Consulting Corporation 1986, revised 1991. All rights reserved.

they are competing with each other at all levels of the pyramid in order to win the game. Specifically, organizations are competing not only in products and technology, but also in their choice of markets, in the resources available and how these resources are managed, their development of operational and management systems, as well as their corporate culture and how they manage it.

Alfred P. Sloan, who guided General Motors to supremacy in the automobile industry during the 1930s,[3] recognized that his company was competing at all levels. Sloan, who was an MIT-trained engineer, assumed the position of president at General Motors at a time when Ford was the number one automobile manufacturer. One of his first steps was to do a competitive analysis of Ford versus GM. He concluded that General Motors was competing with Ford not just in products and technology, but in management philosophy and organizational structure as well.[4]

Another implication of the pyramid concerns the specific levels at which competition tends to occur over the long term. Because many markets can be easily entered and most products can be readily copied or improved on, organizations most often compete at the four top levels of the pyramid over the longer term.[5] For example, a company like Starbucks can identify the market for a café business, but others can enter the same market location and copy their product. Similarly, a company like Visicorp can develop a product like Visicalc, only to have it improved on by Lotus Corporation's "1–2–3." Senior engineers at Hughes Electronics have told us that even the most sophisticated electronics products (such as space satellites) can be reverse engineered (i.e., copied and improved on) within six to eighteen months. In brief, since markets can be entered and since products can be copied or improved upon, competition over the longer term is typically at the top four levels of the Pyramid, even though this is not obvious nor is it well-recognized by managers.

The four top levels of the pyramid can be viewed as composing an organization's infrastructure. There are two aspects of organizational infrastructure: (1) operational infrastructure, and (2) management infrastructure. Operational infrastructure consists of the day-to-day resources and systems required to run the enterprise. Management systems and corporate culture constitute the management infrastructure. It is at these levels in the pyramid of organizational success that a firm can develop its most sustainable competitive advantages. Although any firm can choose to play the same game (i.e., enter the same market as another firm) and can develop similar products or services, it becomes a little more difficult (although not impossible) to duplicate another firm's human, physical, technological, and financial resources as well as its operational systems. It is almost impossible to duplicate the management systems and culture of another firm. In fact, these two levels allow the development of the most sustainable competitive advantages. Unfortunately, it is also at these two levels that managers in organizations have the greatest difficulty finding the time required to develop, implement, nurture, and monitor these important systems.

A Different Perspective

The pyramid of organizational success framework represents a different way of viewing organizations. Instead of looking at all the myriad pieces that make up a business, such as plants, inventory, stores, people, and so on, the pyramid creates a "lens" consisting of six critical factors or building blocks of organizational success. This simplifies the process of visualizing a business. The content of what is looked at in building a successful business is different in the pyramid framework. Specifically, it highlights not just markets, products, and technology, but the entire infrastructure of the business. Often, the factors seen as the driving forces in building successful businesses do not include organizational infrastructure, (i.e., resources, operational systems, management systems, and culture). However, some sophisticated entrepreneurs and managers do recognize the role of infrastructure (as we saw in the example of Alfred Sloan at General Motors and will note throughout) and this enhances their chances of long-term success.

Organizational Size

To be effective, an organization's business concept and pyramid of organizational success must fit its "size" and the "environment" in which it operates. In this context, "size" refers to the magnitude of an organization's revenues. An organization with $10 million in revenues is fundamentally different from one with $100 million. Sometimes an organization is too small to benefit from economies of scale, while other times it may be too large to operate effectively and efficiently. For example, as Robert Allen of AT&T stated in explaining the rationale for downsizing AT&T and spinning off both Lucent Technologies and NCR, "Bigger is not always better."[6] Indeed, there appear to be certain critical sizes that represent transitional points for organizations.[7]

Based on research, we have identified seven different stages of growth that help to differentiate firms of different sizes.[8] These seven stages are:

Stage I:	New Venture
Stage II:	Expansion
Stage III:	Professionalization
Stage IV:	Consolidation
Stage V:	Diversification
Stage VI:	Integration
Stage VII:	Decline/Revitalization

At each stage, one or more of the critical tasks of organizational development (discussed in the last section) *should* receive attention until the organization has reached maturity and success. The only exception to this progression is Stage VII—Decline/Revitalization—which can occur at any point in an organization's life. Chapter 4 deals with organizational decline and the transformation needed to overcome it.

The stages of growth and their related critical development areas, as well as the approximate size (measured in millions of dollars of sales revenues) at which an organization can be expected or should pass through each stage is shown in Figure 2–3.

When an organization has not effectively developed the systems, structures, and processes (i.e., effectively designed its pyramid of organizational success) needed to support its size, it will begin to experience what we call "transformational pains." These are discussed later in this chapter.

While the stages of growth represent the norms concerning the size at

Growth Stage	Critical Development Areas	Approximate Organizational Size ($ Millions of Sales)
New Venture	Markets and Products	Less than $1 Million
Expansion	Resources and Operational Systems	$1 to $10 Million
Professionalization	Management Systems	$10 to $100 Million
Consolidation	Corporate Culture	$100 to $500 Million
Diversification	Markets and Products	$500 Million to $1 Billion
Integration	Resources, Operational Systems Management Systems, Culture	$1 Billion +
Decline	All Six Tasks	Any Size Organization

Figure 2–3. Stages of Growth from a New Venture to Maturity.

which an organization must or should have developed particular levels within the pyramid of organizational success, the success of an organization's infrastructure is also influenced by the environment in which it operates.

Organizational Environment

The fourth major factor influencing the success of a business enterprise is the environment. As used here, "environment" consists of the markets, competition, and trends that have a present or potential impact on the enterprise. Each of these aspects of the organization's environment is examined below.

Market

As previously discussed, a market consists of the set of customers for a product or service. It is the field on which the firm has chosen to play. The market's potential (i.e., overall size) has a direct impact on both the business concept and the need for an organization to build (or have built) a particular infrastructure. A firm that desires rapid growth will need to seek a market that has a large number of customers and little competition. To promote success, a firm operating in an extremely competitive market will need to ensure that it has built an infrastructure that will allow it to outcompete and differentiate it from others in that market. Markets can also be identified in terms of "segments," with each segment describing a component of an overall market. For example, there is not just an overall market for computers; there are different segments of the market, including those for mainframes, mini-computers, and micro-computers. In any market, there are also different segments based upon different combinations of price and quality, (e.g., Cadillac vs. Buick and Chevrolet). We examine the concept of market segment further in Chapter 7.

Competition

Competition represents the set of present or potential competitors for an organization's market share. An organization must be concerned not just with who its competitors are today, but also needs to understand who they might be in the future. Further, to be successful over the long term, a firm must understand the impact a competitor can have on its business and take steps to maximize opportunities and minimize threats created by competitive activity in its markets.

Consumers on the West Coast, for example, have seen air fares between Los Angeles and the San Francisco Bay Area drop dramatically since the entry of Southwest Airlines into this market in the early 1990s. Southwest's low fares, combined with a significant focus on customer service, helped it take away a significant share of the market from such giants as United Airlines, US Air, Delta, and others. United responded by trying to adjust not only its fares, but also its operational systems (including passenger ticketing and loading procedures) in an effort to compete more effectively. Other airlines reacted by minimizing the number of flights offered in this market and/or pulling out of the market entirely.

Just as customers can constitute segments, competitors can be focused upon different market segments. For example, in the computer equipment business, organization's such as IBM, DEC, Apple Computers, and Compaq have each selected different segments to focus on, which will, of course, have some degree of overlap. IBM has traditionally concentrated on the mainframe market, while DEC built its business with a focus on mini-computers. Apple focused its efforts on the personal computer market with special attention to the educational market.

Trends

The third aspect of the environment is trends. A wide variety of trends can influence a business—economic, demographic, technological, cultural, and political. All of these can have an impact on (positively or negatively) the opportunities for a business's growth and development. For example, the trend toward more casual living has led to the widespread demand for automotive sport utility vehicles such as the Ford Explorer and Jeep Cherokee, which are actually classified as trucks. Manufacturers in the United States were able to spot this trend early and get a jump on their competition in Japan and Germany, and, as a result, have dominant market shares in this newly developed but highly profitable category.

To successfully play its chosen game, a firm must be designed to maximize the opportunities and minimize the threats presented by its environment. To do this effectively, a firm must take steps and have systems in place for monitoring its environment and adjusting to changes, as appropriate. Transformational planning is a tool that can help organizations do just that. This will be the subject of Chapter 7.

Designing Business Organizations with Proper "Fit"

When an organization's business concept, six key building blocks, size, and environment, all "fit" together, that organization has a very high probability of success. Paraphrasing Star Trek's Mr. Spock, the organization is likely to "live long and prosper." If an optimal fit is not achieved, the organization will probably experience difficulty, even failure. This explains the success of Compaq versus Osborne, Nike versus LA Gear, and Southwest Airlines versus People Express. It also explains why organizations such as IBM, Chrysler, and Bank of America experienced difficulty and required revitalization. An organization primarily controls this fit through the game it chooses to play (i.e., its business concept) and how it plays that game. This is what we call a firm's "business model" or "business design."

Business Design: The Game We Play and How We Play It

When we combine the concept of a business (its foundation) with the pyramid of organizational success (shown in Figure 2–2), we have a picture of the game the firm is playing (including how they play the game). This is illustrated in Figure 2–4. Operationally, an enterprise's organizational design consists of the business concept plus how the firm is managing the six key building blocks of an organization (i.e., the pyramid of organizational success). Conceptually, an organization's design consists of the business the firm is in as well as the markets it has selected, the products it offers, its resources, its operational and management systems, and the organization's culture. Stated differently, it consists of what its business is as well as the way it does business.

Although we tend to think of businesses in terms of their component parts such as people, plant, equipment, and so on, it is necessary to visualize a business as consisting of its conceptual foundation and the structure built upon that foundation (the pyramid of organizational success) in order to take the next step toward understanding organizational transformations and the need to change the game.

An organization's design can help us overcome the complexity of an enterprise and reduce it into something more manageable. In this sense, the model shown in Figure 2–4 is a "managerial lens." This lens can be used as a tool for planning the design and redesign (transformation) of businesses. Designing (or redesigning) a business involves addressing certain "strategic organizational development issues" at each level of the pyramid of organizational success as well as in the business foundation as shown in Figure 2–5.

Taken together, the following six questions are the core issues that must be answered or resolved to build an enterprise:
1. What business are we in?
2. What customers do we want to focus on?
3. What products and services will we offer?

Figure 2–4. Organizational Design=Business Concept+The Pyramid of Organizational Success.
Source: © Copyright *Management Systems* Consulting Corporation 1986, revised 1995. All rights reserved.

4. What resources do we need to effectively compete and operate our business?
5. What operational systems do we need to effectively manage our business?
6. What management systems do we need to develop, implement and monitor so that we can effectively manage and build our business over the long term?
7. What culture is appropriate for our business?

The Model for Building Successful Businesses

By bringing all the five components previously discussed together, we can create a model for understanding successful transformations or how to effec-

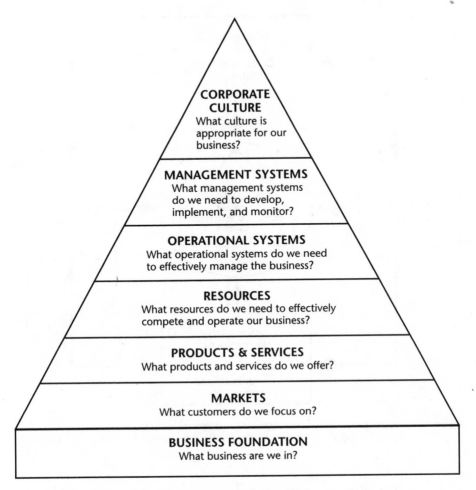

Figure 2–5. Core Strategic Issues for Developing a Successful Enterprise.

tively play the game. Figure 2–6 (which is a modification of Figure 2–1) summarizes the process of designing business organizations with "proper" or optimal fit in schematic terms. It shows that an organization's design (represented as the business foundation and pyramid of organizational success in the center circle) should be influenced by four related factors:

1. The business concept.
2. The six key building blocks of successful organizational development.
3. An organization's size.
4. Factors in the environment such as markets, competition, and trends.

Unfortunately, however, it is not always the case that organizations and their managers design their businesses to maximize the fit of these four factors. When the fit is poor, the firm can begin to experience a series of

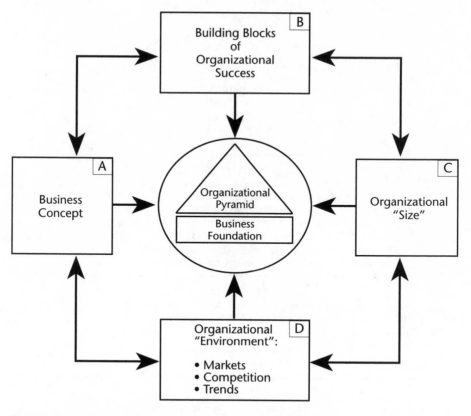

Figure 2–6. Factors Influencing the Design of an Enterprise.

problems. The signs or signals that there is something wrong with the fit between one or more of these factors are called "transformation pains." These are described below.

Organizational Transformation Pains

Most enterprises encounter some degree of difficulty in designing an organization with the optimal fit among the four factors described above. When the proper fit has not been achieved, the organization experiences a "developmental gap." This developmental gap, in turn, produces what may be termed "organizational transformation pains." These transformation pains may be viewed as the symptoms indicating that the organization is experiencing some problems in the game it is playing or how it is playing the game.

Based on the authors' research with companies over the past twenty years, we have identified two different types of transformation pains. Type I, which may be termed "organizational growing pains," tend to emerge in firms who need to transform from an entrepreneurship to a professionally managed firm—for example, they tend to occur in firms that need to make a Transformation of the First Kind. Type II, which may be termed "organizational aging pains," emerge when an organization is in decline and requires revitalization. We will examine each of these two types of transformation pains below. In the following chapters, we will describe these transformation pains further in the context of some examples of firms that have actually experienced them.

Type I: Organizational Growing Pains

Based upon action research and consulting experience, we have identified ten classic symptoms of organizational growing pains, as shown in Figure 2–7. These growing pains are not merely problems in and of themselves, but are symptoms of deeper systemic problems. Specifically, they indicate that an organization has outgrown its infrastructure and must make the transformation to professional management. It must learn to play the game differently. The more severe the growing pains, the greater the likelihood the firm will experience problems and possibly even failure. In Chapter 3, we will provide a detailed example of a firm that experienced many of these growing pains.

---

1. People feel that there are not enough hours in the day.
2. People are spending too much time "putting out fires."
3. Many people are not aware of what others are doing.
4. People lack understanding of where the enterprise is heading.
5. There are too few good managers.
6. Everybody feels, "I have to do it myself if I want to get it done correctly."
7. Most people feel/have begun to feel our meetings are a waste of time.
8. When plans are made, there is very little follow-up and things just don't get done.
9. Some people feel insecure about their place in the enterprise.
10. The enterprise has continued to grow in sales but not in profits.

Figure 2–7. Organizational Growing Pains.

Type II: Organizational Aging Pains

We have also identified thirteen classic symptoms of the need for revitalization which we call organizational aging pains, as shown in Figure 2–8. Like growing pains, aging pains are not merely problems in themselves,

1. We know what's best for our customers; we don't need to ask them.

2. We focus more attention on competing with each other than we do on competing with other companies.

3. People are spending too much time covering their vested interests.

4. We've lost our momentum because we are mired in bureaucracy and red tape.

5. On the surface, we are one big family, but there is a great deal of conflict below the surface.

6. People are increasingly unwilling to take risks.

7. Each manager has his or her kingdom; there's no sense of a unified direction.

8. We have too many people doing the same thing and not enough people doing the right thing.

9. There are too many levels and too many people in the organization.

10. People aren't rewarded on performance; it's who you know, not what you do.

11. Our managers don't know what they are doing and/or don't know what to do.

12. Strategic planning emphasizes form, rather than substance.

13. Although the firm continues to grow in terms of revenue, its profitability has been squeezed for a number of years.

Figure 2–8. Organizational Aging Pains.

but symptoms of underlying systemic problems within the organization's infrastructure. They indicate that an organization has gone into decline and requires a revitalization or business vision transformation. In other words, a firm experiencing organizational aging pains may need to learn to play a different game and/or may need to learn how to play its chosen game more effectively if it is going to continue to thrive (or even exist). In Chapter 4, we will be further explaining these aging pains by providing a detailed example of one firm's experience and what it did to overcome these problems.

Differences in Organizational Design Factors in Each Transformation Type

The model for building successful organizations, shown previously in Figure 2–6, identified four key factors in the design of a successful enterprise. The need for transformations occurs when significant changes have taken place in one or more of these four key factors.

The way in which each factor is defined is different in each of the three principal types of transformations (i.e., Transformations of the First, Second, and Third Kinds). This means that a different "profile" with respect to the four factors exists for each type of transformation, as shown schematically in Figure 2–9 and described below.

Organizational Design Factors in Type I Transformations

A Transformation of the First Kind (Type I Transformation) involves making adjustments to better "fit" with the firm's increased size in some of the six key building blocks of an organization, especially in the operational systems, management systems, and culture. As we will see in the examples presented in Chapter 3, two of the six key building blocks (i.e., management systems and culture) play a major role in Transformations of the First Kind. In this type of transformation, the business concept typically remains unchanged (except in a compound transformation). Taken together, these changes constitute a transformation from an entrepreneurship to an entrepreneurially oriented professionally managed organization.

Organizational Design Factors in Type II Transformations

A Transformation of the Second Kind (Type II Transformation) involves making changes in all six key building blocks and, usually, in the organization's size in order to adjust to in the firm's environment (i.e., changes in markets, competition, and/or trends). Most typically, the cause of revitalization is an environmental change that makes the existing way of doing business (i.e., the firm's design of the pyramid of organizational success) obsolete. Environmental changes (i.e., new competitors or a decline in market size) may also lead to a need to alter the firm's size. In many cases, the first response to

	Transformation Types		
Key Factors Influencing Design of Transformations	**Type I Entrepreneurial to Professional Management**	**Type II Revitalization**	**Type III Business Vision**
Organizational Environment	• Typically involves growth in markets and competition but not major environmental change	• Major change in environment	• May or may not involve environmental change
Business Concept	• No transformation	• No transformation	• Major transformation
Building Blocks of Organizational Success	• Change in culture, management systems, operational systems	• Change needed at all six levels or within all key building blocks	• Change in all six key building blocks
Organizational Size	• Typically involves rapid growth	• Typically changes. • Downsizing may occur	• May involve size change

Figure 2–9. Differences in Key Factors of Organizational Design in Each Type of Transformation

these types of environmental changes is generally to downsize, but ultimately the six key building blocks require a complete redesign, as in the case of IBM.

Organizational Design Factors in Type III Transformations

A Transformation of the Third Kind (Type III Transformation) involves adjusting to changes or opportunities in the environment, which requires changes in the business concept, all six building blocks, as well as organizational size. Business vision transformations begin with the need to change the business concept. In turn, they require changes in the six building blocks, as in the case of AT&T (which we will examine in Chapter 6). Business vision transformations are most typically driven by changes in the environment, but can also result from changes in the firm's own size.

Transformations as "Solutions" for Different Success Factor Profiles

Each type of transformation involves finding a "solution" to changes in equilibrium among the four basic "drivers" or factors influencing the successful design of a business. The process involves assessing the four factors influencing the design of a successful business as "inputs" and "selecting" the appropriate type of transformation process in order to derive the "output" of a transformed business design. We present the method of accomplishing this transformational process in Chapters 7 to 11.

Conclusion

This chapter has presented a framework that can be used as a lens to plan how to build and transform organizations successfully. We have identified four critical factors that influence the design of a successful enterprise:

1. The business concept.
2. Six key building blocks of organizational success.
3. The organization's size.
4. The environment in which the firm operates.

We have also discussed how changes in any of these four factors can lead to the need for transformations or changes in either the game being played or the way it is played.

In the next four chapters, we present several actual examples of firms that have successfully managed organizational transformations (i.e., changed their games), as well as those that have been unsuccessful at changing their games. The framework presented in this chapter will be used as a lens through which we will come to understand and analyze these transformations.

Part II

CASE STUDIES IN CHANGING THE GAME

3

ENTREPRENEURSHIP TO PROFESSIONAL MANAGEMENT

Successful Transformations of the First Kind

This chapter deals with the transformational issues involved in changing the game at entrepreneurial companies. Specifically, it examines three examples of Transformations of the First Kind (i.e., transformations from entrepreneurships to professional management) in three companies in very different industries: health care, mutual fund management, and computers.

The first example provides an in-depth look at Transformations of the First Kind as they are most typically experienced by growing organizations. It describes the problems that signal the need for making such a transformation. It also provides an example of a process that can be used to successfully make this type of transformation. The second case is an example of a company that faces the special issues related to this type of transformation in a family-run business. The third example illustrates the strategy a company can use to prepare, in advance, for such a transformation. After we have examined the three companies, we will discuss the lessons that can be learned from each.

The Transition to Professional Management at MediPro Industries[1]

Roger Goldsmith, the founder of MediPro, began his career as a salesman for a major medical products manufacturing and marketing firm. Roger worked hard to learn everything he could about the industry. He discovered that the company he was working for was not adequately meeting all its customers' needs, and that an untapped market existed for certain specialized urology products. In 1988, he decided to start his own company. Apparently Roger's belief about the demand for his products was accurate, because within a few years MediPro began to experience rapid growth.

By the beginning of 1995, the company had reached more than $20 million in annual revenues, and it was estimated that by 1999 it would achieve $50 million in yearly sales. MediPro's personnel increased from 25 in 1985 to 200 in 1996.

Symptoms of the Need for Transformation

As early as 1993, MediPro was beginning to experience certain organizational problems, or growing pains, that were symptoms of the need for fundamental change in the way the organization was being managed. Some symptoms were more serious than others, but they all signaled that there were deeper problems that eventually could lead to MediPro's failure unless the organization dealt with them. These symptoms (which include a number of those identified in Chapter 2 as classic growing pains) are described below.

People felt there were not enough hours in the day. Most employees felt overloaded. They commonly stayed after hours to complete their work. Departmental managers in particular felt that their workload was too great and that deadlines were unrealistic.This situation resulted, in part, from the lack of adequately developed operational systems to support MediPro's employees' work. The accounting, operational planning, and communication systems were adequate for a small company, but quite inadequate for one as large as MediPro had become. Systems for purchasing, inventory control, and even mail distribution were either poorly developed or nonexistent.

People spent too much time putting out fires. Perhaps the best indication that MediPro needed to change the game it was playing was that employees spent an increasing amount of time dealing with short-term problems resulting from the lack of long-range planning. This was particularly evident in the constant lack of space within the company's headquarters. It appeared to most employees that as soon as the company increased its office space, that space was filled and it was time to begin planning for another move. It seemed that there was never enough space or equipment to support the company's staff adequately. Salespeople, when they worked at the firm's headquarters, usually arrived early to ensure that they would be able to find a vacant desk from which to make their calls. Employees who did not go out into the field attempted to handle the cramped space by creating schedules for using phones, computer terminals, even desks.

Employees began to feel that MediPro never planned, it simply reacted. (An informal joke around the company was that at MediPro, long-range planning means "what I am going to do after lunch.") Changes in the firm's market place partly created the new demands that needed to be responded to quickly. Some managers felt that they just simply did not have the time to plan. This need to respond quickly contributed to the tendency at MediPro for employees and managers to spend most of their time trying to help the firm stay afloat without keeping an eye on the future.

Employees began to think that, simply because "crisis is the norm" at the company, that was the way they should operate. They began to call themselves "the firefighters" and even took pride in their ability to deal with crises. However, there began to be a suspicion that some people were becoming "arsonists" in order to later be seen as "heroic" firefighters.

Many people were not aware of what others were doing. A significant number of people did not understand what their jobs were, what others' jobs were, or what the relationships were between their jobs and the jobs of others. This problem resulted, in part, from a tendency to add personnel without developing formal descriptions of roles and responsibilities. Since employees were added on an *ad hoc* basis whenever a staff shortage seemed imminent, there was often little time to orient them to the organization's operations or train them adequately in what their own responsibilities would be. Indeed there was no formal training program.

Some people were given job descriptions, but did not adhere to their specified roles. Others were given a title, but no explicit responsibilities. Surprisingly, many individuals often did not know to whom they were to report, and managers did not know for which employees and activities they would be held accountable. People learned what they were supposed to do on a daily basis; long-range planning was nonexistent.

Interactions between departments were also a problem. Managers often did not understand what their responsibilities were and how what they were doing fit in with the firm's overall operations. New departments were created to meet MediPro's product and marketing needs, but many managers were not aware of how these departments fit in with the rest of the organization. One manager complained, "People sit outside my door, but I don't even know what they do." Another new manager described his introduction to MediPro as follows: "I was walked to an area and told: 'This is your department. Run it.'"

This lack of formal roles and responsibilities made it easy for personnel to avoid responsibility whenever a task was not completed or performed unsatisfactorily. This situation also led to duplication of effort between departments. Since no one knew precisely whose responsibility a particular task was, two or more departments or people would complete a task, only to find that it had already been accomplished by someone else.

There was a lack of understanding about where the firm was heading. Many MediPro employees complained that not only did they not know what was expected of them, they could not understand where the company was headed in the long term. This resulted from the inability of MediPro's management to articulate and communicate (through a more formal planning process) its vision for the future to the company's personnel. Employees were aware that changes were being made, but were not always sure how these changes would affect them or their departments. Consequently, many people experienced high levels of anxiety. When this anxiety became too great, many left the firm.

There were not enough good managers.   Most managers at MediPro were promoted to their positions in recognition of service. Some were good managers, but most were described by their subordinates as "good technicians who lack people skills." Further, they were seen as clones. Many employees believed that management had one and only one way of doing things and that to deviate from the norm would result in adverse consequences.

Plenty of people had the title "manager," but relatively few really behaved as managers. After promotion, many people simply kept doing the things they had done in their former roles. They were poor in delegating, often doing the work themselves instead of assigning it to others. As a result, employees came to believe that their managers did not trust them.

Roger Goldsmith was a strong individual who wanted things done *his* way, and he wanted to control almost everything. Goldsmith recognized this, referring to himself as "someone who sticks his nose into everything." Few decisions were made without his approval or review. As a consequence, one of two things tended to happen concerning managers: (1) The stronger managers tended to "butt heads" with Goldsmith and ultimately left; and (2) the remaining managers were slowly turned into "managerial eunuchs." Those managers who decided not to leave MediPro tended to not take Roger on, at least not directly, and they had little real authority and certainly no real power. Inadvertently, Goldsmith had created an organization of "managerial pygmies" and was, in effect, the victim of his own need for control. This phenomenon is part of what has been termed the "Entrepreneur's Syndrome."[2]

Everybody feels, "I have to do it myself if I want to get it done correctly."   This symptom was, in part, due to a corporate culture that had been influenced by Roger Goldsmith's own personal style. As we noted, he liked to be involved in everything. As a result, many managers came to feel that they, too, needed to be involved in every detail of their team's work. This allowed them to be ready to address any questions that Goldsmith might throw their way. The message sent by the organization's culture seemed to be that: "If you want to be valued, you need to be on top of (if not do) everything." In addition, there were not always strong people to delegate to. There were plenty of people in the company, but they weren't always the "right" types of people (i.e., with the right skills) to ensure that tasks would be completed in an appropriate fashion. Therefore, many people felt that it was safer to "do it myself."

Most people felt meetings were a waste of time.   People complained that many meetings were held among top managers and not enough among the lower levels of the organization. In addition, those meetings that were held were often inefficient and did not result in resolutions to problems. This was because many meetings had no written agendas or minutes. Many of those attending described these meetings as "free-for-alls." They were at best discussions and at worst fights between departments or individuals. Worst of all, they went on interminably.

People also complained that most meetings were called on an *ad hoc* basis. Since these meetings were unscheduled, people typically came to them without any sense of their purpose and certainly with no preparation. Thus, they tended to have the atmosphere of "bull sessions" in which people shot from the hip. In addition, people felt that they could not plan their work because they were constantly interrupted for "crisis" meetings.

When plans were made there was very little follow-up and things didn't get done. Like many small and growing firms, MediPro had traditionally operated on an *ad hoc* basis. No formal strategic planning system was needed since Goldsmith had provided all of the firm's direction. Further, the informal structure had allowed MediPro's employees the freedom to generate new product and marketing ideas.

As the company grew, however, Goldsmith and his senior management team began to realize the firm needed to monitor its operations. Unfortunately, MediPro had not developed the systems needed to effectively monitor the organization or individual performance against goals. This led to the perception that performance appraisals were subjective and even political.

Some people began to feel insecure about their places in the firm. This problem grew out of the many changes taking place and the large number of problems the firm was encountering as it grew. Some original "founding members" were terminated and replaced. This caused people to wonder who was next. Although many recognized that some employees had not grown as the company grew, they worried about their jobs and their places within the firm. This, in turn, led people to spend an increasing amount of their time "covering their vested interests."

The company grew in sales but not in profits. MediPro, like many entrepreneurial firms, traditionally had been most concerned with increasing sales. It adopted the philosophy of many growing firms: "If we're selling more, we must be making more profits." Unfortunately this is not often the case. The other side of the equation, costs, often increases along with sales, and if costs are not contained, the firm soon may find itself in a position of losing, rather than making money. Thus, although MediPro's sales were increasing at a rapid rate, profits were remaining relatively constant—a classic warning of future difficulties.

MediPro's problems certainly are not unique. Indeed they are the classic symptoms of organizational growing pains, as identified in Chapter 2. It should be noted that while these "symptoms" represent problems in and of themselves, they also suggest deeper, more systematic organizational problems. Specifically, they signal that the organization needs to change the game it is playing to that of a professionally managed firm.

Changing the Game at MediPro

During 1994, Roger Goldsmith recognized that his firm was experiencing significant problems. An astute individual, he realized that more than a tune-up was required. Specifically, he recognized that MediPro needed to change the game it was playing and make what we have termed a Transformation of the First Kind.

Goldsmith sought out and hired a consultant who specialized in helping firms manage growth-related issues. He worked with this consultant to develop a program to help his company successfully make the transition from an entrepreneurship to a more professionally managed firm. Although consultants are not necessarily appropriate in all situations, they can add value in dealing with the complex issues involved in organizational transformations. Management's role is to provide the leadership required and to be the ultimate decision-maker. A consultant's role is to be an advisor, a catalyst to change, and a facilitator of the transformation process.

The consultant Goldsmith engaged had a great deal of experience in helping organizations make Transformations of the First Kind. Working with the consultant, Goldsmith and a small team of advisors designed and implemented a four-step program. The four phases of this program are presented and described below.

Phase I: Assess the company's current state and future developmental needs (i.e., how the firm is and *should be* playing the game).

Phase II: Develop a plan for changing the game.

Phase III: Implement the plan.

Phase IV: Monitor the plan and make changes as needed.

Changing the Game: Phase I

The first step in changing the game involved assessing MediPro's developmental needs using an organizational audit. This audit involved collecting information from employees about their perceptions of MediPro and its operations. The consultant assisted in this effort by conducting interviews with selected employees. In addition, employees were asked to complete an organizational growing pains questionnaire designed to measure the extent to which an organization experiences the need to make a transformation.

The scores on this questionnaire, along with information collected through the interview process, indicated that the company was experiencing some very significant problems that required immediate attention. Specifically, the audit revealed that the company needed to:

- Better define organizational roles and responsibilities, as well as the linkages between roles.
- Help employees plan and budget their time.
- Develop a long-range business plan and a system for monitoring it.
- Increase the number of qualified present and potential managers.
- Clearly identify the direction the company should take in the future.
- Reduce employee and departmental feelings that they always "needed to do it themselves" in order to effectively complete a task.
- Make meetings more efficient by developing written agendas and taking and distributing meeting minutes.
- Become profit oriented rather than strictly sales oriented.

Changing the Game: Phase II

Having identified its organizational problems and developmental needs, MediPro proceeded to the next step: designing and implementing a plan to help focus the company on resolving the problems identified. The process began with a two day strategic planning retreat that was facilitated by the consultant (with Goldsmith's input). During this retreat, the senior management team of MediPro focused on some fundamental issues necessary for guiding the company's future development, including:

1. What business is MediPro in?
2. What are our competitive strengths and limitations?
3. Do we have a market niche?
4. What are the key factors responsible for our past success; to what extent will they contribute to our future requirements for success?
5. What should our objectives be for developing MediPro as an organization?
6. What should our action plans be and who is responsible for each action plan to implement our specific objectives?

In addition to these core strategic planning issues, which are relevant to all organizations, the company also examined issues that were specifically related to how the firm operated and should operate. One involved making MediPro less dependent on Roger Goldsmith; another included the development of a stronger management team.

After the planning retreat, the consultant prepared a draft of a corporate strategic plan (which detailed how the firm was going to change the game it was playing) for management's review. This plan was circulated among the firm's senior managers for their comments and input. It was revised, approved by Goldsmith, and then distributed to all senior managers. The plan provided a "blueprint" for future development, including specific objectives focused on eliminating the problems that had resulted from the company's rapid growth.

A key decision made during the retreat was to be more selective in accepting new business until the firm had built the infrastructure needed to support its current size and anticipate future growth. Therefore, the plan developed by MediPro's management team contained a number of "programs" intended to help the firm build the infrastructure needed to play its chosen game effectively. These programs included:

1. Implementation of a strategic plan that defined where the company was and where it wanted to go (including how it was going to build the infrastructure needed to effectively play its new game).

2. Design and implementation of a management-development program to help people become better managers and overcome the "Doer Syndrome."

3. Strategies for recruiting new professionals with the advanced skills needed to guide the firm.

4. Development of a formal set of job descriptions and a performance appraisal system.

5. Strategies for changing how the firm was led and managed.

Changing the Game: Phase III

After the planning retreat, the firm began to implement the various programs it had outlined in its plan. The specifics of this implementation are described below.

Developing and Implementing a Strategic Plan.   One of the first steps MediPro took to manage its growth was to begin developing a strategic plan. The major goal of this process was to motivate the company's managers to begin to take a longer range view than "what's happening after lunch." A related goal was to affect the corporate culture at MediPro and make planning a way of life.

Management Development.   Goldsmith and MediPro's other senior managers realized that people were MediPro's true asset. The firm's technology, products, and equipment were really not proprietary; the true differentiating factor was the motivation and skills of its people. Recognizing this, MediPro believed the company had to make an investment in building its managerial capabilities to achieve two objectives. First, there simply was not a sufficient number of effective managers. Although many people had managerial titles and could recite the right "buzzwords," relatively few were really behaving as managers. They were spending too much time doing, rather than managing work; there was little true delegation; and insufficient effort was given to planning, organizing people, performance appraisal, and control, which are the essence of management.

Another reason for focusing on management development was more symbolic. Goldsmith recognized that some of the people who had helped build MediPro to its current size were in jeopardy of becoming victims of "The Peter Principle." There was a belief that they had been promoted to their level of incompetence. Goldsmith felt that the company owed its people a chance to grow with it, and he saw management development as a chance to provide them with this opportunity. Quite frankly, he felt that if people had this opportunity and failed to grow, then he could feel comfortable "letting them go" because the firm had done all it could to assist them.

To deal with these issues, MediPro asked a consultant to design a management development program for its personnel. Two programs were developed: one for top managers, one for middle managers. These programs focused on helping participants develop the skills needed to support MediPro in effectively playing its new game of professional management. Managers were introduced to new skills, as well as new ways of thinking and approaching their work. The overall goal of the programs was to produce behavioral change—to grow effective coaches who would take the firm into the future versus having people continue to operate as firefighters.

Recruitment of Professionals. As the company grew, so did its need for greater skills and sophistication in certain areas. A controller was recruited to replace the firm's bookkeeper. A national sales manager was appointed. MediPro also hired a director of human resources and a marketing manager. Moreover, the firm engaged a consultant to serve as its "adjunct" management development advisor. In brief, the firm made a significant investment in its human resources. These people were then responsible for developing the operational systems required to help manage growth in various areas.

Development of Role Descriptions and a Performance Appraisal System. The fourth major step in strengthening MediPro's infrastructure was to develop more formal job descriptions and a performance appraisal system. In the context of the firm's management development program, individuals were trained in how to develop effective job descriptions that could be used as tools in motivating people to perform their roles effectively. They were also trained in how to prepare for and conduct effective performance appraisals.

Following the management development session, individual managers were given the responsibility for creating job descriptions for their own roles and for working with members of their team (who were not participants in the management development program) in creating job descriptions for their individual roles. These job descriptions were designed to reflect what the company needed these position-holders to do versus what they were currently doing.

Once job descriptions were completed, they were shared among members of the management team and changes were made (where necessary) to ensure that no key responsibilities had been overlooked in designing this important part of the organization's structure. In addition, the management team worked so that duplication of effort (i.e., multiple position-holders working on the same task) was minimized.

The performance management system was designed to ensure that employees at all levels were continually focused on achieving MediPro's goals. Forms were created on which managers could work with their direct reports to set specific, measurable, time-dated goals for each individual contributor.

The manager's role was to see that these goals supported what MediPro, as a whole, wanted to achieve (as outlined in its strategic plan); and that the goals were also appropriate, given the person's role. Once goals were set, managers were encouraged to provide regular feedback on performance against goals. This was accomplished through holding regularly scheduled one-on-one meetings with each direct report. At year-end, managers were asked to complete a performance evaluation form on which they would assess the performance of each person on his or her team in terms of meeting the goals that were set at the beginning of the year. The final step in this process was for the manager to hold a year-end formal performance evaluation with each employee to discuss his or her results and set goals for the coming year.

The overall objective of this program was to help people better understand what was expected of them and hold them accountable for results.

Changes in Leadership and Management.   Another key aspect of the transformation at MediPro concerned Roger Goldsmith himself and changes in his leadership and managerial practices. Goldsmith had long believed that it was his role to pay attention to all the details of the business, which had led to conflicts with his strong managers. Now Goldsmith decided that his strength had become a weakness. He began to use a more participative, interactive approach in decision-making. He began to truly delegate authority and accept things being done differently from the way he would have done them. As he changed, so did his management team. People became more comfortable in discussing issues, even when they knew Goldsmith might disagree. They began to accept responsibility when things went wrong and said: "Let us fix it, not you."

The use of a strategic plan and performance evaluation system made it feasible to hold people accountable for results. Employees began to know what was expected and could see how their evaluations were derived. There was no magical change, but the leadership style was becoming more professional and less dependent on Goldsmith.

Changing the Game: Phase IV

For eighteen months, MediPro continued to implement its new programs of organizational development and monitor results on a monthly basis. The firm also held quarterly meetings to review the company's results, compare them with the plan, and make required adjustments. This signaled that the plan was more than merely a "paper plan"—it was a real management tool.

At the conclusion of eighteen months, the firm again administered the growing pains questionnaire to selected employees. Results suggested that although some problems still existed, there was nothing of major concern. A more significant indicator of success was that the firm's profitability increased significantly over this period of time, as a wide variety of inefficiencies were eliminated through the implementation of the programs described above.

MediPro had made a fundamental transformation. It had gone from a firm that was playing the game of a small entrepreneurship to one that was more professionally managed and able to absorb growth and operate profitably and effectively.

The Transformation to Professional Management at American Century Investors

American Century Investors, Inc. ("American Century") is a highly successful, rapidly growing investment management company. Founded as "Twentieth Century Investors" in 1958, the firm has its headquarters in Kansas City, Missouri and employs more than 2,000 people. The company manages a family of mutual funds (both equity and fixed income). American Century's diversified equity funds were one of the top performers over five- and ten-year intervals, as cited by *Business Week* in 1994. In 1995, the company acquired The Benham Group, located in Mountain View, California and in 1996, it changed its name to "American Century."

Background

American Century's founder, James (Jim) E. Stowers, Jr., was a pilot during his service in the U.S. Military. He began his career as an insurance salesman and later got involved in mutual funds. He holds two degrees from the University of Missouri.

Jim Stowers, Jr., started his first fund in 1958 with $100,000 in assets and twenty-four shareholders. By 1996, American Century Investors managed more than $50 billion in assets. In 1972, American Century was a relatively small company when Stowers developed a proprietary computer program for identifying companies with accelerating earnings. This tool became the foundation of American Century's investment management process, together with a team approach to investment decision-making.

In some ways, Jim Stowers is like all classic entrepreneurs; in others, he is quite different. Like most entrepreneurs, he has always had strong beliefs in the value of his product. Moreover, his intent was to help people achieve financial independence by investing in "the best companies in America."[3] Accordingly, he has been a champion of the small investor. Unlike many entrepreneurs, however, he has been willing to make investments in his organization's infrastructure and management team. Also, while many entrepreneurs want to control *everything*, Stowers wanted to control only a few key factors and was willing to leave the detail of the operations to his management team.

By 1988, American Century had grown to more than $6 billion in assets under management. The company had excellent people, products, and day to day systems. It also had a strong culture that emphasized "doing the right thing." However, the company lacked well-developed management systems. It did not have a formal strategic planning process. There was no budgeting process. In addition, although there were several people who, as individuals, had good managerial skills, there was no system for management development.

During 1988, Jim Stowers and the senior management team recognized that the company had begun to outgrow its informal management systems and needed to change the game it was playing from that of an entrepreneurship to a professionally managed firm. They embarked on a program to make a Transformation of the First Kind.

The Catalyst to Change the Game

There were several aspects to the beginning of American Century's transformation to professional management. One impetus was a conversation between Stowers and his neighbor, Jack Jonathan, who had been an executive with Hallmark, concerning the need for strategic planning. In addition, American Century's Vice President of Human Resources, Paris Couturiaux, attended a seminar at UCLA during which he became acquainted with a professor (one of this book's authors) who talked about the role of strategic planning as a tool in helping organizations transform from entrepreneurships to entrepreneurially oriented, professionally managed firms. Couturiaux invited the professor to make a presentation at American Century.

During that session, Stowers asked one of his senior managers, Irving Kuraner, for his opinion about the ideas being presented. Kuraner, who was a graduate of Columbia University's Law School and served as General Corporate Counsel for American Century, was also a valued advisor to Jim Stowers. He replied, "Well, I think he makes a great deal of sense." At the conclusion of that comment, there was laughter throughout the room. Bob Puff, a senior executive and member of the investment management group then said, "You don't know how high a praise that is."

Based on what they learned in the presentation, Jim Stowers and the senior executive team decided to proceed with the transformation to professional management using strategic planning as a major tool or lever in the process. This process also helped the company recognize the need to make changes in its management structure and leaders. This included helping all managers develop the needed capabilities to take the firm into the future and laying the groundwork for transitioning the overall management of the firm to the next generation.

Changing the Game: Getting Started in Planning[4]

American Century was introduced to a systematic planning process in 1988. This process was facilitated by the university professor/consultant and focused not only on helping the firm define its competitive management strategy, but also on setting goals to develop the internal operational and management systems infrastructure required to support the company's future growth. In this sense, the process was more of a strategic organizational development and transformational process than classical strategic planning *per se.*

At first, the planning meetings were difficult both because some contentious issues had to be resolved and because there were problems in American Century senior management's decision making and meeting management processes. The company's senior management group was accustomed to meetings where virtually anything could be talked about. Accordingly, discussions ranged from major issues to how much ought to be spent on holiday party decorations. In addition, these discussions would tend not to remain focused, as one issue led to another. This contributed to a general feeling of frustration about overall meeting effectiveness.

The new strategic planning process began with a focus on some of the core business foundation issues, questions including such as, "What business are we in?" and "What do we want to become in the long term?" Planning for specific objectives and goals focused on a set of "key result areas" (i.e., factors critical to the organization's success), which included all of the six building blocks of successful organizations: markets, products, resources, operational systems, management systems, and culture. In addition, "financial results" was added as a seventh key result area, or "KRA."

From 1988 through 1990, the senior executive group was mastering the skills involved in strategic planning and strategic organizational development. Planning focused on setting goals to build the organization's infrastructure. A key aspect of the overall mission for American Century was to make the transition from an entrepreneurship to a professionally managed firm (i.e., to change the game it was playing). Over this time, American Century's senior managers improved their skills at strategic planning, decision-making, and executive meeting management. Increasingly, planning meetings centered on strategic rather than operational issues. Discussions in the meetings became more focused on "big picture" issues, instead of the day-to-day details of managing the business (although perfection was never achieved or expected).

American Century experienced a period of very rapid growth from 1992 to 1993. The driver for this growth was the exceptional performance of the firm's family of equity mutual funds led by "Ultra," the number one performing mutual fund in 1991 (the fund increased in value by 86.5% in one year). Fund performance led to a great inflow of new assets. The number of customer (shareholder) transactions increased dramatically. This resulted in a corresponding increase in the number of telephone inquiries, the amount of mail, the number of fund prospectuses to be distributed, and increased demand on most of the company's systems. Through its strategic planning process, the company was able to anticipate this growth and plan for the development of its infrastructure, including its resources and operational systems. This, in turn, helped accommodate the growth experienced.

Changing the Game: Management Structure and Leadership

American Century ultimately adopted a relatively rare management and leadership structure. Specifically, it adopted a "team approach" to corporate management. This structure was an outgrowth of the company's approach to managing its core business—portfolio management. Jim Stowers, Jr., the firm's founder and CEO, had built American Century's portfolio management process on the belief that a team decision is better than individual decisions in portfolio (stock) selection. The company was also team oriented in the operations area. Accordingly, it was a natural notion to extend the team concept to the firm's overall management.

Stowers' concept was to use the firm's Executive Committee (which at that time consisted of thirteen people) as a "team CEO." Jim Stowers was the company's official CEO, and he reserved the right to use "his extra vote" on two or three major decisions each year. Beyond that, he expected the Executive Committee to run the company as a team. This meant that all significant decisions and issues had to come to the Executive Committee. Long-range, more strategic issues were resolved in the strategic planning meetings, while operational issues were addressed in Executive Committee meetings.

It is worth noting that the approach was imposed by Stowers on the organization. In effect, he "mandated" group participation and decision-making, as ironic as this may seem. Stowers' method was virtually a "leadership by exception" approach. Specifically, he permitted the group a wide range of discretion on most issues, with the exception of a few "sacred cows." There was (and indeed continues to be) some dissent as to the wisdom and effectiveness of the process, with some people preferring the clarity of leadership from a traditional CEO. However, the team approach actually worked quite well.

A few of Stowers' "sacred cow" issues concerned fund pricing and fund minimums. Historically, American Century had been known as a "no load, no minimum fund," and Jim Stowers, Jr., was known as the champion of the small investor. This "no minimum" practice was based on the belief that individuals would begin investing with relatively little money and gradually increase their investments over time. Since the company would lose money when account balances were very small, and because there were very large numbers of small, unprofitable accounts, the issue was a concern to many people on the executive committee. After several years of analysis and discussion at its planning meetings, the company abandoned its "no minimum" philosophy and adopted one that requires individuals to increase their minimum balances to $2,500 through a monthly contribution plan. This was a *major* philosophical change by Stowers and the company and it suggested to other members of the team that "sacred issues" could be discussed and possibly changed.

Changing the Game: Developing the Management Team's Capabilities

Another key aspect of American Century's program to make the transition to professional management was management development. The firm began a two-part program of development for its senior executives. First, the consulting firm responsible for assisting with American Century's planning process was asked to design and deliver a group-based management development program (MDP). This program consisted of a series of training modules focusing on core managerial skills like leadership effectiveness, time management, effective team decision-making, communication effectiveness, delegation effectiveness, and others. Each "module" or course focused not only on skill development, but also on how to "think" in ways consistent with effectively utilizing these skills. Each module or course was designed to build on the previous course so as to facilitate a process of continuous learning.

One component of the MDP specifically designed to help influence and enhance each individual's managerial behavior was management assessment feedback. Each of American Century's senior managers completed a set of four management effectiveness questionnaires dealing with:

1. The extent to which individuals had, overall, effectively made the transition to their current roles as senior managers.
2. Time management effectiveness.
3. Delegation effectiveness.
4. Leadership effectiveness.

Each executive received a confidential report that interpreted his or her scores and provided suggestions for development. The report also included standard scores or norms for effective management (based on the consulting firm's database) so that people could compare their own scores with the norms to identify any developmental opportunities. In addition, individuals were given information about the "composite" (average) scores of their own management group. Accordingly, they could benchmark their own scores against both the overall norms and American Century Company-specific norms. This information could then be used to help develop goals for improving individual effectiveness.

Another component of American Century's executive development effort was a one-on-one coaching program that was available to each member of senior management. This program involved a series of individual management development-advisory sessions geared to specific developmental issues faced by each manager. The program focused on each individual's role as a senior manager, and was intended to help make the transition from a technical or functional perspective to a true senior-level, general manager's perspective.

This individualized program (termed a "Personal Executive Development Program" or PEDP) also included additional assessment feedback information. Specifically, the five to seven people reporting to each executive completed the same set of management effectiveness questionnaires described earlier, but in this case were asked to respond about *their* senior manager. A report, based on questionnaire results, was given to each executive. This report included the "average" of the scores obtained from all those who completed the questionnaires about the executive, as well as the individual executive's own scores. Not only did feedback from direct reports (i.e., subordinates) really capture executives' attention, but the comparison of how they had rated themselves with the averages of their direct reports' ratings was a definite eye-opener. This specific, tangible feedback seemed to provide the added impetus needed for executives to work seriously with consultants in setting meaningful professional development goals—and then to make good use of the associated individualized training sessions provided. All the people who participated in this process improved as managers.

Changing the Game: The Transition of the Entrepreneur to the Next Generation

One of the most significant aspects of the professionalization of American Century was the transition of leadership from the firm's founder, James E. Stowers, Jr., to the next generation. In this instance, the transfer was both to James Stowers, III, the founder's son, as well as to other members of the company's senior executive team. It should be understood that this process needed to be carefully managed and sensitively handled to avoid problems and maximize the ability of the firm to continue operating effectively.

Jim Stowers III had joined American Century after graduating with a degree in business from Arizona State University. He became a member of both the equity portfolio management team and the firm's Executive Committee. In this capacity, he gained a great deal of experience to help prepare him for senior leadership in the firm. For several years, like other executives, he participated in a Personal Executive Development Program. In his case, this program was designed to help him develop the advanced management skills and ways of thinking required when he ultimately replaced his father as CEO. He was thirty years old when he first began to prepare for this transition in 1989.

In 1993, Jim Stowers III assumed the presidency of American Century. This transition from James E. Stowers, Jr., the entrepreneur who founded the company, to his son was memorialized by a bronze sculpture of one hand passing a relay race baton to another hand, which was kept at the corporate offices.

This story of transition is not merely one of Jim Stowers III developing his managerial skills. It is also the tale of an entrepreneur letting go and turning over control to the next generation—his son and the other professional managers who had been developed into an effective senior executive team. One of the most difficult issues for an entrepreneur is letting go of control over all aspects of operations after years of personally nurturing a firm's growth. When a company is a new venture, the entrepreneur cares for it like an infant and is concerned about every aspect of the business. However, as the company grows and matures, the effective entrepreneur must step back and allow others to develop and assume authority. Unfortunately, many entrepreneurs simply are not capable of letting go to this extent. Examples of those entrepreneurs who tended to retain a great deal of control of their firms include: Jack Tramiel at Commodore Computers, Karl Karcher at Karl

Karcher Enterprises, and Steven Jobs at Apple Computer. Unlike these entre-preneurs, James E. Stowers, Jr. was able to gradually and skillfully relinquish control of American Century.

One reason for the successful handoff from Stowers to the professional management team led by his son involves personality. Like other entrepreneurs, Stowers has strong opinions that are not easy to change. A classic individualist, he believes in doing "the right thing," and once he decides what the right thing is he does not change his mind quickly. Stowers could also be what some might call a micro-manager—he pays a great deal of attention to many details of the business. However, what differentiates him from many (if not most) entrepreneurs and made a transfer of power more likely to be successful were three related factors.

First, Stowers had a passionate belief that teams were better than individuals at making decisions. For example, American Century Investors is one of the relatively few mutual fund families where funds are managed by teams rather than by individuals. The "fund manager" is explicitly designated as a "team" and not an individual "super-star." This belief carried over to the management of the firm by the Executive Team. Second, unlike many entrepreneurs who hold strong views, Stowers is a very good listener. He can sit in meetings for hours, even days, and say little until something special arises. On many issues, his approach is essentially "do whatever you want." He was good at delegating authority and listening to his people. Third, once he made up his mind that the transition was "the right thing" and had to be made, he was fully committed to it, unlike many entrepreneurs who at the deepest level do not want to let go.

Stowers also utilized the consultants who were involved in the planning and management development processes with American Century to help him with this leadership transition. For a period of several years, Stowers had periodic dinner meetings with the two consultants who were working with his firm. The purpose of these meetings was to "touch base" on what was happening, assess the progress being made, and discuss issues involved in the transformation. During these meetings, Stowers could raise his concerns and the consultants could hear his point of view. They could discuss examples of problems experienced by other companies and other entrepreneurs dealing with the same issues. The consultants could also bring up the concerns of the Executive Team, while maintaining the anonymity of team members. In this way, Stowers and the firm had a third party outside the firm's political system and who could serve as a "bridge" to help facilitate the transformation.

Completing the Transformation: "Keeping Them from Falling on Their Own Sword"

In 1994, the six-year transition for James E. Stowers, Jr., and American Century was nearly complete. Now Stowers defined his role as: "Keeping them (the American Century senior executive group) from falling on their own sword." His role in the company had become one of serving as a "safety function" by using his experience in helping the team resolve only the most significant strategic organizational development issues. Accordingly, by 1994 the senior executive team had made the transition from high-level technical professionals to true senior level managers with responsibility for corporate management; James Stowers III had made the transition from a portfolio manager to a president and chief operating officer; and James E. Stowers, Jr., had made the transition from an entrepreneur and portfolio manager to a senior level elder statesman. The firm had become increasingly successful in terms of its growth (assets under management grew from $6 billion in 1989 to more than $50 billion in 1996), increased market share, and bottom-line profitability. In addition, the firm had increased its profile in its industry and positioned itself as an industry leader with a very promising future.

Postscript: Beyond the Transformation of the First Kind at American Century

Over the years, the senior executive group became increasingly sophisticated at management. In 1994, as they planned for the future of the company, they set ambitious, strategic, and growth-oriented goals. The firm's management began to articulate a new vision—they began to embark on a Transformation of the Third Kind. Part of this vision was to diversify the company's product line from a very substantial emphasis on equity mutual funds to a more balanced "portfolio" of fixed income as well as equity funds. This new vision grew out of management's continued focus on strategic planning as a tool in effectively managing the business.

This strategic decision led American Century to acquire the Benham Group in June 1995. The Benham Group consisted of mainly fixed income funds and was a perfect strategic fit with American Century's existing funds and new strategy. The Benham Group had more than $10 billion in assets under management, which brought the combined organizations to more than $40 billion in assets just after the acquisition was completed.

In August 1997, J. P. Morgan, the Wall Street giant, acquired a 45% stake in American Century for $900 million. This investment implied an overall value of $2 billion for American Century (45% of $2 billion = $900 million). In assessing whether this was a "good deal" for J. P. Morgan, an article in *BARRON'S*[5] commented on the value of a computerized system that American Century has developed for record-keeping. It noted that American Century's system was among the best in the business. One of its key features is optical imaging—this system can scan in and store every piece of written correspondence an investor sends to American Century. The article also noted the key role that such a system would play in attracting 401K pension business. In brief, it should be noted that this type of system is part of American Century's infrastructure, not its product *per se*, and in turn, the focus on and development of the company's infrastructure was a result of the type of planning process used by the firm, a planning process based upon the pyramid of organizational success presented in Chapter 2.

This business combination has positioned the firm for further growth and transformation, but that is another story and another transformation.

The Transformation to Professional Management at Compaq

Compaq Computer Company was founded in 1981. The company's experience in making the transformation from an entrepreneurship to an entrepreneurially oriented, professionally managed firm was quite atypical. Specifically, from the start, Joseph (Rod) Canion and his senior management team focused on building a sound organizational foundation and an organizational infrastructure that would allow Compaq to grow into a large, successful computer company. By 1983, when its first computers were released, Compaq had all the resources, systems, and structure needed to handle the hypergrowth that followed. It was, in many respects, an entrepreneurially oriented, professionally managed firm throughout its formative years. There are two distinct periods in Compaq's history to date. The first (1981 to 1991), was a time in which the company moved very rapidly from a new venture to effectively playing the game of an entrepreneurially oriented, professionally managed firm. We will focus on this time period here. In the second period of the company's life (1991 to 1994), Compaq experienced a period of sharp decline and revitalization. We will examine Compaq's experience with revitalization in Chapter 4.

Changing the Game: Compaq's Strategy

In 1981, IBM introduced its personal computer and was extremely successful. IBM was so successful, in fact, that within a year and a half of its release, the firm could not meet customer demand for its product. Recognizing that there was a great demand for personal computers that could run IBM software (which rapidly seemed to be becoming the industry standard), Compaq began to design one of the first IBM-compatible PCs. In addition, the firm decided to differentiate its product by making it portable.

Compaq's strategy was to focus on being IBM-compatible (so much so that they were almost slapped with a copyright infringement suit and had to re-engineer the product at the last minute) and acting as a technological leader who could, as a result, command a premium price for their products. Given the environmental condition cited above and the product the firm would be offering, Compaq's management team believed that within a very short time the firm would grow to at least $500 million. They therefore set about developing an infrastructure to support this goal.

Changing the Game: Development of Operational Infrastructure

The acquisition and development of adequate resources are often problems for entrepreneurial firms. Compaq solved this problem well. From the very beginning, Compaq got its financing primarily from private investors, including Ben Rosen, a venture capitalist who became chairman of the board. After resounding success in their first year of sales (they grew to $111 million in one year), financing was accomplished through profits and stock offerings.

Compaq also paid close attention to acquiring human resources. From the start, Compaq attracted a cadre of young, talented, energetic, and committed professionals and managers. Through their policies of pushing decision-making down the hierarchy and emphasizing teamwork as well as offering competitive salaries and benefits, Compaq was successful in attracting and keeping people. In acquiring the physical resources needed to support its growth, Compaq looked beyond the United States, becoming a multinational producer. By the mid 1990s, Compaq had three manufacturing sites in Singapore, Scotland, and Houston. Unlike most start-ups, Compaq instituted strong operational systems from its very inception. Meaningful financial controls and excellent forecasting systems were in place when production began. Unlike traditional product development where a new product progressed from marketing through design and engineering and then passed on to manufacturing, Compaq used teams of professionals from the various areas working together from the start to develop the products. Turf battles were minimized using this approach and the lead time shortened dramatically. The teams were responsible for making most product decisions; only rarely was top management involvement needed to resolve conflicts. The team-oriented approach was known internally at Compaq as "the process."

The company directed its advertising on key products and placed its ads for PC decision-makers and enthusiasts interested in high-performance state of the art through business and PC-oriented publications. To maintain quality, Compaq chose to do all assembling itself and did not subcontract any subassembly work. Sophisticated forecasting systems were used to estimate future demand for scheduling production. The dealers, not Compaq, were responsible for handling the delivery process. Every company operation was based on an official list of priorities that served as a guide to that operation's actions.

In the early 1980s, Compaq had numerous competitors vying for the same customers. Compaq forged a strategic alliance with its dealers to strengthen the visibility of its computers with customers. Unlike IBM and others who sold through dealers and also directly, Compaq committed to exclusively selling its products through dealers. To strengthen dealer relationships, Compaq trained each dealer's staff in selling and servicing its products. It also has helped dealers finance its inventory and accounts receivable. In return, Compaq got more shelf space and enthusiastic marketing of its products. Compaq was a new company with no existing sales staff. Since the company chose to use dealers, this became a strategic advantage for Compaq instead of a liability.

Changing the Game: Management Systems and Culture

From its inception, Compaq paid attention to its management systems and culture. Top management treated planning as its most important function, including the communication of results to all employees. Since decision-making was pushed down the hierarchy, Compaq realized that the key to a coordinated effort relied on keeping all players informed. Control systems were geared to measuring the results that the decision-maker could influence. Since timely development of new products is critical in an industry where the product life span is shortening all the time, the organization's structure reflected these needs with the extensive use of teams. Compaq also tried to have people with strong management capabilities who would help contribute to the firm's success. As already discussed, the firm's culture emphasized teamwork and team decision-making. It also supported the focus that Compaq had on understanding and serving the business customer (an absolute necessity if the firm was going to compete with IBM).

However, one key weakness in Compaq's management system would ultimately prove costly. Specifically, the company did not have a well-developed planning *process*; it had a plan developed from the very beginning, and did a great deal of ongoing, operationally oriented planning. But it lacked a true strategic planning process. This limitation made Compaq vulnerable, as we will see in Chapter 4.

Results

The preparation Compaq did and its ability to create the infrastructure needed to support its growth even before it needed it (i.e., it had operational and management systems to support a $500-million firm *before* it released its first product) greatly contributed to its success. In fact, some industry experts estimate that Compaq was more successful (based on estimated profits) than IBM during the first computer shakeout, which occurred in 1987.

Lessons to be Learned from the Transformation of an Entrepreneurship to a Professionally Managed Organization

This chapter has discussed three different companies and the transformations they have made to become professionally managed organizations. Each organization faced somewhat different circumstances.

With MediPro Industries, we saw a small company facing the classic transformation from an entrepreneurship to a professionally managed firm. In this case, there was no change in leadership. American Century Investors illustrates the special situation involving a family business transformation as well as the transformation to a professionally managed firm. Compaq Computers presents the unusual example of an organization that prepared to become a professionally managed enterprise from its inception.

In all three examples, the transformation was relatively successful. Taken together, these companies illustrate the different aspects of Transformations of the First Kind and learning to play the game of professional management effectively.

What can we learn from these actual experiences? If we step back from the details of each example, we see that the classic problem that occurs in all entrepreneurial firms and creates the need to change the game from an entrepreneurship to an entrepreneurially oriented professionally managed firm, is growth. As an organization grows in size, there is a need to change the organization's infrastructure to better support the larger organization it has become. This includes making changes in the enterprise's resources, operational systems, management systems, and culture—the top four levels or building blocks of the pyramid of organizational success.

Stated differently, as an organization grows, changes in size create the necessity for a different organizational model. Instead of an informal entrepreneurial model, the organization must change the game to that of an entrepreneurially oriented, professionally managed enterprise model. In terms of the four factors influencing the design of a business model, shown in Figure 2–1, the key factors in the transformation are size (Factor C) and the six building blocks (Factor B).

Unfortunately, many managers are so caught up in the details of day-to-day operations that they cannot see that the fundamental issue is the need to make a Transformation of the First Kind (i.e., a transformation from entrepreneurship to professional management). There are, however, some identifiable symptoms or early warning signals of the need for this transformation. These are the growing pains cited in Chapter 2 and defined in more depth in the example of MediPro Industries.

Another key lesson from these three examples is that when classic symptoms of organizational growing pains are experienced, more than an organizational tune-up is required. Instead, a comprehensive program designed to make a complete overhaul or transformation is necessary. Unfortunately, most entrepreneurs, by their nature, want a quick fix or magic pill. However, Transformations of the First Kind typically require two to three years or longer to accomplish.

Since these transformations do demand a major organizational tune-up, an organization will frequently require outside assistance to plan for, implement, and monitor the changes required. Consultants who specialize in helping firms manage growth-related issues can be of great assistance to the entrepreneur, senior management team, and others in managing this transformation. They bring an outsider's perspective, as well as the lessons of other organizations with similar experiences. This can be quite valuable to organizations (and their leaders) who are struggling to make sense of "what's wrong" and "what do I do about it?" Given the complexity of the transformation process, some organizations may find it difficult to execute it without outside consulting assistance. At a minimum, experienced consultants can reduce the risks involved in transformation.

A final lesson is that entrepreneurial transformations to professional management *can* be accomplished with the existing entrepreneur and management team remaining in place. Some people believe that transformation is only possible if the founder or existing management team is replaced. In fact, this view has been stated in academic literature.[6] One of the most frequent occurrences when a rapidly growing entrepreneurial company "hits the wall" and exhibits symptoms of growing pains is the replacement of the CEO. Sometimes this is precipitated by venture capitalists or bankers, who fear the loss of their investment or the potential opportunity cost of the aborted development of a business. Although replacement of the entrepreneur may be necessary in some instances, the examples presented in this chapter show that Transformations of the First Kind can be accomplished by an existing management team, if they are willing to change their own behavior and support the needed change in the firm itself.

The next chapter examines the challenges faced by several firms in need of revitalizing their operations and what steps they took to do so—Transformations of the Second Kind.

4

SUCCESSFUL REVITALIZATIONS
Transformations of the Second Kind

This chapter examines examples of three very different organizations that have had significant success in managing revitalization transformations. Two of our examples are entrepreneurial companies (a company we call "Miller Brothers" and Compaq Computers), and the third is Chrysler, a long established enterprise that involves one of the great revitalizations of the twentieth century.

The Revitalization Transformation at Miller Brothers, Inc.[1]

One of the first things that catches your eye when you enter Harry Miller's office is a cartoon hanging on the wall behind his desk. It shows a little boy who appears to be peeing, but his eyes are raised upward. An inscription states: "Please let there be one more real estate boom, and I promise not to piss it away this time!" This symbolized the situation at Miller Brothers, Inc., in 1988, after the firm had experienced more than twenty years of success but still found itself in a very troubled situation.

The Name of the Game at Miller Brothers: "Let's Make a Deal"

In the real estate development and management industry, the Miller Brothers were known for their flamboyance and their integrity; even after a loudly contested negotiation with a potential partner or an important anchor tenant, a handshake had always been as good as a signed agreement from the early days of the business. With a lot of foresight and hard work, Sam Miller had developed his first strip center in the early 1950s in a small midwestern town. His youngest brother, Harry, had joined him a few years later and together they had built one of the nation's major real estate development and management companies.

As Miller Brothers, Inc. (MBI), they formed alliances with department store giants, like May Company and Macy's, experienced great success building regional centers as well as community centers, and expanded from the Midwest to the East, South, and finally to the West.

The 1970s and 1980s were boom years for MBI, when opportunities seemed endless and the company could not add development, construction, marketing, and management staff fast enough to keep pace with the demand for new malls and strip centers. By 1988, annual revenues had reached about $750 million and the company had about 3,600 employees in the home office and its nationwide centers.

Sam and Harry thrived on the adrenaline of the deal-making process. They were fast moving, quick decision makers, who lived for the action of the deal. They were neither interested in operational details nor very involved in them.

The Catalyst for Transformation

During the late 1970s and throughout the 1980s, Miller Brothers experienced all the classic growing pains described in Chapter 2 (see Figure 2–7). During this period, as a result of rising real estate values, it was feasible for the Miller Brothers to refinance their properties and take out cash to reinvest in their business. These reinvestments consisted of monies both for new developments and operational expenses. The nature of the business was that the company could increase in value and assets as long as real estate appreciated, even if it broke even or incurred operational losses.

In the late 1980s, the development boom ended and the challenges facing Miller Brothers were daunting:

- The country was becoming saturated with shopping centers.
- Department stores were collapsing or consolidating, and cutting much tougher deals than ever before.
- In the West and East, increasingly stringent environmental standards were required, affecting all aspects of the development and construction process.
- Cities were requiring more and more concessions from developers for the right to build.
- Money was getting tight, with interest rates rising significantly.

As a result of these and other changes in their environment, the company no longer had the slack financial resources to continue with its aggressive, if sometimes poorly planned, developments and its other operational inefficiencies. Although it seemed as though the Miller Brothers had lost the "Midas touch," the reality was that the environment had changed and the company that had been created did not fit well in the new environment.

In addition to experiencing growing pains, Miller Brothers now began to experience many of the classic organizational revitalization pains, shown in Figure 2–8, and described below.

Strategic planning emphasizes form, rather than substance.   In very large firms, sometimes strategic planning becomes an end in itself (or an "event") versus a means to the end of serving as a guide for future organizational success. At Miller Brothers, it was not that strategic planning had evolved into such an event, but that it was not really done.

The type of planning that did occur at Miller Brothers focused on the analysis of deals, instead of planning for the growth and operation of the overall business. The culture and mind-set at Miller Brothers concentrated on "the deal on the table. " As a result, there was no long-range strategic plan, no contingency plans, and very little planning within the company's divisions of Development, Property Management, and Corporate Support.

As a result of this lack of planning, a number of Miller Brothers' personnel expressed several concerns about the business that are summarized in the following comments:

"We don't know which developments are targeted for completion, much less where the company is heading over the next five years."

"We don't know who has the ultimate authority to make decisions on deals with a given city, mall design, or tenant concession. One time a decision might be made by the Leasing VP, and another time Harry or even Sam might step into the middle of the negotiations."

"Is anyone captain of the ship?"

Indeed, Sam commented to one of the authors, who also served as a consultant to Miller Brothers beginning in the late 1980s, that he "stopped understanding his company more than twenty years ago."

The prevailing attitude among many Miller Brothers executives was: "You can't plan in this business, because it is a deal-driven business and we are entrepreneurs." In addition, some people argued, "We've been successful for many years without planning, so why do we need it?" Some also stated: "That's bureaucratic or too 'academic'."

However, not all the executives felt this was true. A small minority had begun to believe that Miller Brothers was headed for serious difficulties and it was no longer appropriate for business-as-usual tactics to be used. They believed that Miller Brothers had grown too large to operate in the informal, unplanned, unmanaged, "seat-of-the-pants" manner so often characterized as "entrepreneurial." Actually, some felt that the absence of a plan was leading the firm much closer to chaos.

Our managers don't know what they are doing and/or don't know what to do. Most senior managers knew their functions, such as Leasing, Property Management, Development, and Marketing, but they were not true managers. In fairness to them, they had never been asked to be managers or given the type of training that would have permitted them to develop the level of managerial skills required for an organization of the size and complexity Miller Brothers had become.

Each manager has his or her own kingdom; there's no sense of a unified direction. In addition to the lack of systematic planning and management development for the business as a whole and to a great extent as a consequence of it, there was also a lack of coordination and integration among the different organizational units at Miller Brothers, especially the core operational units of Development, Property Management, and Leasing.

To a very great extent, this aging pain was exquisitely characteristic of Miller Brothers. The company was development driven, and property managers sometimes felt like second-class citizens. Although a few developers worked hard to incorporate Property Management input into the decision-making process during a center's development, others did not. Developers could make decisions that met their short-term needs to bring the project in on time and within budget—without adequately considering the long-term needs of the mall management team who would be responsible for day-to-day operations and annual budgets for decades to come.

In contrast, because of the nature of their job and the Property Management reward system, property managers *had* to focus on longer-term planning as well as more systematic handling of operational issues. In frustration, they developed a collection of horror stories about how their annual budgets had been devastated by costly corrections that had to be made during the first year or two of operations, as a result of "bad decisions" by architects or construction vice presidents. One mall had been opened with the latest in lighting fixtures, elevated so high above the floor that no MBI equipment could reach them. In addition, Development had saved money by using inadequate asphalt covering for parking lots, causing some mall managers to invest thousands in resurfacing within the first few years of operations. There was no incentive or reward system reinforcement for Development and Property Management to set shared goals.

People are spending too much time covering their vested interests. When things went wrong, significant effort was invested in trying to figure out who was at fault versus working together to solve the problem. This was, in part, due to a lack of unified direction (resulting from an underdeveloped planning process) as well as the tendency for each manager to develop his or her own kingdom that tended to work in isolation from the rest of the organization. People frequently described the situation as one in which there was "a lot of finger-pointing" versus problem-solving.

We focus more attention on competing with each other than we do on competing with other companies. While there was a certain amount of political behavior occurring at MBI, the firm did not lose sight of their competition. The Miller Brothers and their management team were acutely aware of what competitors were doing in their markets and had taken steps over the years to secure and maintain strong relationships with their customers. Internally, however, the competition that existed between the different kingdoms was taking its toll on the ability of the firm to effectively and efficiently meet *all* its customer needs.

There are too many levels and too many people in the organization.   Another problem of the Miller Brothers organization, and a classic organizational aging pain, was that there were too many people and too many levels. As the organization had grown, people were literally "thrown" into and at new tasks. At one point, Sam asked the company's consultants rhetorically and somewhat plaintively: "Where did all these people come from and what do they all do?"

We have too many people doing the same thing and not enough people doing the right thing.   Another classic symptom of the need for revitalization at MBI concerned the paradox of simultaneously having "too many and too few people." In effect, the company seemed to be overstaffed in some areas while understaffed in others. This was attributable to the lack of overall organizational planning as well as the political atmosphere created by the independent kingdoms in the firm. Managers tended to protect *"their* people," regardless of the firm's overall needs. In addition, it was not always clear that MBI had enough people with the skills needed to effectively meet its long-term goals.

Some of the specific comments expressed by Miller Brothers' managers about this issue included:

> "Every MBI developer has a different way of doing business, and there is no standard process for any aspect of mall or residential project development. This leads to confusion when you have multiple project responsibilities for different developers."

> "Our computer and financial systems are in shambles. Different systems are used in different areas of the company; the systems don't interface, and multiple people are performing the same reporting tasks."

People aren't rewarded for performance; it's who you know, not what you do.   In MBI's political culture of independent kingdoms, people tended to be rewarded for loyalty to their managers. It sometimes didn't matter what an individual's actual performance was (relative to what goals *did* exist), as long as the individual continued to do what his or her manager said needed to be done. Questioning the authority of certain managers could result in being publicly humiliated or, at the extreme, psychologically or physically banished from the organization. Thus, the prevailing sentiment throughout much of the organization was: "It's who and what you know, not what you do."

People are increasingly unwilling to take risks.   As a key part of their personalities, Sam and Harry were very vocal, sometimes loud, and very comfortable
with "verbal combat." The brothers were also very colorful in meetings,
many times challenging and poking fun at each other. The naive outsider
might assume that there was hostility and even conflict going back and forth,
but this was simply part of their communication process; they were playing
with each other. Nevertheless, some people were intimidated by Sam and
Harry. After all, they were the owners, and they could, at times, also become
verbally aggressive toward other people in the firm. Although this behavior
was actually a sign that the person had been accepted and welcomed into
their corporate family, it was not always pleasant to be on the receiving end
of one of their verbal barrages. Sam, in particular, was comfortable with
hyperbole and might say that "everything is all screwed up," which really
meant that there simply was a problem or issue he wanted to discuss.

Even though their bark was far worse than their bite and people were
rarely terminated from Miller Brothers, many employees were unwilling to
confront Sam, Harry, and certain other senior executives. This contributed to
a situation in which people were unwilling to take risks. Therefore, most of
the issues regarding the need to change how the game was being played at
MBI were discussed in the halls rather than at corporate meetings, where
decisions could be made to actually do something about the current and
anticipated future problems facing the firm.

This unwillingness to take risks created a situation where, to a certain
extent, a resistance existed to new ideas and innovation at Miller Brothers,
especially if there was the possibility of affecting the way the firm operated.
This was especially true when it came to implementing new ways of operating that might increase the accountability of certain executives who had
enjoyed being left alone to manage their own kingdoms. Accordingly, there
was resistance to the idea of introducing systematic corporate planning in
the firm.

*On the surface, we are one big family, but there is a great deal of conflict below the
surface.*   Within the company, there were two different groups of managers
with very divergent views of the current state of the company's overall
health and how it ought to be managed in the future. The most powerful
group, the developers, who were nominally led by Sam and Harry, liked
things as they were. However, another group led by Gil Strom, who was in
charge of the property management function, felt that unless there were significant changes in how MBI operated, they were all poised for a sharp reversal of fortune. This Property Management group was frustrated not only with
the lack of a corporate plan articulating a clear sense of the future direction
for the company, but also with the lack of a forum for the open and candid
discussion of their views about the current state of the company as well as its
goals. In early 1988, they were merely a silent minority at the corporate
table, but this was to soon change.

In brief, on the surface MBI was still "one big happy family," but there was a great deal of conflict brewing below that surface. In a sense, it was possible to differentiate members of the two groups in terms of who "had it made." The developers got a piece of all of the deals and virtually all of them were affluent, if not truly wealthy. The people on the administrative side of the business had less of the "action" and depended to a great extent on their salaries and bonuses, which were both generous. In a sense, the latter group had a greater degree of self-interest in the long-term survival of MBI because their personal livelihood still depended on the firm's prosperity. If necessary, the developers could go out and do deals on their own, as a result of the financial and human capital they had acquired over the years. In addition, in the way deals were structured, a potential upside existed for a developer but no real downside, since Sam and Harry ultimately bore the financial risks. Accordingly, there was a great deal of motivation for administrative people to have the organization change its mode of operations, while there was a significant incentive for developers to keep "business as usual."

We've lost our momentum because we are mired in bureacracy and "red tape." One of the organizational aging pains shown in Figure 2–8 that certainly did *not* characterize MBI was the extent to which red tape affected the firm's ability to move quickly to take advantage of market opportunities. Miller Bothers actually tended to move too fast, and its planning could sometimes be characterized as "Ready, Fire, Aim" instead of the "Ready, Aim, Fire" of an entrepreneurially oriented, professionally managed firm.

We know what's best for our customers; we don't need to ask them. This was another aging pain that was not obviously present at MBI. Given the focus that Sam, Harry, and their management team placed on deals, there continued to be a strong focus on meeting the needs of current customers. In the context of the planning process, however, it was not always clear that the firm was taking a longer term look at this issue. It was unclear whether, in light of environmental changes, the firm had decided who its *future* customers might be and what steps they might take to meet these customers' needs.

The company's revenues were beginning to level off, and its profitability starting to decline. For many years, MBI had made more and more deals and used the refinancing opportunity provided by appreciating real estate values to fuel their growth. At the end of the 1980s, however, real estate values were either stagnant or in decline, and this tactic was no longer as easily available. Since Sam and Harry had to personally guarantee all loans, their own assets as well as the assets of the firm were at risk. The wolf, if not quite at the door, was beginning to prowl the neighborhood, and even Sam and Harry sensed this. However, they continued to operate in much the same fashion as they had in the past.

Initial Leadership for Changing the Game: Managing Upward

As Executive VP of Property Management and Administration, Gil Strom recognized that problems with internal operations were placing the firm at risk. He felt that nothing short of a complete transformation of MBI was required. He also believed that it was unlikely that, left to themselves, Sam and Harry would change the company. He, therefore, decided to try to be a catalyst for transformation.

After doing some research by checking with colleagues in other companies, he engaged a management consulting firm to assist with the revitalization of his own area, Property Management. After discussing the situation at MBI with the consultant, they adopted the strategy of helping the Property Management Division become a "model" of how the business ought to be managed, and, in turn, trying to "manage upward" by being a role model for the rest of the firm.

The consulting firm began its work by conducting an organizational audit of the strengths and limitations of Property Management. Gil assisted the consulting team in obtaining as much access as possible to other parts of the company as well. When the audit was completed, Gil arranged for Sam, Harry, and the entire senior executive team to attend the presentation of audit results. There were specific recommendations for dealing with the transformational pains managers had identified, but what most caught the Miller Brothers' attention was a slide prepared by the consultant. It showed a simple cartoon: a cement truck pouring dollar bills down the manhole of a city street. This image was intended to represent what was happening at MBI; as they saw it, the color drained from Sam and Harry's faces—at a gut level, they had recognized the validity of what the consultant said. However, while Gil Storm proceeded with implementing many of the consultants' recommendations in the Property Management Division, Sam and Harry were not quite ready to make any wholesale changes in the entire firm yet.

Further Catalysts to Change the Game

Two key events happening nearly simultaneously finally caught the Miller Brothers' attention. First, one of the company's primary competitors and a previously unassailable giant in the industry, Campeau, faced bankruptcy. If that could happen to Campeau, why not to MBI? Second, three long-term friends, business associates, and advisors to Sam and Harry confronted them with a friendly prediction: either they bite the bullet now, make some tough decisions about budget-cutting and foregoing deals where profit could not be guaranteed, or the brothers could watch while their *personal* wealth was siphoned away into the company at an ever increasing rate. These friends and advisors included a past bank president, a senior partner in a prominent local CPA firm, and a president of an investment company. They were *not* members of a Board of Directors.

Recognizing what had just happened to Robert Campeau's firm, the consultant decided to write a memo to Sam and Harry suggesting that MBI was facing a potential crisis and offering his assistance, since he was already on retainer in connection with work for Property Management.

Leadership to Change the Game: The Eight Hundred-Pound Gorilla and Supporting Leaders

Sam was the person who had started the firm. He was a classic entrepreneur: creative, hard-working, highly intelligent, and able to make quick decisions. Although the firm was a partnership between both brothers, Sam was the spiritual leader and "the 800-pound gorilla." Harry called the consultant and said, "Your memo worked. Sam says, 'Let's do it'." This was critical because nothing would have happened without Sam's blessing and support.

As a first step, the consultant suggested that he facilitate a joint meeting of the Miller brothers with their three friends/advisors to identify the top few issues to be addressed. Given the long history of trust with these advisors, the consultant felt that they might help keep Sam and Harry's feet to the fire when the brothers made commitments. The group called itself the Arizona Group, because they often spent time together in their Arizona vacation homes.

At this time, Sam's son, Robert, an MBA from an Ivy League university with a very successful six-year track record on Wall Street, joined MBI as Chief Financial Officer. As an MBI owner and senior manager, he also joined the Arizona Group in meetings every six to eight weeks. Perhaps most important, in his role as CFO, Robert began a detailed assessment of the firm's financial agreements overall and on a property-by-property basis. This was the start of the financial transformation that allowed MBI to survive a time of tremendous industry upheaval.

Changing the Game at MBI: Delegation of Leadership and "Getting Our House in Order"

There is a saying in management lore: "Lead, follow, or get out of the way." At one of the first Arizona Group meetings, Sam articulated his concept of his role in the organization's transformation process. He said:

> I am not the person to lead these changes. I am a deal maker, not a manager. This process must be led by Harry—as much as I hate to admit it—since he is only slightly better than me as a manager and his deals have gotten us into as much trouble as mine. But he is the one who is best for what we need to do now.

Sam's statement was couched in humor, but it contained wisdom as well. In brief, Sam stated that he knew that management was not his forte and therefore someone else should assume the responsibilities of directing the transformation that had to be made at MBI. It was his opinion, supported by other members of the Arizona Group, that this role should be filled by his brother, Harry.

Harry, like Sam, was a quintessential deal-maker. He was not the most structured individual in the world, but he had the willingness to assume the responsibilities of being the coordinator of the overall effort to restructure the company. Like his brother, Harry had a large personal stake in the company and he was motivated to do whatever he had to do to protect the family's assets. In this context, he was a "600-pound gorilla."

The third senior player, Robert brought a tremendous set of skills and motivation to the team. He also brought a fundamentally different perspective from other family members. He had been trained as a professional manager and a financial manager, and, accordingly, his orientation was critical to helping the firm complete a successful transformation.

During an initial meeting with the consultant, Harry summarized the immediate MBI mission as "getting our house in order." This would require a multistage process. As identified by the Arizona Group, the first stage of this process would involve:

- Drafting the broad outlines of a mission and strategic direction for MBI.
- Helping clarify the roles of Sam, Harry, and Robert.
- Addressing the company's liquidity situation (including moving toward a smaller, more efficient organization that reflected the decrease in new development opportunities).
- Evaluating the strengths and limitations of the current MBI senior executive team and redefining their roles.
- Developing accountability (and a more professional management mind-set).
- Developing improved operating systems.
- Involving the executive team in a more comprehensive strategic planning process based on the direction set by Sam, Harry, and Robert, with input from the Arizona Group.

Changing How the Game Was Played at MBI Through the Development of New Systems

Harry decided to request that the consultant team conduct structural reviews of Development and Construction and all financial departments companywide. His ultimate goal was to help ensure that each development project was run as cost effectively as possible. Other goals were to have the optimal development project team in size and composition in place for each project, and to professionalize the management of the business's entire development and financial sides. Harry made his decision despite Robert's vocal objections about the expenditure and the more subtly stated objections of the Executive Vice President of Development, who potentially had the most to lose from a study of his department; he could lose personnel *and* his own appearance of invulnerability. Robert simply did not want consultants involved. He felt that they (MBI) could do the required work themselves, without incurring consulting fees.

While the consulting team began the structural audits, MBI's senior executive team started the strategic planning and role clarification processes critical to MBI's first phase of organizational development. A third component of organizational development at MBI was one-on-one coaching for Harry to assist him in performing some of the critical functions of a corporate president that he had been neglecting in favor of deal-making and development responsibilities.

Changing How the Game Was Played Through Leadership

During different phases of the transformation process, "different" leaders emerged to help make the process a success. Gil Strom's leadership was to help initiate the transformation at MBI. Sam's was to bless the process and take it company-wide. Harry's was to oversee "the big picture." Now, in the next phase, another dimension of leadership was required: leadership to implement required change in day-to-day operations at MBI. Here, the best person for the job was Robert, Sam's son. Robert was extremely task oriented and he understood, perhaps better than anyone else, the long-term consequences of the ongoing drain in the company's financial resources. This led to an almost single-minded focus on reducing costs and getting things under control. Thus, while Harry led the charge in looking at some of the longer range issues, Robert's primary focus was to get MBI's financial agreements and operations under better control.

One of his major contributions involved the corporate budgeting process. Robert had each executive in the organization prepare detailed budgets and give a budget presentation. Initially, Robert examined these budgets almost on a line-by-line basis in order to reduce overhead. On the one hand, he might have been accused of micromanagement. However, given MBI's near-crisis state (brought about by significant environmental changes combined with MBI continuing to operate with a "business as usual" mind-set, even in the face of a crisis), this approach led to a total reorientation of the mind-set and attitude of people at MBI.

For years, costs had been out of control. Managers had been unwilling to significantly decrease spending. Robert's approach challenged MBI's corporate culture and behavior. However, since people do not like "takeaways," this aspect of culture change was not comfortable and Robert was not the most popular senior executive. He was willing to stand firm for the short- and long-term interests of the company. Robert was also involved in several other aspects of operational improvement. He assumed considerable responsibility in dealing with bankers and others to restructure financial deals and transactions. He brought in a new senior executive to assume responsibilities for the MIS area and provide better financial information to managers. He led the team that focused on the "work-out work" on MBI's "difficult" properties, deciding whether properties should be refinanced, renovated and remarketed, or sold. Both leading this effort and training others to consider a broader range of alternatives were critical to MBI's revitalization.

Results of the Revitalization Transformation

In early 1993, about three years after Gil Strom had asked for consulting assistance in professionalizing Property Management, Harry could feel proud of the transformation at MBI that he and his team had accomplished. Observable results of this effort included the following:

- Management had finally accepted the fact that a more cost-conscious and systematic approach to doing business was here to stay. MBI's culture was beginning to change to reflect this new understanding.
- MBI was in a better financial position than it had been a year before. New financing had been negotiated on some properties and company overhead had been reduced through Roberts' examination and elimination of budget items.
- Structural changes had reduced duplication across departments, and Harry now had a new Management Committee that he hoped was the right mixture of "old" and "new" blood.
- A major "bet the company" project was on track, getting the executive attention it required.

The executive team through Robert's organization and elimination of budget items, had gone through a shared planning process and completed the first corporate plan. While MBI's financial crisis had dictated a short-term focus to the plan, in the next planning cycle, they could do a better job of focusing on long-term strategic issues.

Coordination among VPs and their respective departments had improved, partially as a result of the strategic planning process.

The Property Management Division continued to improve operations in ways that directly affected the bottom line. Gil Strom, in fact, had begun implementing the processes that would make this a reality shortly after he and his team had received the results of their audit. These included implementing a strategic planning process and a management development program.

Despite resistance at the highest levels of Development, other Development personnel were designing and adopting more standardized processes for managing development projects.

For someone who had no inherent desire to be president, Harry felt he had done a respectable job of "getting our house in order." He had been assisted by Sam's blessing, Robert's financial acumen and discipline, the consultant's skills at revitalization transformation, and the efforts of many people throughout MBI. Under his leadership, the team had done their job: the foundation for MBI's future was now in place.

The Revitalization Transformation at Compaq

During the period from 1983 (which was its first year of sales) to 1991, Compaq's revenues grew from $111 million to over $3 billion. In 1991, due to changes in the environment and changing customer needs, Compaq suffered its first loss. Compaq responded swiftly to the challenge, and in less than two years had grown into a stronger and more effective organization. This startling and successful turnaround was possible because Compaq's infrastructure for organizational effectiveness had been consciously developed and managed from its inception. Compaq only needed to change its focus; it did not have to develop a new infrastructure. Without this sound infrastructure, it is highly unlikely that Compaq could have met the challenge as quickly and effectively as it did.

The Changing Environment for Compaq

By 1990, events were taking place that changed the PC market. The product life cycle was shorter than ever before while demands from customers for more timely and sophisticated support were rising. In addition, Compaq's competitors like Dell Computer and Gateway were lowering their margins and prices, offering products that were technologically comparable to Compaq, and going after market share. The market was segmenting into new configurations of customers with unique needs. Competitors responded with more and more product introductions to meet the needs of customers in these new segments.

Compaq, which had designed its entire infrastructure around the notion of providing technologically superior products at premium prices, essentially "got caught" by other IBM-clones who offered very similar technology at lower prices. Consumers began to, in essence, ask: "Why should I pay for a Compaq machine, when I can get something very similar at a significantly lower price?" By 1991, the world was well into a recession, and Compaq suffered its first loss: $71 million on sales in excess of $3 billion. In addition, Compaq laid off 1,700 employees (14% of its workforce) when it announced the loss.

Leadership of the Revitalization

Unfortunately, a significant difference of opinion existed between Rod Canion and Compaq's Chairman of the Board, Benjamin Rosen. Rosen had helped provide the venture capital required by Compaq when it was a new venture—he was more than a figurehead on Compaq's board. He believed that the environment had changed, and, in turn, Compaq needed to transform itself to the new realities of greater competitors and lower margins. Rod Canion disagreed.

Compaq's board response was swift; Rod Canion, co-founder and president, was asked to resign, and Eckhard Pfeiffer, who had developed the international operations, became president. Pfeiffer immediately initiated a revitalization process for Compaq, which involved changes in all six key building blocks of the business.

Changing the Game: Markets and Products

Pfeiffer quickly set to the task of returning Compaq to profitability. His message was simple: the market was now far more price conscious than before and was unwilling to lower quality expectations. Compaq's costs for design and production were too high, expenses and overhead costs were also too high, premium pricing was untenable in the new market, customer support was inadequate, distribution was too narrowly focused, and customer communication was poor. Compaq had to change its strategy to meet the new market conditions. To succeed, Compaq had to focus on the total PC market, not just the high-end segment. In brief, the company needed to reposition itself regarding price, promotion, and place. From a high-priced, high-cost, low-volume company, Compaq transformed to a low-priced, low-cost, high-volume producer while maintaining its focus on quick product development using leading edge technology.

Less than eight months later, Compaq announced forty-five new models. It also drastically lowered its price structure so it met the desktop and portable PC clones head-on. In response to complaints by potential customers that its products were hard to find as well as to challenge Dell's increasing market share, Compaq greatly expanded its distribution channels. It upgraded its service and support programs, even providing support for other vendors' products. It also began to implement plans to offer bundled PCs, where the product is offered with software already installed to meet specific segment needs.

Changing the Game: Resources and Operational Systems

Compaq was overstaffed, given its new market and product strategy and existing market conditions. As a result, to lower costs, the company laid off 17% of its employees. Because Compaq responded so quickly to its first loss, the negative impact on financial resources was minimized. Although there was excess production capacity, if the new product offerings proved successful, it would be needed.

The company's operational systems were re-engineered to meet the new cost goals. In the past, the processor boards, the heart of a PC, could go through fourteen redesigns because designs of the other components were constantly changing. This was reduced to three redesigns of processor boards. In the production process, the high cost of the burn-in process— where each PC is run for ninety-six hours to detect any defects before the unit leaves the factory—became a target for scrutiny. By analyzing the data on actual failures, engineers determined that two hours of burn-in was more than adequate.

For purchasing, lowering the costs of materials became the top priority because they accounted for 80% of the company's manufacturing costs. Compaq's emphasis on quality had led to the production of components that were excellent, but whose costs were very high. Compaq changed its strategy and began to use components that were being purchased by other manufacturers.

More radical was the edict to lower production costs 50%. To achieve that goal, the entire production process was re-engineered around a new list of priorities. This was done by a team approach. Every step in the production process was scrutinized and redone to achieve that goal. Efficiencies in the utilization of existing resources were experienced everywhere. Factories that traditionally ran only one shift were now running two and three. When bottlenecks appeared in the distribution of goods to its distribution channels, Compaq took over the transportation function because the increase in output more than covered the costs of assuming this function.

Changing the Game: Management Systems and Culture

With the exception of its planning process, Compaq had and was utilizing fairly effective management systems and a fairly well-developed culture management process. The company was able to build on these capabilities in its revitalization process.

Eckhard Pfeiffer kept and even expanded the teamwork concept that was the linchpin of the firm's culture by insisting that conflict resolution was now each team's responsibility. In the past, conflicts between the various functions were often resolved by the president. One sign of the success of Pfeiffer's policy of not tinkering with the culture is that very few managers left the organization after he became president. Pfeiffer did make one change in culture and the firm's performance management system: he began basing executive compensation on such criteria as product profitability and reduced cycle times. This was intended to transform management's behavior and help keep them focused on bottom-line profit.

While Pfeiffer does not have a charismatic style of management, his leadership in focusing Compaq's energies is very impressive. He understands that his role is to provide direction and goals that everyone clearly comprehends. His role is also to ensure that mechanisms are in place to expedite and monitor the efforts made to meet those goals. Although he inherited an organization that had a superb foundation for meeting the challenges of change, his successful management in keeping the key elements of the culture and systems is exemplary.

The Results of Revitalization

The results of the changes made to meet the challenges created by new market conditions is that sales increased to $7.2 billion by the end of 1993, representing an astounding 75.4% increase over the previous four quarters; net profits increased by $462 million, up 116.9%; and return on equity is now an impressive 17.4%. This profit was more than the combined profits of IBM and Apple. Compaq's market share was 10%, up from the 3.8% when Pfeiffer took over. Compaq is now producing products for the entire personal computer market, from pocket communicators to home computers to sophisticated servers.

At present, Compaq is the market leader based on market share. The company's stock (after a split) had substantially increased during the period from 1994 through 1997. The revitalization transformation led by Pfeiffer was successfully completed.

The Revitalization Transformation at Chrysler

Chrysler is one of the largest industrial enterprises in the United States and the world. In 1978, it had more than $17 billion in sales and a market share of 13.6%. It was one of the Big Three automobile companies, and it had a long history.

In terms of both its size and the nature of its business, Chrysler was very different from Compaq and Miller Brothers. However, in terms of the problems it faced, a considerable amount of similarity exists among all three companies. Despite its size, its substantial resources, and even its storied tradition as one of the earliest and greatest automobile companies, Chrysler was on the brink of failure and required a complete revitalization transformation.

Chrysler at the Time of Lee Iacocca's Arrival

To put it mildly, finances were precarious when Lee Iacocca arrived at Chrysler in 1978. Although Chrysler had sales of $17 billion, the company lost $159 million in the third quarter, and $248 million for the year. These losses could not be attributed to general market conditions, because both Ford and General Motors (GM) were enjoying handsome profits in 1978.

The company was facing a Catch-22. Its costs of production were the highest among the Big Three, while it had the lowest profit margins because most of its sales were in the low end of the market. Chrysler was also paying the price for actions taken during the recession of 1973 to 1974, when thousands of engineers and designers had been laid off. This, in turn, delayed the introduction of new models, giving the competition the advantage in 1978. It also cost Chrysler, which had been known for its engineering, one of its key intangible assets and long-term sustainable competitive advantages.

Markets and Products

Chrysler's position in the market was relatively weak because its products appealed to older, conservative, blue-collar customers who tended to buy basic models with few high-profit options. These customers were extremely price conscious, and the products competing for their attention were used cars. In comparison, Chrysler's competitors enjoyed the support of more affluent customers who were willing to spend on options and sophisticated styling.

Resources and Operational Systems

The financial resources needed by Chrysler for new product development and regulatory compliance were strained. Many of Chrysler's physical resources (plants and equipment) were aged and inefficient. Chrysler's human resources were also relatively weak when compared to its competitors. Human capital in engineering, design, and management had been depleted as a result of layoffs and downsizing. The morale of the assembly-line workers in inner-city, antiquated plants was very low.

Chrysler's relationships with suppliers were weak, too. While GM and Ford could play suppliers against one another, Chrysler's orders were much smaller (because they also tried to have multiple suppliers for a given item) and they therefore lost leverage in their dealings with suppliers. The relationship with dealers was also poor. Dealers did not commit to car orders. They would hold off orders, waiting for massive discounts that would typically arise when inventory levels became too high because of Chrysler's inability to adjust production to demand on a timely basis.

Lee Iacocca arrived to find virtually no controls, accountability, or discipline. This resulted, periodically, in abnormally high inventory levels of finished goods that then became part of what was termed the "sales bank"—a euphemism for the inventory of unsold merchandise.

Management Systems and Culture

Planning was a very new phenomenon at Chrysler. The very first company-wide, long-range plan had been completed in late 1976 under John Riccardo. Prior to 1976, planning had been done informally and on an *ad hoc* basis by top management. The management development function was not a formal part of the organization. Little or no formal training was offered to groom managerial talent.

In terms of structure, Chrysler was a model of "organizational chaos." In principle, the company was functionally organized. However, each function at Chrysler (e.g., engineering, manufacturing, sales) operated as a separate fiefdom with no central authority, direction, or coordination. Oddly, each function took pride in treating the other functions with contempt. For example, purchasing avoided communicating with manufacturing, engineering would not deal with marketing and production, and so on. Consequently, decisions were made by each area in splendid isolation.

Chrysler's control systems were also weak. Managerial financial controls were virtually nonexistent. Top management could tell that money was lost, but not how it was lost.

Chrysler's culture was also dysfunctional. There had long been an engineering-dominated culture at Chrysler, one that ignored product planning and marketing. Cooperation between the functions was disdained; each function perceived other functions as natural enemies.

Confrontation was the norm. The pie was considered finite, and resource allocation was a zero-sum game. Whatever one group got had to be at the expense of the other groups. Compromise was considered a sign of weakness. Each group considered the other with suspicion. There was a perceived conflict of interest between white- and blue-collar workers, and the same was true of suppliers, dealers, and Chrysler. Each unit of the firm jealously protected its prerogatives against the encroachment of others.

In brief, there was not a team or community of interests at Chrysler. It was a war of all against all. Accountability and responsibility for decisions made and actions taken were also alien concepts.

Beginning to Change the Game at Chrysler

John Riccardo brought Lee Iacocca in as president of Chrysler Motors. One of the inducements Riccardo offered was the promise to make Iacocca Chief Executive Officer after one year, because he felt so strongly that Iacocca's skills were really the answer to the problems Chrysler faced. This was a courageous decision because Iacocca had been fired by Henry Ford and had a reputation as somewhat of a loose cannon. But Riccardo, like Sam Miller, perceived the need for a revitalization transformation, and believed that someone else (notably Lee Iacocca) was the person to do it.

When Iacocca came on board in November 1978, his immediate goal was to return Chrysler to profitability. The first steps involved changes in operational and management systems. These steps included:

- Reorganizing by separating sales from manufacturing.
- Placing purchasing with manufacturing instead of engineering.
- Reducing the number of dealers.
- Improving quality through creation of joint UAW-Chrysler "quality" programs, as well as instituting Quality Control systems with suppliers.
- Instituting meaningful financial and managerial control systems.

The long-term goal was to become a low-cost producer through downsizing and better supplier relations.

In 1979, Chrysler faced an oil crisis and economic recession that was combined with spiraling interest rates. The result was plummeting auto sales. Chrysler's losses reached $1 billion! After unsuccessfully seeking regulatory relief from the federal government, Chrysler then received the famous "bailout," or loan guarantees.

As promised when he was recruited to join Chrysler, Lee Iacocca assumed the CEO position after Riccardo retired in September 1979, a few months earlier than originally anticipated. Shortly thereafter, Iacocca made a spectacular gesture of sacrifice by downgrading his salary to $1 a year. This was a critical step toward changing the "everything for me, nothing for Chrysler" culture that had previously existed.

Changing Leadership at Chrysler

One of Iacocca's major steps in beginning the transformation process was to assemble a new senior management team. Some of the key players are noted below. The new leadership group operated as a team, but with each individual had specific responsibilities and objectives that would help the company develop the infrastructure needed to operate effectively within its new environment.

Paul Bergmoser was a former Ford vice president in charge of purchasing and an expert in material control. His task was to put quality-control people back into purchasing while developing reliable relationships with suppliers. He had joint responsibility with Hans Matthias (whose roles and responsibilities are discussed below) for putting product development on track with better scheduling.

Richard Dauch was recruited from Volkswagen of America as Executive Vice President of Manufacturing in 1980. His mission was to bring quality and reliability to the manufacturing and assembling of vehicles. He automated the manufacturing and assembly processes and increased robot usage from 300 to 1,242. He was responsible for initiating rigorous training programs for line workers. He also introduced line sequencing where an item stays in line until it meets the specs. He was responsible for the implementation of a "just-in-time" inventory system that resulted in higher inventory turnover rates, thus reducing production costs.

Gerald Greenwald was recruited from Ford Motors as controller in April 1979. His task was to develop the financial managerial accounting systems needed to establish control, accountability, and discipline throughout Chrysler. He centralized accounts payable so that it was now feasible to manage cash flow and analyze costs. In addition, he put in controls to track warranty costs. He was later promoted to Executive Vice President of Finance with a seat on the Board of Directors.

Gar Laux was a former Ford executive in charge of marketing and sales. He was hired first as a consultant in 1979, and then became Executive Vice President of Sales and Marketing. He was responsible for establishing sales training programs for dealers. He also began systematic market planning, eliminated the dysfunctional "sales bank" (over the protests of dealers), and separated the sales forces of the Chrysler/Plymouth product lines from the Dodge lines.

Hans Matthias was a former Ford vice president in charge of manufacturing. He was also hired first as a consultant in 1979, and then came on board as the Executive Vice President of Manufacturing. His mission was to improve quality. To achieve this, he instituted the joint "UAW–Chrysler Quality Program," in which quality task forces were responsible for a particular system from conception to realization. In addition, he reduced the firefighting syndrome on the production line by making quality verification an integral part of the process. Finally, he established a system to resolve disputes between designers and manufacturing *before* production began. He also had joint responsibility with Bergmoser for putting product development on track.

Hal Sperlich was a former Ford executive and friend of Iacocca. He was hired as Vice President of Products and Planning early in 1978, and later promoted to Group Vice President of Product Planning, Design, and Engineering. His task was to get the front-wheel drive K-cars launched on schedule with acceptable quality.

This team, under the leadership of Lee Iacocca, focused on all the six key building blocks required by successful organizations, as we will see below.

Changing the Game: Markets and Products

The year 1979 was a disastrous one for the auto industry, with Chrysler suffering its worst sales since 1974. While the Big Three automakers were all committed to providing a full range of products for all segments of the passenger car market, Chrysler had no viable products to compete with the very popular front-wheel drive "X cars" from GM. As a result, Chrysler experienced greater losses in market share. In addition, Japanese automobile manufacturers continued to gain share in the smaller car segments at the expense of the Big Three, especially Chrysler.

Because the costs of producing new products were very substantial and Chrysler had limited financial resources, it searched for a joint venture partner to design and manufacture a new small car. Chrysler was unsuccessful in finding a partner for this project, even though GM and Toyota did have luck in a similar joint venture.

Chrysler continued to have sales and product problems during the period from 1979 to 1981, but it began to make some progress. In 1979, the Dodge Omni/Plymouth Horizon subcompacts sold well due to the oil embargo. In September 1980, the K-cars were introduced (eighteen months after the very successful X-cars from GM). Although these cars were impressive to the public and critics, sales were weak because the production mix was weighed heavily toward "loaded" cars that were priced too high.

During the period from 1982 to 1984, Chrysler's share of the truck and car market increased. More important, Chrysler began to attract more of the most economically desirable market segments ("Yuppies"), who were able to purchase more expensive and more profitable cars. These segments had traditionally avoided Chrysler products, but Chrysler began reaching out to them with new products.

In 1982, Chrysler successfully introduced the LeBaron and Dodge 400 convertibles, which were the first American-produced convertibles in ten years. In 1983, the company launched the Chrysler Laser/Dodge Daytona sports cars and the Voyager/Caravan minivans. The minivans were extraordinarily popular: 148,000 minivans were sold without benefit of advertising. By introducing the minivan, Chrysler had created a new automotive market segment. By 1984, Chrysler's break-even point was less than 1.2 million units, a significant improvement from prior years.

Changing the Game: Resources and Operational Systems

As much as Lee Iacocca and his management team accomplished, one of the keys to Chrysler's successful revitalization was the now famous federal loan guarantee or "bailout." In 1979, these federal loan guarantees kept Chrysler from bankruptcy and gave it the "breathing room" it needed so the revitalization process could take effect. Other financial factors were at work as well. In 1981, lenders converted $686 million of their debt to preferred stock while suppliers and workers made financial concessions.

During this period (1979 to 1982), Chrysler was able to obtain new credit in the form of a $500-million refinancing package from thirty-nine major banks. The firm also received $239 million from the sale of its defense subsidiary. Twenty of the company's plants were also closed or consolidated; the remaining 40 were modernized.

Downsizing (through layoffs of white- and blue-collar workers) continued to bring Chrysler's cost structure into line with industrial standards. By 1982, Chrysler had cut its total workforce from 160,000 to 80,000 with its white collar staff cut from 40,000 to 21,000. The number of dealers was also reduced significantly.

A key factor in Chrysler's success in reducing its workforce and thus its labor costs was a partnership relationship with the UAW. During the period from 1979 to 1982, the UAW accepted concessions amounting to savings of $1.1 billion. As part of this new relationship between UAW and management, Douglas Fraser, head of the UAW, received a seat on the Chrysler Board of Directors.

In 1983, a new contract was signed with the UAW where workers regained $400 million that was given up during the crisis. During this period, executives and managers started to receive many of the perks that were sacrificed during the crisis and the profitability of the firm's remaining dealers increased substantially.

Chrysler also improved its relationships with suppliers. First, it reduced the number of its core suppliers. This, in turn, increased Chrysler's importance as a customer for the remaining suppliers. Chrysler and its suppliers also began cooperative programs on quality issues. For example, a quality program was implemented where knowledgeable Chrysler retirees were placed at suppliers' plants to advise them on the needs of Chrysler's assembly line.

In addition to focusing on its resources, Chrysler also revamped its operational systems. A major area of improvement involved the systems associated with production of cars and trucks. These included the actual production on the assembly line, the procurement of inputs to the production process, the systems for assessing how well products met specifications, and systems determining how much and when items should be made. The rationale was that with simpler, better production systems, Chrysler would make better cars for less money, thereby lowering its break-even point.

Chrysler simplified its production process by using a single-car "platform" (the K-platform) for most models. Using this approach, the number of parts required were reduced from 75,000 to 40,000, resulting in a $1-billion saving in inventory carrying costs. Another technique of production simplification involved bundling options into a limited number of packages. For example, electric door locks were always offered with electric windows.

Chrysler also implemented rigorous quality control systems on arriving components from suppliers as well as on finished products before they left for dealers. In addition, the production function increased its use of automated processes, such as robots, allowing for a higher level of consistent quality. Line workers received rigorous training programs so they could also monitor the quality process. Chrysler also implemented the "just-in-time" (JIT) inventory system where supplies arrive when needed rather than using the stockpiling system. This, in turn, reduced inventory carrying costs.

By 1982, Chrysler had developed the ability to match factory output to market demand. Production increased from 1.2 million units in 1982 to 2 million in 1984. The joint quality program with UAW was spread throughout all Chrysler plants.

Chrysler's long-term goal was to become the low cost producer of the Big Three. Ironically, since Chrysler was less vertically integrated than either Ford or General Motors, it was able to use this "weakness" to its advantage by contracting with suppliers who gave the lowest bids and then involving them in its quality program. More recently, GM and Ford have been trying to emulate Chrysler in this practice. By the mid-1980s, Chrysler met its goal.

Changing the Game: Management Systems and Culture

Soon after Iacocca's arrival, many long-tenured Chrysler executives retired. Their departures speeded up the transformation to professional systems of planning and budgeting because there was less resistance to change. A new performance appraisal system was introduced. Performance appraisals were now performed against standards that were understood by both manager and employee. The design of the organization was also streamlined: two layers of management in manufacturing and several layers in administration were eliminated.

In the new Chrysler, executive bonuses were based on quality, productivity, market share, and profits rather than on political skills and clout. In 1983, the Office of the Chairman was created to strengthen Chrysler's management. It was composed of Iacocca, Gerald Greenwald (Vice Chairman), Harold Sperlich (President), and Bennett Bidwell (Executive Vice President) who was hired in 1983 from Ford to run Sales and Marketing. One of the purposes of this office was to decentralize some of the decision-making away from Iacocca.

The compensation of both white-collar and blue-collar workers increased. Management received very large raises and bonuses, along with stock option plans. However, the cooperative spirit that was so dominant during the crisis began to weaken to some extent. Specifically, the UAW complained that the executives and managers received a larger share of the bounty than its members did.

The culture of Chrysler also had to change significantly to facilitate its revitalization and survival. First, cooperation had to replace confrontation. Thus, the fiefdoms had to be dismantled. Under Iacocca's leadership, there was a significant turnover in top management. This enabled Iacocca to change the composition of Chrysler's management significantly. In addition, the culture of focusing on "splitting the pie" had to change. By reducing his own pay to $1 a year, Lee Iacocca sent a powerful message to all stakeholders, including employees, unions, and suppliers, on the need to sacrifice. Another key cultural dimension that helped Iacocca at Chrysler was the "cult of strong leaders." Iacocca achieved the status of a "savior" during this period. He was willingly followed and personified the nature of the transformation at Chrysler; he benefited from a culture that accepted and even revered strong leaders. A key aspect of Chrysler's culture was the willingness to follow the CEO and never question decisions. This culture preceded Iacocca and Riccardo and actually originated in the days of Walter Chrysler.

Results of the Transformation: The New Chrysler

By the mid-1980s, Chrysler had completed the first phase of its corporate transformation, and results were significant. In brief,

- *1982* saw a return to profitability (from the gain on the sale of its defense subsidiary) after losing $3.3 billion since 1979. Unfortunately, continuing operations still experienced a loss.
- *1983* saw profits of $700.9 million with $301.9 million coming from continuing operations. Chrysler was now able to repay $1.2 billion in loans guaranteed a full seven years early, saving $392 million in interest and fees. Lenders swapped preferred stock for common stock, which strengthened Chrysler's capital base. Warrants held by the federal government were bought, eliminating the threat of stock value dilution.
- *1984* saw profits of $2.4 billion. Chrysler now reclaimed its position as one of the world's top fifty firms. Reflecting the return to financial health, dividend payments resumed and the firm bought back 20% of its outstanding common stock, increasing its share value. It also reduced its unfunded pension liability by two-thirds, and was able to get a revolving credit agreement of $1.1 billion with fifty-seven banks.

Clearly, the crisis was over and there was a "new" Chrysler.

Epilogue

The ultimate test of a successful transformation is that it lasts. In 1978, when Lee Iacocca joined Chrysler, it was a step away from the "corporate graveyard." However, on January 13, 1997, *Forbes* magazine declared Chrysler its "Company of the Year." As stated in the *Forbes* article: "You want numbers to justify our calling Chrysler Company of the Year? It probably finished 1996 on the sunny side of $5 a share, on $60 billion in sales. The return on net sales is above 6%—fantastic for a metal bender. . . . Chrysler's return on capital is 20%—again fantastic for a company in a capital-intensive business." Company of the Year! Chrysler? $7.5 billion in the bank. Chrysler? One out of every six vehicles sold in the United States. Chrysler? An innovation in the automotive Industry (i.e., the minivan). Chrysler? Superior management. Chrysler? A modern day Rip Van Winkle would think it was a dream; but, no, it was merely one of the most successful (if not *the* most successful) revitalization transformations in U.S. history.

Lessons from the Transformations at Miller Brothers, Compaq, and Chrysler

In terms of the framework for the design of successful organizations presented in Chapter 2 (see Figure 2–1), the need for revitalization occurred in all three companies when a change took place in the environment (factor D) attributable to changes in the market, competition, or trends. These changes led to the need to redesign or revise one or more of the six key building blocks that compose the pyramid of organizational success (factor B) and were accompanied at Compaq and Chrysler by changes in the organization's size (factor C).

If we step back from the details of these companies, we can see some overall patterns that provide lessons for identifying and managing Transformations of the Second Kind. One lesson is that the need for revitalization can be masked for quite some time. For the Miller Brothers, the 1970s and 1980s were boom years. Although problems were continuing to develop, there was no perceived need to deal with them until the company was facing a crisis. When the boom in real estate ended, the Miller Brothers were caught in a "scissors effect." There was less financial slack to offset operational inefficiencies.

The Miller Brothers were not the only ones to ignore problems until a crisis was perceived. The same situation was also encountered at Compaq Computers and Chrysler. In Compaq's case, the crisis was a loss that led to a sharp drop in the company's stock price. However, Compaq's loss was only the final warning that the environment had changed. At Chrysler, the crisis was precipitated by the recession of 1974 and the "oil shock" of the late 1970s, as well as increased competition from Japan.

Another lesson from these companies is that this type of transformation takes time. There is no quick fix because revitalization requires a comprehensive overhaul of the entire organization's infrastructure. Even in the case of Compaq Computers, where the revitalization process was exceptionally fast, the process still took two years. At Miller Brothers and Chrysler, it required three and five years, respectively. Revitalization demands a comprehensive overhaul of the entire organization's infrastructure.

Several other key lessons concern the leadership of a company in revitalization. One is that leadership can come from very different places to initiate a revitalization process. It came from a divisional manager at Miller Brothers, from the Chairman of the Board at Compaq, and from a CEO (Riccardo) at Chrysler. However, once a revitalization is initiated, other people can lead the process. Sam Miller took the first steps at MBI and then delegated the process to his brother Harry. The Board chose Eckhard Pfeiffer at Compaq. John Riccardo brought in Iacocca, who developed his own team at Chrysler.

Another key leadership lesson is captured in the phrase: "lead, follow or get out of the way!" In the example of the Miller Brothers, Sam, the oldest brother, was the "800-pound gorilla." He had the power to stop the process or direct it in any way he wished. However, he also had the wisdom and ability to control his ego so that he did not have to be in charge. He blessed the process, observed it, and got out of the way. His reward was that it worked. Another of the lessons concerning leadership of a revitalization transformation is that leadership does not have to reside in a single individual. For example, at Miller Brothers, leadership came from Sam, Harry, Robert, and Gil Strom at various points in the process. It should also be noted that leadership *teams* were just as important in the process (especially at MBI and Chrysler) as individual, charismatic leaders.

A final key lesson is that effective revitalization requires letting go of old ways of doing things, even if they have been successful in the past. Unfortunately, the longer these ways have been successful, the more difficult it will be to truly give them up and try something new and different. Nevertheless, making a successful Transformation of the Second Kind is not consistent with "business as usual."

Final Comments and Conclusion

As we have seen in the examples of Chrysler, Compaq Computers, and Miller Brothers, the need for revitalization transformations can occur in a wide variety of organizations of all sizes. We have also seen that it *is* feasible to manage a Transformation of the Second Kind without changing the basic business the organization is in. At times, it is appropriate or necessary to change that business. In the next chapter, we will examine a very different type of transformation—business vision transformations, which we have termed Transformations of the Third Kind.

5

SUCCESSFUL VISION TRANSFORMATIONS COMPLETED AND IN PROGRESS

Transformations of the Third Kind

This chapter deals with organizations that have either completed or are in the process of making Transformations of the Third Kind. Specifically, these transformations involve a metamorphosis from one kind of business to another based on differences in business vision. They involve changing the game that the firm is playing. Unfortunately, although several organizations have embarked on this type of transformation, there are relatively few completed "success stories."

Shooting Stars:
The Business Vision Transformation at Starbucks Coffee

Starbucks Coffee is one of the truly great entrepreneurial success stories of the past two decades. The scope and speed of its success are reminiscent of Apple Computers, Microsoft, Compaq Computers, and Nike.

The Company's Origin

The original Starbucks Coffee Company began as a local roaster of coffee. It opened its first store near Seattle's Pike Place Market in 1971. Another was located in a shopping center across from the University of Washington's campus in 1972. The original Starbucks' stores did not sell coffee drinks. They sold fresh-roasted coffee beans, imported teas, and spices. However, sometimes the individual behind the counter would brew a pot and serve free samples in Dixie cups.

Starbucks' founders were three individuals who shared a passion for gourmet coffee: Jerry Baldwin, Zev Siegl, and Gordon Bowker. By the end of the 1970s, they had four retail stores, a mail-order unit, and a wholesale company. Their sales were $2 million per year. Zev Siegl sold out in 1980, while Baldwin and Bowker continued to own the firm.

Unlike many entrepreneurs, who do not know what they do not know, Baldwin and Bowker realized they needed someone with greater business experience to help run what they had grown into a serious enterprise. They became acquainted with Howard Schultz, and invited him to run Starbucks. Schultz, who is now Chairman and Chief Executive Officer of Starbucks Corporation, joined the company as Director of Retail Operations and Marketing in 1982. Schultz grew up in Brooklyn and had begun his career in the marketing department at Xerox. At the age of twenty-six, he headed the American Division of Hammerplast, a Swedish housewares firm, before he joined Starbucks.

A Journey to Italy and the Seeds of the Transformation

Howard Schultz had been with Starbucks for approximately one year when he visited Milan to attend a trade show. While walking Milan's streets and going back and forth from his hotel to the show, he marveled at the ubiquity of the Italian coffee bars. After a few days, he began to be drawn into them himself, because, in his words, "It was so romantic."

In describing his experience, Schultz states: "I saw the same faces and the camaraderie. The coffee bar was an extension of peoples' homes and was *truly* part of the fabric of the Italian culture. It struck me right across the head, this is something dynamic and unusual."[1] What struck Howard Schultz was, in part, irony and insight. Starbucks *was* in the coffee business but: "I thought we had missed it completely, because we had not given people the romance of the beverage and the personal interaction of creating an environment outside their homes where they could enjoy the beverage in a personal, unique way." That notion was what Howard Schultz brought back to the United States.

Predictably, the founders of Starbucks, who had been doing very well for a local company, viewed Schultz's insight with disinterest and a lack of enthusiasm. It took him a year and a half to convince them to allow him to test his idea. He went back to Italy to do more research and when he returned, he was more convinced than ever that he was on to something. In April 1984, they tested the idea by opening up a small coffee bar inside a new Starbucks store.

Changing the Game: The Business Vision Transformation Begins

Overnight, an instant transformation took place. The store changed. The customer count became higher. The beverage became a treat while, more than that, the relationship with the customer changed. Starbucks people were able to develop closer relationships with customers because of the instant gratification and romance people received from the beverage served in this environment.

Starbucks had suddenly transformed its business from a purveyor of whole bean coffee to something very different. While whole bean coffee remained the core business, Howard Schultz had changed the game at Starbucks. It was the juxtaposition of two simple elements to create a more complex and, in some ways, more wonderful thing; just like the combination of hydrogen and oxygen creates water.

Despite the "experiment's" success, the owners of Starbucks balked at adapting their company to the vision Schultz articulated: an American version of the Italian coffee bar. Schultz decided to create his own company and left Starbucks. He called his company Il Giornale, which was founded in 1985.

Within a year, one of the founders of Starbucks acquired another company, Peet's Coffee in Berkeley. After the acquisition, the debt to equity ratio of Starbucks was 6 to 1, which was very high. This occurred because the founder was averse to issuing equity, which meant a dilution of ownership.

In August, 1987, Howard Schultz went back to Starbucks with a buy-out offer and a vision of taking the concept well beyond the boundaries of Seattle. The high debt burden on the owners of Starbucks made them receptive. Il Giornale acquired the assets of Starbucks and changed its name to Starbucks Corporation.

Shultz's vision was not only to build a national retail brand; it was to "recreate the paradigm" and transform coffee from a commodity product to a "truly exquisite product" with brand equity. Another aspect of Schultz's vision concerned his concept of the kind of organization he wanted to build. He had a strong commitment to company-owned stores. To support this idea, he articulated a set of five "Guiding Principles" that was intended to serve as the basis of Starbucks' culture. Subsequently, a sixth guiding principle was added to the initial five: "Embrace diversity as an essential component in the way we do business." Figure 5–1 lists all six guiding principles.

- Provide a great work environment and treat each other with respect and dignity.
- Apply the highest standards of excellence to the purchasing, roasting, and fresh delivery of our coffee.
- Develop enthusiastically satisfied customers all of the time.
- Contribute positively to our communities and our environment.
- Recognize that profitability is essential to our future success.
- Embrace diversity as an essential component in the way we do business.

Figure 5–1. Starbucks Corporation: Six Guiding Principles.

Schultz believed that the kind of organization that Starbucks was, and, in turn, the way it did business would become a source of sustainable competitive advantage. In his words, "The values of the company and the guiding principles became a unique sustainable competitive advantage." In effect, Schultz understood the role of culture as a building block of organizational success, but he did not know of the concept "corporate culture" *per se* as a management tool. Instead, it was an intuitive insight.

One critical feature of Starbucks' culture concerned the treatment of people. Schultz wanted everyone in the company to have a stake in Starbucks' success,in effect, he wanted everyone at Starbucks to be and behave like owners.

From 1987 to 1995, what energized Starbucks were the twin pillars of: (1) the commitment to the quality of its coffee, and (2) the quality of its values. They were synchronized and in Schultz's word, "seamless." As he states,

> That's what attracted people to the company. That's what sustained us, and that's what gave us our stake in the ground and we were able to measure our decision against that. Why don't we franchise? Because it wasn't part of our value system. Why don't we sell flavored coffee? Because it is a bastardization of the product. Why do we give everyone health benefits? Why do we give everyone ownership? Because these things are central to our value system and the way we treat people.

As in any true entrepreneurship, Howard Schultz is the embodiment of the company. A great deal of what characterized Starbucks is derived from Howard Schultz's own background and values. His commitment to Starbucks' treatment of people, all of whom are called "partners," was derived from how he saw his own father treated in the business world. Actually, it was the *reverse* of what his own father experienced.

Leadership's Role in Changing the Game

The chemical formula for water is H_2O. It represents the combination of two different elements (hydrogen and oxygen) to create something very different, water. At Starbucks, H_2O represents something even more different: the combination of two "H's" or "Howards" (Howard Schultz and Howard Behar) and an "O" (Orin Smith) to create a great company. It was more than a mere play on words. The H_2O notion at Starbucks implies a team effort.

Howard Behar joined Starbucks to help build its retail operations. When he arrived in 1989, Starbucks had thirty retail stores. He brought with him years of experience from other larger organizations, as well as a passionate commitment to building a different kind of organization. Behar is a right-brained creative type who also has an appreciation for the role that process can play in building a company like Starbucks. He is the kind of person who can "go either way," right-brained or left, entrepreneurial or professional manager. He is a high energy, very creative type of person, who was perfectly suited to manage Starbucks' hypergrowth retail strategy.

Orin Smith, the O-element, joined Starbucks as CFO in 1990. He brought not only a strong financial background, but a lower-key, more deliberate decision-making and managerial style. This was a counterpoint to the two H's, who tend to be passionate, with a strong orientation for immediate action. Howard Schultz stated, "Orin had a great gift to be able to tolerate my recklessness." Smith was seen as solid and dependable.

Howard Schultz is the first to say that he alone did not build Starbucks. He states that: "I was very fortunate to hire wonderful, gifted people to balance out the weaknesses and the strengths that I had as a business person." Schultz also stated, "We've made each other better like a basketball team. They've allowed me to do what I do well."

The chemical formula for hydrogen peroxide is H_2O_2, but it has a different meaning at Starbucks. The second "O" stands for Olsen, Dave Olsen, who is also known as "Mr. Coffee" at Starbucks. Olsen, currently Senior Vice President of Coffee for Starbucks, opened his own espresso bar in Seattle's University district in the mid-1970s. He was always a "coffee guy" and his search for the perfect espresso led him to Starbucks. Together, Olsen and Starbucks formulated the original Starbucks "espresso roast." Although Olsen's title is Senior Vice President of Coffee, his role is to be the keeper of the "coffee flame." His personal passion for coffee along with his quest for the perfect coffee have helped reinforce the overall corporate coffee culture. He is the company's conscience.

To fully understand the role that leadership played in Starbucks' development and its transformation into the retail coffee business, it is essential to examine what happened during the three-year period from 1989 to 1991. When asked if there was an untold secret to the Starbucks story, Schultz stated that, "Starbucks lost over $3 million during the period from 1989 to 1991." He noted that there was tremendous pressure on him from investors and the Board of Directors to change the strategy and the vision. They believed that Starbucks was hiring "too far ahead of the growth curve"; that the infrastructure investment was too great for a company as small as Starbucks; that company owned stores were too expensive; and that the concept wasn't going to work outside Seattle. George Bernard Shaw has stated that, "The reasonable man adapts himself to the world. The unreasonable man does not. Therefore, all progress is made by the unreasonable man."

What should Schultz and Starbucks do? A "reasonable man" might have changed the strategy and stopped hiring the kinds of people that Starbucks was recruiting. Maybe the company should have started franchising as a way to create capital. Maybe they should have looked at Starbucks as a regional company. Howard Schultz was not a reasonable man. His vision was to build a national company. He stated:

We could not have gotten where we are today if we had not had the commitment to build a national company with a national brand from the beginning. If you're going to build a 100-story building, you've got to build a foundation for 100 stories; but people were getting very nervous.

Schultz had to continually raise more money. He had to keep saying: "It's going to work, and we will turn profitable. It was a very tough time, a very vulnerable time." Howard Schultz's Board of Directors thought he was being very unreasonable, until Starbucks became very successful.

Why did Howard Schultz see opportunity where others did not? Why did he see the possibility of transforming coffee from a commodity into something very different after visiting Milan, a city visited by countless others for many, many years? Typically, after an entrepreneur like Schultz has had a brilliant insight, others can recognize the concept and think that it was "obvious." But it was not. If it was so obvious, why did Schultz have difficulty convincing the original founders of Starbucks about the merits of the idea? Why did it take a year and a half to persuade investors to provide the $1 million? Why did he have to struggle to keep the support of his Board of Directors? Schultz's vision, although expressed clearly and simply in retrospect, had great subtly and texture. It had the same subtly that allowed Nike to transform "sneakers" into "athletic shoes" and Disney to transform animated characters into theme parks.

Starbucks and the Pyramid of Organizational Success

Starbucks did not explicitly use the pyramid of organizational success in designing an organization to support this new vision. Schultz had a vision for the development of the business, and he set about to grow a company that would fulfill it. We can, however, use the pyramid as a lens to examine what Starbucks did and did not do well in building the company, in designing a firm to play its chosen game effectively.

Markets and Products

The foundation of Starbucks was its vision of the market and product. Schultz envisioned a large, national company. He knew that although the core of his company's product was coffee, the real "product" was the store itself. It was what Starbucks conceptualized as "a third place to be" (or, more simply, "the third place.") As stated in the 1995 Annual Report of Starbucks Corporation,

> Ever since diners and pubs and plazas and town halls we've needed places to gather outside of home, outside of work, rather [a third place to go]. Coffee ... community ... camaraderie ... connection. ... It seems we all just need the warmth.[2]

Schultz also understood that service was an integral part of the "delivery" of his product, and that the person Starbucks calls a "barista" (the person who tends the coffee bar) was critical.

Resources and Operational Systems

Once the market and product for Starbucks were identified and designed, the next steps in building the organization involved the acquisition of resources and the development of operational systems. As we have already discussed, Schultz spent considerable time identifying investors. In this regard, it was fair to state that, "No bucks, No Starbucks!"

The financial resources were used to hire people capable of building Starbucks as a national company. In contrast to many entrepreneurships, where there is a relatively strong senior team but not strong people at the next level, one of the reasons for Starbucks' success and its ability to manage its rapid growth was a relatively strong team of functional specialists in such areas as real estate and retail operations. This reduced the severity of the usual growing pains identified in Figure 2–7.

Management Systems and Culture

The final building blocks of successful organizations are its management systems and culture. As we have already discussed, corporate culture was very important to Schultz. Unlike many other companies at a comparable stage of development, there was an explicit statement of Starbucks culture in its "Guiding Principles. However, the one area of the pyramid that was significantly underdeveloped was Starbucks' management systems. Until 1994, there was planning and strategy but not a formal strategic planning process. There was training for customer service personnel but no management development. In addition, there was an incentive system for people but no well-developed "performance management system" (see Chapter 11). In a sense, the development of Starbucks Corporation's pyramid of success was very typical of most companies in which there are very well-developed markets and products, somewhat developed resources and operational systems, relatively underdeveloped management systems, and a well-defined culture.

What's Next for Starbucks?

Starbucks has never forgotten that the entire company is about coffee. However, the name Starbucks has developed brand equity. The brand of Starbucks is likely to become more a part of people's lives. What does Starbucks want to be when it grows up? Howard Schultz's answer is, "I don't know yet. There are a lot of things we are capable of doing beyond our core business."

When asked if there are any companies that he admires, Schultz replied, "Nike is a model, because they took a commodity product (sneakers) and they have become bigger than their product. They are known worldwide. The Gap is also a model. They execute city by city, flawlessly. They are great merchants." What Schultz noted about Nike and The Gap, can also be said about Starbucks. They are in the process of becoming bigger than their product. Their growth is phenomenal and, most important, they represent a classic example of a successful business vision transformation.

Changing the Game at the Walt Disney Company

Once upon a time, the Magic Kingdom of Walt Disney, one of the great entrepreneurial geniuses of the century, could do no wrong. Disney had created an empire consisting of movies and theme parks. It influenced television as well as American and international culture with its proprietary characters, such as Mickey Mouse, Donald Duck, and Pluto. Alas, all fairy tales must end, and Disney's seemed about to come to an ignominious finale in 1984. Walt Disney was now beyond the Magic Kingdom, and the company had lost its way.

Walt Disney, a classic entrepreneur, had been larger than life. His successors were unable to create a new second act to the play he had written. They often wondered aloud: "What would Walt have done in this situation?" Roy Disney was Walt's brother and "partner" in building the Walt Disney Company. His son, also named Roy, led a shareholder revolt to bring in new creative leadership. The transformation at Disney began with the arrival of a new leader, Michael Eisner.

Eisner found a company, like many other entrepreneurships, that had been unable to make the transition from a strong, creative, paternalistic, autocratic leader to a more professionally managed firm. Ron Miller, Walt Disney's replacement, had tried to move the company into different directions. For example, he started Touchstone Pictures, which enabled Disney to get into the adult movie market without compromising the image of Buena Vista films. Touchstone produced *Splash*, starring Daryl Hannah as a mermaid and Tom Hanks as the man who finds her. The movie was a financial success, but not sufficient to stop a decline in corporate profits.

Miller also had to contend with financier Saul Steinberg, who began to buy the company's stock, which, like profitability, was declining. After a period of turmoil, management paid Steinberg a premium of $52 million to sell his stock back to Disney and let the company alone. When Eisner joined Disney from Paramount Pictures, where he had been president, he already had a string of hits, including *Terms of Endearment* and *Saturday Night Fever*. He was able to step into the creative vacuum left by Walt Disney.

Nature of the Transformation

Eisner's transformation of the business focused on changing the game from a motion picture company to a global entertainment business. One of the first things Eisner did was recruit new members to supplement his management team. He brought Jeffrey Katzenberg, head of production at Paramount, to head up its movie and TV studios. Although Katzenberg is no longer at Disney, he left a lasting impact. Under Katzenberg, efficiency and cost effectiveness became the strategy for motion pictures. For example, Touchstone's first project under the new team was *Down and Out in Beverly Hills*, which starred a group of "name" actors (including Richard Dreyfuss,

Bette Midler, and Nick Nolte), who were no longer "hot" and who agreed to work for far less than superstar compensation. The film grossed $62 million at U.S. box offices, and cost only $13 million to produce.

From 1984 to 1992, Disney invested a great deal of money in revitalizing animation-based films. The company was successful with *Aladdin, The Little Mermaid, Beauty and the Beast,* and *Who Framed Roger Rabbit?* This success has had multiple payoffs. The new characters have led to profitable merchandising agreements, as well as providing for new "faces" at Disney theme parks. Today, Roger Rabbit, the Beast, and the Genie join Mickey Mouse at Disneyland. Building on this success, Disney also produced *The Lion King* (1991), *Toy Story* (1996), *The Hunchback of Notre Dame* (1996), and *Hercules* (1997).

In addition to the transformation of the motion pictures group, Disney used its film library to become a force in video. The Disney Channel has become a major pay-TV enterprise. The company also updated its theme parks, which still constitute the lion's share of its revenues. In addition to its U.S. theme parks, Disney now operates Tokyo Disneyland and Euro-Disneyland near Paris. After struggling for several years, Euro-Disney has become a modest success following a financial restructuring.

Building upon the worldwide recognition of its Disney characters, the company moved aggressively to license merchandise. In addition, it has opened a series of Disney stores. The company now accompanies the release of its animated features such as *The Lion King, Pocahontas,* or *Toy Story* with a multitude of items designed by artists at Disney's consumer products business segment.

Disney is organized into three major product groups: (1) theme parks and resorts, (2) filmed entertainment, and (3) consumer products. Although the word is much overused, Disney has achieved true synergy among its units because of its characters. For example, some of Disney's recent movie hits such as *The Little Mermaid, Aladdin, The Lion King,* and *Pocahontas* have been equally successful in merchandise. The films themselves might even be viewed as very sophisticated commercials for the merchandise. In 1996, Disney completed the acquisition of Capital Cities/ABC, which provided the company with a non-cable television network that was already airing several Touchstone Television produced programs (like *Home Improvement).*

Results of the Transformation

The results of the transformation led by Eisner have been impressive. The company's strategic mission is "to sustain Disney as the world's premier entertainment company from a creative, strategic, and financial standpoint." The Walt Disney Company achieved revenues of more than $18 billion in 1996, with net income of $1.2 billion.

Michael Eisner and his management team have transformed the Walt Disney Company and once again made it a magical kingdom not only for its customers, but for its shareholders as well. In almost a decade (1987 to

1996), Disney's stock increased from a low of $10 a share to $63 at the end of 1996. By the end of 1997, it appreciated further to $99 a share, an increase of about 900% over the eleven-year period, for a truly "magical" return to share holders.

Successful Vision Transformations in Progress

The previous section has examined some successful business vision transformations. Several other organizations are currently in the process of making similar promising transformations, and we will examine some selected examples, including Navistar, SCE Corp., Hughes Electronics, and Nike. Although any "work in progress" must, by definition, be incomplete, we can still benefit from a review of these transformations.

The Transformation of International Harvester into Navistar[3]

We now describe the metamorphosis of International Harvester, an old-line industrial company and a component of the Dow-Jones Industrial Index, into Navistar. This example is of interest for a variety of reasons. First, it is a classic case of a compound transformation (revitalization and business vision). In addition, it is an example of a transformation at a company that is more than one hundred years old. Finally, it represents an enterprise that narrowed (rather than broadened) its business focus. This transformation occurred in three phases, as we will see. Although we discuss each phase of the transformation, our principal interest is in the third phase (which began in 1987) for the purpose of illustrating the business vision aspects.

Who Is Navistar?

Navistar International Corporation is in the transportation business. The company manufactures heavy and medium trucks, buses, and diesel engines. Navistar, the largest U.S. truck company, was once the truck division of International Harvester and became the surviving company when the farm machinery division was sold. The existence of Navistar as a company is the result of a series of revitalization and business vision transformation efforts that have taken place in three phases since 1971, culminating in a company very different from the original International Harvester.

International Harvester

The old International Harvester company was founded in 1831 when Cyrus McCormick invented the McCormick Reaper. The initial Harvester products were all agricultural implements, but by the early 1900s the company produced a motorized tractor. It also produced a truck for farm use.

The development of nonfarm trucks began during World War I; heavy-duty trucks became a separate product line in the early 1920s. By the mid-

1920s, International Harvester was the leading producer of trucks in the United States. Another product line that was an outgrowth of agricultural equipment was construction equipment. By 1950, International Harvester had sales of almost $1 billion and employed about 90,000 people. The company was not merely headquartered in the midwestern United States, it was strongly rooted in midwestern culture. It was paternalistic, with a tradition of people joining when they were young and spending their entire career there.

The Onset of Decline

International Harvester was at the apex of its strength after World War II. From there, it began a decline that ended with the sale of the farm equipment and construction divisions. A number of problems led to the company's decline, including a poorly conceived strategy of diversification into the home appliance industry, failure to focus on its core agricultural business to maintain its competitiveness, poor labor relations resulting in a number of strikes, and a lack of management sophistication appropriate to the size, scope, and complexity of International Harvester's business. The company had no long-term planning, no job descriptions, and poor management systems.

Changing the Game: Phase I

The first attempt at revitalization of International Harvester was begun by Brooks McCormick, great grandnephew of Cyrus McCormick, who became president in 1971. The company's organization and management systems had not changed significantly since the 1940s, even though sales were more than $2.7 billion in 1970 and had been less than 10% of that amount in 1940 ($248 million).

McCormick set out to revitalize International Harvester. He engaged a consultant to review the company and define its problems. The consultant concluded that the company was paternalistic, centralized, bureaucratic, and inbred. It lacked focus on long-term goals as well as a system for individual accountability.

McCormick proceeded to develop the focus and management systems required by a company of International Harvester's size and complexity. A consultant was engaged to help establish a corporate strategic planning process. Another was hired to set up a system of job descriptions and individual accountability. Incentive-compensation was linked to individual performance, while previously it had been based on overall corporate performance. Another consultant was also engaged to do an organizational structure study, and a complete reorganization was recommended. The company was reorganized around five product groups: trucks, agricultural equipment, construction equipment, engines, and components (which supplied the other groups). Each group was managed by a "group president." Under this approach, the intent was to have the company decentralized with accountability for performance assigned to each group. This would lead to a diminished role for the corporate staff. However, because the culture at International Harvester was based on a very centralized, autocratic tradition, the transformation was not completely successful.

In 1977, Brooks McCormick recruited Archie McCardell, who was CEO at Xerox, to continue the revitalization. Although McCormick had made changes at Harvester, the company was unprepared for McCardell and his changes. McCardell began with a budgetary review process in which he asked questions that his managers were unable to answer. He rejected all budgets and sent the group presidents back to do them over. This was a culture shock for International Harvester. He also instituted the process of having the company benchmark itself vis à vis competition. This encouraged people to look outward. One of McCardell's priorities was to get the company to reduce its costs. McCardell also changed certain aspects of the management process. Under Brooks McCormick, the company had an Executive Committee composed of group presidents, executive vice presidents, and selected corporate staff. There was also a "management council."

By 1979, International Harvester had made some progress in its efforts toward revitalization. Unfortunately, McCardell felt that one of the long-term problems he was facing concerned the company's relationship with its union, UAW. International Harvester's contract with United Auto Workers expired October 1, 1979. On November 1, 1979, thirty-five thousand UAW workers struck against International Harvester Company over a conflict involving work rules.

McCardell viewed the strike as a challenge to the union, believing that contract changes were essential for reducing the firm's huge cost problem. The resulting strike was the longest and most contentious in the firm's one-hundred-forty-nine-year history and it significantly weakened International Harvester's financial position. Given the bitterness created by the strike and the financial reverses suffered by the company, the Board of Directors decided that McCardell needed to be replaced.

In early May 1982, McCardell was terminated as CEO and replaced by Louis Menk, a Director of International Harvester and retired head of Burlington Northern Railroad, who was asked to fill in on a temporary basis. During the period from 1980 to 1984, Harvester lost $3 billion. As a result of these losses, management began a process of selling off any available assets to raise cash, reducing costs, and negotiating a series of debt restructurings with Harvester's banks.

Changing the Game: Phase II

The second phase of revitalization at International Harvester began in the early 1980's.[4] The company was on the brink of bankruptcy. The plan for the company's survival involved a major transformation in its business vision. In contrast to most vision transformations that involve broadening a business's scope, the transformation of International Harvester into Navistar involved a *narrowing* of vision. Unfortunately, strategic planning had never been one of Harvester's strong suits, and the process of changing the game actually involved a series of decisions rather than a "grand plan."

International Harvester bought some time by negotiating a financial restructuring with its creditors. Even though it avoided Chapter 11 bankruptcy proceedings, the company realized that changes in its markets were not merely temporary cyclical declines, but actually longer term structural changes. This led to a series of divestitures.

The "Death" of International Harvester

Although the details of management's thinking are not available, we can summarize the logic that led to the business vision transformation at International Harvester as follows: International Harvester no longer had the resources to compete in all its businesses. The company's position had eroded in several businesses, including turbines, construction, and trucks. In addition, even though the company had been a founder of the agricultural equipment business, by the early 1980s it was no longer a market leader in this industry, which was now dominated by Caterpillar and John Deere.

Unlike a stronger company, such as General Electric, which had the deep pockets to keep a weaker performing business afloat, Harvester found itself in the unenviable position of facing decline in most of its core businesses. The businesses that had the greatest relative strength were trucks and diesel engines. Accordingly, management, with the Board's approval, decided to focus the company on trucks and engines and divest itself of all other assets. The intent of the divestiture was both to provide a source of cash to finance the revitalization of the truck business as well as to eliminate other businesses that were incurring operating losses.

Beginning in 1982, International Harvester began to divest itself of what was once considered its core assets. With a sense of loss and regret, the Fort Wayne axle and transmission plant was sold to Dana Corporation. The Solar Turbine Division was sold to Caterpillar Tractor, and the Construction Equipment business was sold to Dresser Industries. The most profound and traumatic change, though, involved the sale of the agricultural equipment business to Tenneco in 1984. The original business on which International Harvester was founded was now gone, and with it International Harvester's sense of identity and heritage. The remaining businesses were trucks and engines.

The "Birth" of Navistar

As a result of the sale of the agricultural equipment business, the company not only changed its game, but also changed its name as well. On January 7, 1986, the company announced that its new name would be Navistar International Corporation. The company had transformed itself by narrowing its focus to the business components with the greatest chance of long-term survival and profitability: heavy-duty and medium trucks, buses, and diesel engines. The Navistar name symbolized the company's metamorphosis from International Harvester to something "new and different."

Unfortunately, the company's problems were not over. Navistar faced still another period of revitalization in the late 1980s and early 1990s.

Changing the Game: Phase III

In the late 1980s, John Horne became the President and Chief Operating Officer of Navistar. Horne, who had an engineering background, had been the head of the company's Engine Division. He was selected by James Cotting, who was Chairman and CEO of Navistar. Cotting, who had a strong financial background, became "Mr. Outside" and dealt with the banks and Wall Street; Horne, who had an operations background, became "Mr. Inside."

At that time, Navistar was facing three key problems that needed to be resolved to facilitate the next phase of its revitalization. One concerned its "legacy costs," the pension and health care costs associated with its former employees from the Agriculture and Construction Divisions. The second problem involved the costs of benefits for active workers. The third included the overall management processes and structure of the company. The first problem was addressed by a strategy of getting retired employees and unions to accept reduced pension and health care benefits in return for shares of Navistar's common stock. This plan called for reducing Navistar's total liability for post-retirement benefits from $2.1 billion to $1 billion in return for an equity share in the company financed by additional stock.[5]

Leadership of the Transformation Process

The stereotypical concept of leadership in a transformation process is that of a "great leader," such as Lee Iacocca at Chrysler, who single-handedly creates the motivation for change and the vision and then guides the process to a successful completion. Clearly, this does occur. However, leadership in the process of transformation is sometimes more diffuse and elusive.

As we have seen, sometimes the initial leadership for transformation does not come from the formal, "number 1" leader in a firm (as in the case of Miller Brothers), but from someone else (Gil Strom) with limited power, but who has mastered the ability to be a catalyst for change. In other instances, it is not really feasible to identify a single leader; rather, the impetus for transformation occurs, almost by osmosis, from the cumulative initiatives and efforts of a loosely defined group of people. This was the case at Navistar. There the impetus for transformation had become part of the culture. It was part of the process of survival at the company, an ongoing factor that was not really centered in the acts or responsibilities of a single individual such as the CEO. Navistar had been struggling to survive for so long that leadership for change was simply part of how things were done, not a part of a special program.

Changing the Management Game at Navistar

At Navistar, a process of organizational development had been going on for quite some time. The overall purpose of this program was to improve Navistar's operational and management effectiveness. As part of this process, a unit of Navistar focused on helping Navistar's more than 600 independent dealers (who owned and operated the stores that sold and serviced Navistar's line of "International" trucks) improve their effectiveness. In 1987, the Dealer Advisory Council, which was intended to be the liaison between Navistar Corporate and the dealers, requested training for dealers in how to *manage* their dealerships. Stated differently, the dealers wanted training in how to run their dealerships as businesses. In response, Navistar's training group decided to offer such a program, and they began a search for a firm to deliver it.

One of Navistar's dealers, who was also a member of the Advisory Council, decided to attend a seminar offered at UCLA entitled, "How to Make the Transition from an Entrepreneurship to a Professionally Managed Firm." The seminar was conducted by Dr. Eric Flamholtz, one of this book's authors. The dealer then proposed that Flamholtz and his firm, *ManagementSystems* Consulting Corporation, conduct the Navistar Dealer Executive Development Program. After considering several organizations, Navistar awarded the contract to *ManagementSystems*.

The concept was to deliver a two-year program designed to enhance the managerial capabilities of Navistar's largest dealership owners as well as help them develop the management systems required for operating their firms. Participation in the program was voluntary, and although it was anticipated that about twenty or twenty-five dealers would get involved, forty-two actually enrolled.

The program was well received by the dealers, who began to ask whether something similar was going to be offered to Navistar's corporate managers. One dealer stated: "You have helped us, but unless Navistar changes the way it is managed, this won't be enough." After discussion among themselves, the dealers decided to sponsor *ManagementSystems* as a firm that could benefit the corporate structure.

Eric Flamholtz was invited to present an overview of the dealer executive development program at the Navistar Senior Leadership Conference. A few months later, John Horne, the new CEO at Navistar, asked *ManagementSystems* to assess its organizational structure, focusing especially on the organization of its truck operations.

Prior to the study, "Truck" was organized in a functional form (this structural form is further explained in Chapter 8). In this structure, Horne basically acted as the head of all truck operations and had all major functions (e.g., Manufacturing, Research and Development, Sales, etc.) reporting to him. Based on the results of the study, Navistar's senior management team decided that the company's effectiveness would be increased by adopting a matrix structure consisting of three "strategic business units." These units would focus on three different subunits of the truck market: (1) heavy truck, (2) medium truck, and (3) bus.

The next phase of the organizational development process was to implement a new strategic planning process. Prior to this time, Navistar had had a corporate strategic planning function, a staff department that had the charter to do corporate planning. The expectation was that the plans developed by this department would serve as a guide for the efforts of all managers and employees within the company. The problem was that in many cases, these plans were disconnected from the company's line managers. Further, if line managers did not follow the plans, there were few repercussions.

As a result of the organizational development program, a new process of strategic planning was initiated that involved having members of the strategic business units' operating management create the plans that would guide the efforts of people within their unit. Consultants assisted the firm's senior management in designing the planning process that would be used and assisted in facilitating unit planning meetings. The objective was not merely to develop a plan *per se*, but also to have operating managers learn and adopt the new approach.[6]

Another aspect of the overall organizational development program was leadership effectiveness training. This included a series of management development sessions designed to help create a new type of Navistar manager. A key part of the leadership training effort was the participation of John Horne and other members of Navistar's top management team, who were the program's first participants. It was, using Navistar's truck-related language, then "rolled out" to the rest of the organization.

One of the principal reasons for the successful implementation of these programs (and a key lesson for other transformation efforts) was the strong support of Navistar's President, John Horne. The planning process became "John Horne's planning process," and the "Leadership Effectiveness Series" became "John Horne's Management Development Program," rather than just "a program." Cloaked with the authority of Navistar's president, the planning process became "Navistar's Planning Process," the way "we do planning" rather than just a "program of the month."

No single individual or even a small group was the leader of the process. Instead, a number of people played significant roles at various points. In a very real sense, leadership was now part of the Navistar culture.

Results of Changes

Taken together, all the major initiatives for the revitalization of Navistar have resulted in the first signs of a turnaround. One specific bottom-line result is that in 1993 Navistar achieved a net profit for the first time in many years. Although the revitalization of Navistar is not yet completed, the preliminary results of this phase show promise. By 1993, some investment analysts had actually begun to express favorable opinions on the company's stock.

Year	Revenues[a]	Net Income[a]
1991	3,460	(164)[b]
1992	3,875	(146)
1993	4,694	(272)
1994	5,305	102
1995	6,292	164

[a] In millions of dollars.
[b] ( ) indicates loss.

Figure 5–2. Navistar International Corporation Revenues and Net Income (1991–1995).

The "bottom line" of the revitalization is in the earnings of an enterprise. Navistar's revenues and net income for the period from 1991 through 1995 are shown in Figure 5–2. During this period, revenues increased from $3.5 billion to $6.3 billion. The company incurred losses in 1991, 1992, and 1993. However, it earned a profit in 1994, 1995, and 1996. As a result, Navistar actually had a P/E ratio (price/earnings ratio) for the first time since 1989. It should be noted that to have a P/E ratio, an enterprise must have a positive "E" (or earnings)! By the end of 1997, Navistar's stock price was almost $25 a share, and the P/E ratio was 15, marking great progress in the transformation of a company that had been on the brink of bankruptcy just a few years before.

The Transformation of Southern California Edison into Edison International

Another example of a business vision transformation in progress involves Southern California Edison, an electric utility that has been in the process over the last several years of changing the game it is playing. In 1995, the transformation was marked by its name change from SCE Corp to Edison International.

We have included this example because it illustrates a company that has engaged in a dual aspect of transformation, involving both its core business as well as the development of new ventures. Our intent in this example is to describe a concept of how a game can be changed, rather than all of the specific "moves" involved and the leadership dynamics of the transformation process.

Edison's Business Concept and Environmental Changes

In 1977, legislation was passed (the Public Utility Regulatory Policies Act) to deregulate the energy industry. This occurred in response to the energy crisis of the early to mid-1970s and was intended to encourage the development of alternative sources of energy, such as solar, wind, geothermal, and waste fuel. It was also intended to decrease the public's dependence on utilities with virtual monopolies in defined geographic areas. Specifically, state governments assisted independent energy producers in negotiating contracts with existing utility companies. The government's efforts were successful and by 1987 more than 60,000 megawatts of independent power facilities were approved by the Federal Energy Regulatory Commission.

By the mid-1980s Edison found that their business environment had changed from a virtual monopoly to a more competitive marketplace[7] brought about by the emerging independent power companies. This was one of those times when the nature of the changes occurring in the environment was obvious to all within the industry, and Edison's CEO, Howard Allen, the Board of Directors, and the company's senior management were all aware that Edison could no longer continue with business as usual. They could see that Edison was on the cusp of changes in the environment that would transform electric utilities from sleepy monopolies to something totally different. In response to these changes, Edison began to transform itself from a provider of electric energy as a commodity, to what might be termed an "energy solutions business."

Steps Toward a New Vision

Some companies respond to environmental changes by developing a grand vision of what they are going to become. Others react by taking a series of incremental steps. Southern California Edison was one of the latter. One of the first steps it took to survive in a deregulating environment was the creation of the Mission Group companies in April 1986. The Mission companies are subsidiaries operating in nonregulated, energy-related businesses in national and international markets. The original Mission Group companies consisted of: Mission Energy Company, Mission First Financial Company, Mission Land Company, and Mission Power Engineering Company. Mission Energy was the largest of the four nonutility subsidiaries; its goal was to pursue cogeneration projects, from ownership to development and operation.[8] Mission First Financial Company primarily provided venture capital services to energy projects. The Mission Land Company owned and operated six industrial parks in California and Arizona and was involved in industrial real estate transactions. The Mission Power Engineering Company provided consulting in the field of energy engineering and construction.[9]

Another major step in response to environmental changes occurred in 1988 when the parent holding corporation SCE Corp was formed. SCE Corp was established as the parent company of Southern California Edison and of the Mission Group companies. This new structure enabled a definite, clear-cut separation of the utility Edison operations from the "nonutility" subsidiary operations. The major subsidiary of SCE Corp remained the Southern

California Edison Company (a utility company serving approximately four million customers living in Central and Southern California).

Changing the Game at Southern California Edison

As part of Edison's transformation from a producer of electrical energy as a commodity to an energy solutions business, the company has continued to pursue alternative ways of generating energy through research and development programs. In April 1990, Edison and Texas Instruments announced a breakthrough in cell technology. Other promising technologies are desalinization, waste-to-energy ("Advanced Integrated Recycling" or turning 200 tons of refuse daily to a clean-burning gas), fuel cells, smart meters (two-way communications linking the utility to customers), and composite transmission towers.

Role of the Mission Group in Changing the Game

The creation of the Mission Group companies has given Edison International not only a competitive advantage, but has also been a factor in its overall transformation. The Mission Group positioned SCE Corp in a high-growth segment of the nonregulated energy market. The earnings of this group in 1992 were $109 million. Some of the components of the Mission Group were successful; others were not. Both Mission Energy and Mission Financial First were successful. The Mission Power Engineering Company discontinued its operations in 1990. Mission Land was also phased out.

One of the most interesting and significant aspects of the transformation at SCE Corp has been the success of Mission Energy. Since many companies establish new ventures as part of their business vision transformations, we will examine this example to identify any lessons that are relevant for others.

Edison Mission Energy

Mission Energy is the largest independent power producer in the United States and one of the largest in the world. In 1993, it had more than 1,500 megawatts of generating capacity in thirty operating domestic and foreign projects. It also owns 1,970 megawatts in another eleven projects that are underway.

Edison Mission Energy company develops, owns and operates "cogeneration" (a process of producing electricity using waste energy by an industrial facility) and independent power plants and supplies low-cost wholesale electricity to customers. As an independent company, it would rank in the top 150 of the *Fortune* 500 and in the top 50 of the magazine's fastest growing list. It is an entrepreneurial company existing as a component of a large, established business. What is particularly interesting about Mission Energy is how it was developed as a new venture by Southern California Edison.

Seeing an opportunity in the unregulated energy market, Edison chose Ed Meyers to be the "entrepreneur" or "intrapreneur" to develop a business in this area. Meyers, a long-time Edison employee, was someone who might have become its CEO. However, when this did not occur by the mid-1980s, he was looking for a new challenge. This came in the form of an invitation to head a start-up venture within Edison dealing with opportunities in unregulated energy. Meyers was intrigued; he accepted the opportunity as a final chapter in his career.

In a sense, the whole process was very informal. There was no strategic plan for the new venture. It was just an idea: "There is an opportunity in unregulated energy. Let's see what we can do with it." In addition, Meyers was an interesting choice as an "intrapreneur." Although he had been seen as someone who might ultimately become CEO of the utility, he did not have any previous experience as an entrepreneur. To some people, his appointment as CEO of Edison Mission Energy might be seen as a consolation prize. However, Meyers saw it as an opportunity to do something significant and "have some fun."

Meyers was told that he would be funded by Edison and could recruit a small core team from Edison's employees. He put together a team of seven "Merry Men," as he called it. This small band established a business that has grown from ground zero in 1986 to what is now one of the world's largest, unregulated energy companies.

It is of interest that none of the original members of Meyers' team was a classic entrepreneur, all were career Edison employees. As one of them stated, "I saw an opportunity to leave the safe, secure world of Edison and go out and build something. It was exhilarating for a guy in mid-career."

Results of the Business Vision Change

What are some of the results of the transformation in progress at Edison International? At present, Edison International is the second largest U.S. utility company and Edison Mission Energy is the largest U.S. unregulated power producer; it operates nationally and internationally.

Edison International is an example of an organization that is in the process of making a significant transformation successfully. This company was able to understand that times were changing and acted on its new environment by recognizing opportunities. It has diversified, but remained primarily within its main expertise and experience, a realm offering significant future growth potential.

The transformation of Edison International is interesting and significant for several reasons. One key dimension is the dual aspect of the transformation involving both the core electrical utility business as well as new ventures such as Mission Energy. Another concerns the way in which the new ventures were formed and organized.

The Transformation at Hughes Electronics Corporation

Hughes Electronics Corporation (Hughes) was founded by the legendary entrepreneur Howard Hughes. From its inception, Hughes has been engineering driven. In 1992, one third of the company's 68,000 employees were engineers. This example is not intended as a comprehensive illustration of a business vision transformation, but a highlight of the role of certain critical aspects, including culture change, business concept, and management practices. Accordingly, we will present only a limited description of how Hughes changed its game.

Historical Background

To understand the nature of the transformation that has begun at Hughes, we must understand the organization's culture. People at Hughes describe the company as "a hobby shop." The traditional approach to recruiting new engineers at Hughes was to ask them to "come work with us on interesting problems." The focus was on engineering, not profitability. The projects acquired by Hughes were a means to the end of providing opportunities for engineers to solve interesting problems and, in turn, support them. Profit, *per se*, was not the raison d'etre. In contrast, most companies are in business to make a profit, and the work they do is simply a means to that end. This difference between Hughes' historical culture and most companies is critical in understanding the transformation it must make today.

Throughout its history, the major market for Hughes' products and services has been the U.S. Government, especially the Department of Defense (the DOD). This is an unusual situation for most businesses: a small number of customers or even a single customer with an ongoing relationship to its supplier. The mechanism for contracts is the RFP, request for proposal. Since Hughes has had a reputation for solving difficult problems, it had a niche in the aerospace market. Consequently, it had the ability to command significant fees. These fees were well earned, but over time the company's successes led to a level of confidence that some saw as complacency and others viewed as arrogance. It also led to a belief that Hughes' engineers knew what was right for all programs. Throughout the company it was widely recognized that when some programs called for a Chevrolet Nova Hughes engineers delivered a Cadillac. This mind-set was well established in the Hughes culture. While many engineers were proud of it, others recognized that it was not always a strength.

Hughes' practice of focusing on quality regardless of cost was not a problem for many years. In the old structure of government cost-plus contracts, the belief was that "no matter what we did, someone would pick up the bill." Since the work that Hughes did was of very high quality, there were relatively few complaints. In addition to government contracts, Hughes also had some commercial business. Many of Hughes' commercial contracts (e.g., for satellites) were also won through procurement contracts similar to government RFPs.

Taken together, Hughes' engineering-oriented culture and its RFP-based business had created a situation in which there was little experience in determining what customers really wanted or needed and *then* developing products to meet those needs at a competitive price. In brief, Hughes culture was based on reaction: customers came to Hughes with problems to be solved and Hughes responded. The classic commercial venture requires a different mind-set and skills, as well as a different culture.

Prior to 1985, Hughes was a nonprofit organization, which served to reinforce the "hobby shop mentality." After General Motors acquired Hughes, there was a growing recognition that the organization would have to change. However, for the first few years after the acquisition, GM itself adopted a hands-off approach, and the impetus to change was based more on a feeling by Hughes' personnel that they needed to do things differently. Interestingly, it was the mere presence of GM, in a sense its shadow, rather than its actions, that acted as a catalyst for change.

Changing the Game at Hughes: Current Actions and Future Challenges

Given the decline in governmental defense budgets since the late 1980s, Hughes has begun the process of transforming itself from a giant hobby shop to an organization capable of competing in the commercial marketplace. In the future, Hughes hopes to generate 50% of its revenues from commercial sales.

At present, Hughes does not appear to have a broad vision that is guiding its transformation. Instead, it is engaged in a major effort to diversify away from the defense industry by leveraging some of its defense-related technology for commercial uses. For example, Hughes has developed and owns the satellite network that has become "DirectTV—Hughes Electronic's New Satellite Broadcasting Network." This is the first compact digital satellite system, a billion-dollar venture, that is considered a serious threat to cable TV and the video rental business. The system consists of an RCA receiver and an 18" diameter satellite dish that receives about 150 channels of movies, sports, news, and pay-per-view features through a high-resolution digital signal transmitted by DirectTV. The product was introduced in the fall of 1994 and received a promising response from the public.

Although this is an excellent step in the beginning of Hughes' transformation, experience from other organizations suggests that there will need to be a broader vision of what Hughes wants to become for the ultimate transformation to be completely successful.

Hughes' management knows that there are opportunities in Asia and Europe as well as in new markets such as broadcasting and commercial telecommunications. The company needs to foster the skills to identify customer needs and develop (or refine) products to meet those needs. These are the tasks at the first two levels of the pyramid of organizational success presented in Chapter 2.

Changing the Way the Game Is Played: Future Challenges

This transformation from a company that was largely dependent on government defense contracts to one that gains a very substantial portion of its revenue from commercial business will also require a variety of organizational changes. At the resources and operational systems levels, Hughes will have to build a sales and marketing organization. In the "old Hughes," this function was not necessary. At the management systems level, Hughes will also have to make some significant changes. The company has historically lacked a strategic plan for Hughes as a whole. As a government contractor, Hughes was project oriented. The importance of long-term strategic planning has become clear as Hughes has moved more into competitive commercial markets.

Hughes may have to change its organizational structure as well. Historically, Hughes' business units were encouraged to be independent. They were responsible for "keeping their own buckets filled." This led to several independent fiefdoms that were often in direct competition with each other for resources. There is a need to create a greater sense of teamwork across the company. GM has helped Hughes to form teams with cross-divisional representation. The system of control at Hughes also must be changed. Historically, people have not been held accountable and rewards have not been linked to performance.

Perhaps what must undergo the most fundamental change at Hughes is its culture. In transforming itself from a hobby shop to a profit-oriented, competitive enterprise, Hughes must make a number of specific cultural changes. The culture has tended to reward firefighters, who are often seen as corporate heroes. Historically, managers who planned and achieved their projects without fanfare were not as readily recognized and rewarded. Coupled with the firefighter mentality, Hughes has had a culture that emphasizes individual performance instead of teamwork. There has also been an emphasis on engineering rather than management, and perhaps even a subtle contempt for management. Strategic planning has neither been valued nor practiced. Organization has occurred by chance, not rational design.

Hughes has begun to change its culture. Historically, Hughes had a no-layoff policy. After its acquisition by General Motors, there were several layoffs. The company is taking steps to create a culture that values planning and teamwork, and a process has begun to chip away at the kingdoms.

The process of transformation at Hughes is significant not only for the organization itself, but also because Hughes is a kind of national treasure. It consists of a group of highly trained, highly skilled individuals who are oriented to solving complex engineering problems. This is the type of organization that we all should really want to see succeed in transforming itself and continuing to exist.

Epilogue

In January 1997, Raytheon Co. agreed to acquire the defense business of GM's Hughes Electronics for $9.5 billion in stocks and debt. The satellite broadcasting business will remain a part of Hughes. Since GM originally paid $5.4 billion for Hughes, it will have recovered all its initial investment, reap a profit on the sale, *and* still hold the assets of the nondefense component of the company's business.

Changing the Game at Nike

Nike is another example of an organization that has made, at least partially, a successful business vision transformation. Nike, which began as an athletic footwear company and grew to dominate this market, is currently in the process of transforming itself into a "sports and fitness wear" company. Our interest here is simply to describe the concept underlying Nike's business vision transformation, rather than the whole process by which it is being executed.

In the early 1960s, Phillip Knight, a middle-distance track runner from the University of Oregon, set off for Japan after graduation to pursue an idea of promoting high-quality/low-cost athletic shoes. Knight had been heavily influenced by his favorite track coach, Bill Bowerman, who "had a fascination with customizing shoes."[10] The running shoe was an important piece of equipment for track and field athletes, and, at the time Knight was running at Oregon, there wasn't a product on the market that focused on the needs of these "authentic athletes."

It wasn't long before Knight established relations with a Japanese manufacturing company and began selling running shoes at various track meets in Oregon under the company name "Blue Ribbon Sports." The subsequent ten years brought a new name to the company and rapid growth. The name Nike came at the suggestion of one of Knight's friends, who liked it because it was the name of the Greek goddess of victory. It stuck. Sales grew at exponential rates and profits nearly doubled each year. By 1980, Phil Knight had built a billion-dollar company.

Success had been founded on the company's value of sport and fitness and a commitment to "keeping the magic of sport alive."[11] Functionality at an acceptable price was what Nike delivered in their shoes. What Nike offered however, and what 80% of their customers bought, was the fantasy associated with sports. Nike deftly created an image based upon association with superstar athletes such as Bo Jackson and Michael Jordon.

Internal and external changes took place beginning in 1980. In December 1980, Nike went public and a few of the original people opted to leave the company in light of the new organizational ownership structure. The corporate culture had changed. Outside the company, there was a new player on the rise, Reebok. Reebok cashed in on the aerobics trend and, in 1986, became the number one shoe company in the United States. Reebok also developed a niche with women buyers, which was especially ironic since Nike's namesake is a goddess.

As a result, Nike went through a period of transformation from 1985 to 1987 and the company had to take a new look at its business. The idea that emerged was to create market segments by selling packages that would include shoes, colors, clothes, a logo, and athletes, and focusing on heavy TV advertising.[12] Examples of these "packages" include Air Jordan, Air Force, and Cross-Trainers. Underlying them, however, was a more subtle concept of making Nike more accessible to people. Historically, Nike had oriented itself to "authentic athletes." Now, Nike repositioned itself for "the rest of us," as symbolized by its "Just Do It" campaign.

Today, Philip Knight, the company's founder as well as current Chairman and CEO, visualizes Nike as a "global power brand." The company's product is seen all over the world as well as on television, in advertising, and at athletic events. Many athletes wear Nike and such display contributes to the building of brand equity. Nike has transformed its image from the shoe for "authentic athletes" to "the people's choice." The company has leveraged its brand equity by developing a line of athletic apparel. The company has also begun to open Nike outlet stores.

A key lesson provided by Nike's transformation concerns the nature of the vision. It is based on a different notion of what the product is. The ultimate "product" is sports and athletic fitness, not athletic shoes. Accordingly, Nike defines itself as a sports and fitness company, not an athletic shoe or even athletic wear company. This vision has positioned the company for future growth even as the product category of athletic shoes has become more competitive. A related lesson concerns Nike's transformation from a niche player to a global "power" brand through its creative use of advertising and the "Just Do It" theme.

Lessons to be Learned

This chapter has described several examples of business vision transformations. Some of these transformations have been successfully completed (i.e., Starbucks and Disney), while other are still in progress (Navistar, Edison International, Hughes Electronics, and Nike).

The most fundamental, and possibly the most significant, lesson is that business vision transformations require creating a new business. It is difficult to "graft" or superimpose a business vision on an existing organization, although many have tried to do this unsuccessfully as we will see in the next chapter. The creation of a new business involves incorporating the six key building blocks of the pyramid of organizational success into the new business foundation.

Some people believe that business visions must be dramatic new ideas that offer "breakthroughs." In fact, as seen in our examples, the basis of a new vision can be profoundly simple, yet elegant. For example, coffee has been around for a long time and so have coffeehouses and cafes. Yet Howard

Schultz brilliantly recreated the idea and used it as a foundation for developing one of the great entrepreneurial success stories of the 1990s. Similarly, Disney was Disney before Michael Eisner arrived on the scene. Yet he saw possibilities for leveraging the intellectual property and brand owned by Disney and created a fully integrated entertainment company. Nike did not invent athletic shoes, but Philip Knight created a new vision of their role in society.

Others have already learned these lessons and are in the process of applying them to build successful businesses. For example, Kirk Perron, founder of JAMBA Juice, recognized that juices and smoothies are not new, yet he is creating a successful new business around this concept.

The next lesson is more of a hypothesis. Specifically, it seems as though the development of successful new visions requires an outside or outsider's perspective. Howard Schultz was not the founder of Starbucks and was not tied to a single way of doing things. He was personally open to change. Similarly, Eisner was an outsider who came into Disney with a mandate for change. He could see Disney differently from someone who has spent years inside the existing Disney paradigm. At International Harvester, Archie McCardell also was an outsider (he came from Xerox). In his case, another advantage was that he did not have the political debts of an insider when he assumed the top job. Similarly, although John Horne was technically an insider at Navistar, he had run the Engine Division and was not really a "truck man" in the sense of others at the company. In a sense, the role of the outsider is to be a maverick and think and do things differently. This was actually hinted at by Ed Meyers of Edison Mission Energy in his use of the phrase "Merry Men." If we analyze Meyers' metaphor, we can recall that the merry men were Robin Hood's band. They took from the rich (Southern California Edison) and gave to the poor (Mission Energy). They were also outlaws, but good-hearted ones. Mission Energy was operating outside the normal boundaries of Edison.

Another lesson concerns the possibility of reverse diversification in creating a new business vision. Most people tend to think of new business visions as broadening. Yet Navistar has shown that it is possible to benefit from narrowing a business concept as well.

These companies demonstrate that it is not only feasible to create a successful Transformation of the Third Kind, but also give us insights into how it can be done. In the next chapter, we examine the experiences of some companies that could have benefited from these lessons. As we will see, these companies were unsuccessful in learning to play their chosen game effectively or in changing the game they were playing to more effectively "fit" with their environments and/or size.

6

ANATOMY OF UNSUCCESSFUL TRANSFORMATIONS

In Chapters 3 to 5, we examined a number of organizations that have made successful transformations, or are at least in that process with the promise of future success. Unfortunately, not all organizational transformations succeed. Many companies have tried to transform themselves and have failed, while others have experienced significant difficulties. We can learn a great deal from their experiences. In some instances, the concept or vision behind the intended transformation was good, but there were problems with the execution. In other cases, the vision itself was faulty.

The Unsuccessful Entrepreneurial Transformation to Professional Management at Osborne Computer

Just as some individuals can expect "15 minutes of fame," so can some companies. This was the situation for Osborne Computer, which had a fleeting moment of glory in the early 1980s and is a good illustration of the dire consequences of the failure to execute a successful Transformation of the First Kind.

Origin of Osborne Computer

Osborne Computer Corporation began when Adam Osborne recognized the market for a microcomputer that was relatively low-priced, easy to use, and also portable. His idea was a spin-off of the personal computer concept pioneered by Apple Computer, but Osborne identified a new market niche when he made his computers easy to carry. Despite skepticism, Osborne produced and marketed his machines and, in doing so, created a new market.

The firm experienced extraordinarily rapid growth. In 1981, the firm's first full year of operation, its sales were $5.8 million. By 1982, sales had grown to $68.8 million. During 1983, they were growing at an annualized rate of more than $100 million per year.

Osborne's success was the classic entrepreneur's dream come true, but it turned into a classic nightmare when the firm experienced its now well-publicized difficulties. When some suppliers sued to collect $4.5 million, Osborne filed for bankruptcy under Chapter XI of the Federal Bankruptcy code in September 1983. In his book entitled *Hypergrowth: The Rise and Fall of Osborne Computer Corporation,* Adam Osborne stated, "For Osborne Computer Corporation the game was over."[1]

What caused the fall of Osborne Computer after its meteoric rise? Although the answer is complex, a key to the basic problem was stated by Adam Osborne himself in reflecting on what had happened. The firm "had existed only eighteen months in terms of operation—hardly time to get my feet wet; all of a sudden the job was a whole different order of magnitude. I realized it was no longer an entrepreneurial operation in any conceivable way."[2] Despite this recognition, Osborne was unable to make the required changes in himself or his company.

Some of the problems faced by Osborne Computer were present from the company's earliest days, but they were masked or at least made less acute by its rapid sales growth. Engineering problems and manufacturing disputes were buried under an avalanche of orders created, in part, by a very successful advertising campaign. Money flowed into Osborne Computer and the firm received a great deal of visibility, but it was actually a profitless prosperity. Although revenues were $5.8 million in 1981, the firm incurred a loss of $1.3 million. The next year, when sales exploded to $68.9 million, the company still incurred a loss of $1 million. During the first quarter of 1983, sales were $34.4 million, for an annual running rate of more than $137 million, but the firm still had a loss of $600,000 for the quarter or $2.4 million on an annualized basis. Clearly, something was wrong with its operations.

Adam Osborne recognized that he was in over his head as a manager. As he stated,

> Growth had taken Osborne Computer Corporation to a size where I had to question my own qualifications. I had no professional training whatsoever in finance, management, or business administration, the very disciplines within which I was making critical business decisions every day.[3]

In May 1982, Osborne began looking for a seasoned professional manager to become president. The search process was not completed until the second week of January 1983, almost nine months later.

Unfortunately, when a company experiences the kind of rapid growth that Osborne Computer did, it is analogous to "dog years" (or years in a dog's life). Each year of rapid growth may not be equal to seven in a more stable company, but they are experienced as though they were. For example, Osborne was aware of the need to bring experienced, talented managers and supervisors into the company and did so. Yet, in the three to six months required for employees to learn their jobs at Osborne, the jobs had out-grown them.

Unless an organization has the infrastructure (including resources, operational systems, management systems, and the managerial capabilities) required to support this kind of rapid growth in advance of when it is actually required, the company is playing a very dangerous game. As long as revenue continues to increase and cash flow is there, the company can keep on going, even though there are great problems, inefficiencies, even losses. However, if anything breaks the momentum of increasing revenues and cash flow, the firm will then be caught in a situation where all its problems will no longer have the financial slack to mask or overcome them. This is exactly what happened to Osborne Computer in 1983.

In April, 1983, Osborne was in the middle of a product transition from its original core product, the "Osborne I" to a new product, the "Executive," an IBM compatible machine. Even though the Executive was a very promising product for the future, and the company had already received orders amounting to more than $25 million from dealers, the company still needed the revenues and cash flow from sales of the Osborne I. Unfortunately, the sales of this machine collapsed following the end of a sales promotion that gave a free copy of "dBASE II" software with each Osborne I purchased. The company also had some 15,000 Osborne I's in inventory, waiting to go into a dealer network already choking with unsold machines. In brief, the life-sustaining flow of cash slowed sufficiently to bring Osborne to the verge of collapse.

There were several other contributing factors, including the inability of the firm to arrange sufficient financing to give it time to try and survive, the unsuccessful entry of a new president (Robert Jaunich from Consolidated Foods), the unsuccessful attempts to sell Osborne to another company, and the company's aborted attempt to go public. There were also questions about Osborne's vision and strategy. We can speculate that the desktop computer, first with the MAC and then with the IBM PC, became more sophisticated and less expensive. Customers were no longer as tolerant of Osborne's small, hard-to-read screen. In addition, many competing machines were IBM compatible, which Osborne's were not.

The ultimate failure of Osborne Computer was attributable to a combination of factors, but was precipitated by the slowdown in orders and cash that exacerbated all its other problems. The root cause was its inability to change the game it was playing as well as the way it played it. Osborne failed to make the transition from a pure entrepreneurship to an entrepreneurially oriented, professionally managed organization. This would have given it the tools to manage its rapid growth. It also failed to adjust to market changes that eventually would have caused other problems.

The Unsuccessful Transformation

Adam Osborne recognized the *need* to make a Transformation of the First Kind (as described in Chapter 3), but it is not clear that he knew what that meant or what to do. He did not have a "template" for making the required transformation. We believe that if Osborne had used the lens presented in Chapter 2, he would have had a better understanding of what needed to be done at Osborne Computer to continue its initial success. He was experiencing what he himself termed hypergrowth, and he could simply not implement the concept of this type of transformation.

Drawing on the lens for building successful organizations presented in Chapter 2 (the pyramid of organizational success), Osborne had successfully "built" two of the six key building blocks: his market position and his product. Unfortunately, his business was much less developed at the other four levels of the pyramid: resources, operational systems, management systems, and culture.

One of the key weaknesses of his company was its underdeveloped operational and management systems. Osborne Computer did not have adequate financial, information, and control systems. For example, in an article on the rise and fall of Adam Osborne, Steve Coll stated: "In retrospect, it seems clear that the company's accounting procedures were so slipshod that no one knew how bad things were."[4]

To help us better understand why Osborne was unsuccessful as well as what must be done by a company like Osborne to ultimately succeed, we will compare the process of developing an organization at Osborne and Compaq Computers. This "paired comparison" will help clarify why Osborne ultimately failed, while Compaq became one of the world's leading companies. It will also illustrate the role of the pyramid of organizational success as a managerial lens in planning for the development of a business enterprise.

A Comparison of Osborne and Compaq

Osborne and Compaq, two companies who entered the personal computer market around the same time with products geared to similar users, had very different outcomes. Part of the reason for Compaq's success and Osborne's decline can be seen in their respective approaches to key developmental tasks at each stage of their growth.

Compaq successfully met the challenges of growth (as described in Chapter 3). It was what might be called a professionally managed entrepreneurship from the beginning. Attention was directed toward securing adequate resources and developing a tight infrastructure. Compaq's founders were able to see the pressures beyond market and product development and plan for their response. As Rod Canion, one of Compaq's founders and former president, remarked, "If you're growing slowly, problems can sidle up on you almost unnoticed. With high growth, if you don't get out of the way first, they knock you down flat."[5]

Identifying a Market and Developing Products. Osborne and Compaq chose the same arena—the portable personal computer market—in which to attempt to carve out a business segment. Initially, both new ventures were highly successful. Osborne saw a need for a portable, inexpensive computer for the naive, first-time user that brought the cost of personal computing within reach of the consumer. Osborne reached $1 million in sales in the first two months and was generating more than $5 million per month the next year. Keeping a focus on the market, Osborne launched a subsidiary in the United Kingdom a month after the first computers were shipped.

Osborne's early days were fully focused on market and product development. The first computer was presented after just four months of development, and four months later the first units were shipped. This rush to market, however, resulted in over $140,000 of associated costs, since Osborne had to fix bugs that appeared in the field. Getting the product to the customer is an important part of productization, and Osborne acted to ensure availability. To guarantee adequate shelf space for its product, Osborne emphasized dealer relationships. Osborne Computers offered the dealerships attractive terms and did not compete with a direct sales force of its own.

For Compaq, the business segment was based on creating a portable computer completely compatible with the IBM PC, the industry standard. The firm correctly identified a market for a small, compact, relatively lightweight computer that could be carried almost everywhere. Like Osborne, Compaq experienced phenomenal growth, and recorded sales of over $111 million in the first year after its product was released (1983).

The need to get the product to the customer was met successfully by Compaq with a strategy similar to that of Osborne's. Compaq stressed the development and maintenance of good dealer relationships. Despite this similarity, Compaq dealt with the developmental task of productization in a fundamentally different way from Osborne. The product was not the sole concern at Compaq during its early days. Before production even began, attention was directed toward the infrastructure that would support the organization as it grew.

Acquiring Resources and Developing Operational Systems. The differences between Osborne and Compaq in handling key developmental tasks are most noticeable in the two key issues to be faced in the next two levels of the pyramid of organizational success. Osborne hired personnel and developed systems on an as-needed basis. The first financial person was not brought in until February 1981—a month after incorporation and just six months before the first shipment of the product. Market planning problems were the impetus for development of control systems. Quality control problems a year after the company was founded led to the addition of a Vice President for Engineering. This was followed a short time later with a major restructuring in response to manufacturing problems. Instead of anticipating needs, Osborne Computer was caught responding to problems. Its resources and systems were inadequate for handling the industry's fast-paced environment and the company's explosive growth.

Compaq took a longer view of its needs and invested in its operational infrastructure (resources and systems) in order to support its future growth. It hired computer programmers who averaged fifteen years of experience and drafted the best sales and marketing professionals possible, some from their competitors. In establishing operational systems, Compaq again demonstrated the importance of professional management. According to John Gribi, Compaq's Vice President and Chief Financial Officer, financial controls and forecasting systems were in place well before production began.

Both companies successfully achieved the first two challenges of growth. They were able to establish a new venture that provided a product to a market previously untapped. Compaq had the comparative advantage in its ability to successfully acquire the resources and develop the operational systems necessary for supporting its growth. While Osborne ended up in bankruptcy, Compaq built a multibillion-dollar company that is now included in the *Fortune 500* and has challenged IBM for technological leadership in the personal computer market.

Leadership of the Transformation Process

Unfortunately, although Adam Osborne may have been a good entrepreneur who was able to successfully establish Osborne Computer, he was not an effective leader of the transformation to professional management. By definition, leadership requires vision. Osborne did not realize the need to make a Transformation of the First Kind until it was too late (or, if he did realize this need, he was unable to initiate the changes necessary to ensure success). In addition, it does not appear that Osborne had adequate advisors, such as consultants, to help him. The proper role of a consultant would have been to alert Osborne to the impending need to make a transformation to professional management well before it hit him in the face. As a leader, Osborne recognized his own limitations, and sought to bring in a professional manager to run his company. However, by the time this individual arrived, it may have been too late.

Lessons from Osborne Computer

What can we learn from the failure of Osborne Computer to make the successful transformation to professional management? The first lesson is that this transformation is a *necessity* for long-term survival of a business enterprise. It is not just something that might be nice to do. Second, the more rapid the rate of growth experienced by a company, the more rapid the need for this type of transformation. In addition, the more rapid the rate of growth of a business, the less time there is for a transformation. There is less clock-time in terms of months or years to accomplish the transformation in rapid growth businesses such as Osborne Computer, Apple Computer, MaxiCare, Starbucks, and Boston Markets.

Another lesson can be derived from the comparison between Osborne and Compaq. Like an outfielder who is playing shallow and does not have enough time to react to a line drive, Osborne did not anticipate the need to make a Transformation of the First Kind early enough. He was focused on products and markets and did not appreciate the need (or did not have the time or resources) to develop the other key building blocks of organizational success until too late. In contrast, Compaq did just what we have described as the appropriate way of building a successful enterprise.

The management team at Compaq knew what to do because of their prior experience. Many members of the original founding group were experienced professional managers from Texas Instruments. They understood what was necessary and did it. In effect, Compaq did what we have been suggesting must be done to build a successful organization. Compaq's successful development does illustrate the power and value of the frameworks presented in Chapter 2 as a lens and template for guiding successful development and transformations of businesses into other enterprises. Indeed, the way the authors initially developed the frameworks was, as noted in the Preface, to study "best practices" of successful organizations such as Compaq.

We should point out, however, that Compaq did have some important advisors. One of the original investors and Board members was a venture capitalist named Benjamin Rosen who had a history of successful entrepreneurial start-ups. It is clear that he played a significant role in the company's successful development, not just as an investor but as an advisor as well.

Different Strategies for Playing the Game, Different Results

As a result of the way it played the game from its inception, Compaq Computer Corporation achieved $14.8 billion in revenues and net income of more than $1 billion in 1995. As a result of the way it played the game, Osborne Computer Corporation no longer exists in a market that it helped identify. As Adam Osborne stated in reflecting on his experience, "When you become an entrepreneur, you can go up awfully fast, but you can go down just as fast. It's so ephemeral, like actors who end up committing suicide. One day they're famous, the next nobody knows who the hell they are."[6]

The Unsuccessful Revitalization Transformation at Eastman Kodak

Photography was invented during the 1840s. By the 1880s, most photographs were taken by professionals because the equipment was difficult to use and processing was complex. George Eastman, the founder of Eastman Kodak, was interested in photography, and began experimenting with developing better and easier processes for taking and developing photos. He started manufacturing photographic development equipment based on his own inventions in the 1870s.

Eastman Kodak Company was formed in 1888 with the introduction of a roll film camera for the amateur. The company later began processing film in its factories at Rochester, New York. With the introduction of the immensely popular Kodak Brownie in the early 1900s, an industry was born. Kodak was the major player, and the company had little competition until the 1980s, almost a century after its inception.

The Decline

Eastman Kodak was an extraordinarily successful company for a very long time. Unfortunately, its own success ultimately contributed to its decline. Specifically, Kodak's success led to a culture that began to expect continued success as an entitlement. It also led to a belief that the company "should avoid hasty action." Kodak proceeded cautiously and watched competitors develop new products and pioneer new market segments that were natural extensions of its own core business. Specifically, Kodak avoided haste while competitors developed instant photography (Polaroid), 35-mm cameras (Canon, et al.), and VCRs (various Japanese companies).

In addition, while still the leader in the film market, Kodak's market share dwindled with the onslaught of competition from Fuji and discount film manufacturers. Kodak also saw its market share in cameras shrivel. More ominous was the threat from digital imaging technology that could make film photography obsolete. Although digital imaging is still in its infancy, the threat to Eastman Kodak is real.

In brief, Eastman Kodak, an organization with a long history and more than $10 billion in revenue, faced a decline that necessitated a major revitalization transformation.

In 1984, Colby Chandler, then Chairman, recognized that Kodak needed more than a tune up. He embarked on a program to revitalize Kodak. Although this need was perceived correctly, the process of transformation actually undertaken was poorly conceived and ultimately led to its failure.

Kodak's Initial Attempt at Revitalization and Leadership

Chandler began the revitalization process by engaging a consultant to review Kodak's management structure. This was based on the assumption (either explicit or implicit) that Kodak's problems were internal and related to its inability to diversify. This was, at least in part, correct. After the consultant's report was received and reviewed, the next step was to attempt to gain broader agreement among Kodak's management about what needed to be done. This was accomplished by a series of meetings among "ever widening groups."

Kodak's management system had in fact contributed to the failure to develop new products. Specifically, the company was organized into a functional structure for its core business—photography. A classic limitation of the functional form of organizations is that it tends to inhibit, rather than facilitate, the development of new products.

Unfortunately, Kodak's difficulties in new product development were a symptom of its decline and not the core problem to be solved. The real problem seems to be that Kodak and Chandler did not ever articulate a true vision for what Kodak was to become, but, instead based their revitalization on a strategy of diversification. Kodak's revitalization plan seems to have grown from the notion that the key issues were its structure and lack of new product development.

The company's strategy was to diversify into areas based on Kodak's core competencies. To implement this strategy, Kodak did an assessment of those competencies. Since it was essentially a photography business, the company had to have competencies in three key areas: (1) optics, (2) chemistry, and (3) electronics. Kodak then attempted to leverage the three core competencies by developing new products. The new products covered a broad range of areas from bottle-feed nutrients to electronics.

As part of the strategy of revitalization through diversification, Kodak made several acquisitions. The largest acquisition was Sterling Drugs, which was intended to complement the development of pharmaceutical products to be leveraged from Kodak's core competency in chemistry. Kodak also acquired a number of start-up firms. It entered a variety of markets, including the videotape, floppy disk, and alkaline and lithium battery markets. It also entered the instant photography market with its own product line, but was sued by Polaroid for patent infringement.

To support the company's growth and diversification, Kodak restructured and formed seventeen autonomous business units, largely within two segments of its business (imaging and information). Business unit managers were encouraged to act "entrepreneurially" and compete aggressively—not only for new business but for the company's finite resources. Although initial results were promising, the costs of this type of "helter skelter growth strategy" and decentralized form of organization would become increasingly apparent, as we will see below.

Problems with the "Lens" Used for Revitalization

To a great extent, the problems Eastman Kodak ultimately faced were attributable to the lens it used in planning its revitalization. During the 1980s, the lens typically employed was the "market share growth" matrix, as originally developed by the Boston Consulting group.[7] Although there are several versions of this matrix, Figure 6–1 illustrates the basic concepts. The matrix (or table) consists of two dimensions: (1) market share, and (2) growth potential.

In this context, "growth" refers to cash flow and profitability. Under this paradigm, businesses are classified into one of four possible categories: (1) "Dogs," (2) "Cash Cows," (3) "Stars," and (4) "Rising Stars." Businesses in quadrant 1 are termed "Dogs" because they have low market share and growth potential. Businesses in quadrant 2 are called "Cash Cows" because they have high market shares but low growth potential. The connotation of a Cash Cow was that the business would be "milked" or used as a source of funding for more promising investment opportunities. Businesses in quadrant 3 are "Stars" because they have relatively high market shares and high profit growth potential, while those in quadrant 4 are termed "Rising Stars"

**Growth
Potential**

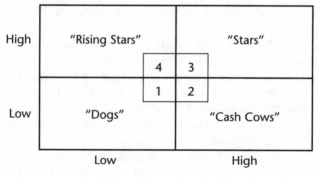

Market Share

Figure 6–1. Market Share–Growth Potential Matrix.

because they have low market shares but high growth potential. If successful, "Rising Stars" became "Stars." This lens suggests that cash cows are to be treated as sources of funding to invest in question marks to help them become rising stars.

Another version of this matrix is shown in Figure 6–2. In this figure, the variables used are "Cash Generation" and "Cash Use." Figure 6–2 shows "Cash Cows" as businesses with high cash flows, which can be used to fund investments in other, developing businesses. Stated differently, they are

**Cash
Use**

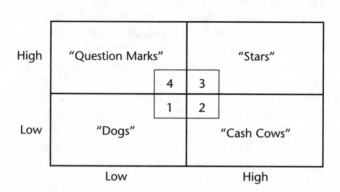

Cash Generation

Figure 6–2. Cash Use/Cash Generation Matrix.

"harvested" (managed to generate cash). "Dogs" are weak businesses, which have little growth or cash-generating potential. They should be "harvested" to generate cash or "divested." "Question Marks" are businesses that require high investment or cash flow. Finally, "Stars" are businesses with high cash generation that require high cash flow investment.

The reason for illustrating the cash flow aspect of the growth-share matrix is to bring out the nature of its underlying paradigm. Explicitly and implicitly, this approach views businesses from an investment perspective. Under this lens, businesses are "managed" like a "portfolio" of stocks. The crucial issue is not so much how they are managed on a day to day or even longer term basis but how *cash* is managed and allocated among business units. Implicitly, this approach treats a business as (what engineers term) a "black box"—something that functions in an unknown way.

One problem with this deceptively simple approach is that it requires complex judgments about what businesses are: dogs, cash cows, and so on. Corporate management must evaluate a business and determine whether it has growth potential, in both an absolute sense and relative to other business units in the company's "portfolio." In the case of Eastman Kodak, it was assumed (in 1984) that the core photography business had limited growth potential and therefore that ought to be treated as a cash cow to fund more promising growth opportunities. Unfortunately, this premise was not correct (as shown by subsequent events). In addition, Kodak's acquisitions of various new businesses as investments and the management of the overall enterprise as a portfolio of investments did not work out very well, as shown in Figure 6–3.

In using this lens for planning what to do to revitalize its business, Eastman Kodak assumed, at least implicitly, that the core photographic business was a mature business with low growth potential. Based on this assumption, the company chose a strategy of continuing to grow through diversification. This, in turn, had two negative results. First, it led to a relative neglect of the core photographic business at Kodak. Even though it was a slow growth business, it continued to generate substantial profitability, as

	Revenues (billions)					Net Income (millions)				
	1989	1990	1991	1992	1993	1989	1990	1991	1992	1993
Kodak	18.4	18.9	19.4	20.2	20.1	1,591	2,844	772	2,147	1,924
Imaging	7.0	7.1	7.1	7.4	7.3	821	1,611	489	1,216	1,109
Information	4.2	4.1	4.0	4.1	3.9	(360)	5	(688)	(151)	(137)
Chemicals	3.5	3.6	3.7	3.9	4.0	643	602	538	494	392
Health	4.0	4.3	4.9	5.1	5.2	487	626	433	588	560

Figure 6–3. Eastman Kodak Financial Summary (1989–1993).

shown in Figure 6–3. Second, it allowed Kodak to lose its focus as a business. By building on its so-called core competencies and diversification, Eastman Kodak's business concept became blurry.

Results of the Revitalization Transformation

Eastman Kodak's attempted revitalization transformation under Colby Chandler was not successful. This attempt transformed it from a photographic business into a conglomerate with four business segments: (1) imaging, (2) information, (3) chemicals, and (4) health. As Figure 6–3 indicates, the result of this diversification was very uneven during the period from 1989 to '93. The core imaging business grew very modestly from $7 to $7.3 billion during this period. Net income for this segment was very uneven, and earnings in 1993 were well below their peak in 1990. The information business segment was clearly a "dog," with losses incurred in four of five years. Kodak's chemicals grew modestly in revenues, but profits were decreasing from a peak of $643 million in 1990 to $392 million in 1993. The health business was a bit more healthy. Revenues increased from $4 to $5.2 billion, but profits were uneven. Net income in 1993 of $560 million was less than the $626 million earned in 1990. Clearly, Kodak did not achieve the steadily increasing revenues and earnings stability required by a growth company, such as General Electric, Merck, or Coca-Cola.

Kodak's Revitalization: Stage II

By 1990, there were already hints about the need for a more coherent business concept and strategy in the comments of Kay R. Whitmore, who was then CEO of Eastman Kodak. As Whitmore stated, "The formation of our Commercial Imaging group combines in one organization not only our centers of excellence, but all of our Information Segment Units. This will enhance our research, product development, and manufacturing efforts, while intensifying our focus on customers."[8]

In 1991, Eastman Kodak experienced a very difficult year. Although revenue increased slightly as shown in Figure 6-3, net income declined by 73% from $2,844 million to $772 million. Profit declined in all of Kodak's business segments, but there was a staggering loss of $688 million in the information unit. Faced with these results, Kodak, under the leadership of Kay R. Whitmore, made a significant change in its strategic direction and organizational structure.

Beginning in 1992, the company began to refocus on its core business of imaging. First, it redefined its business concept or business foundation. As Whitmore stated, "Our principal business, we concluded, was in images and not in every form of imaging. Recording, storing images, transmitting images and delivering image outputs—this is our competitive advantage."[9] Accordingly, Kodak sold a number of what it described as peripheral businesses. The company used the proceeds to reduce its debt as well as fund a

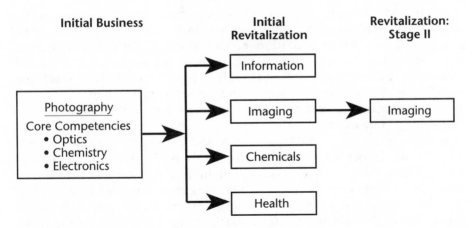

Figure 6–4. The Transformation of Kodak.

renewed emphasis on research and development in image-related technology. For example, investments in silver-halide technology resulted in twenty new photographic products (announced in 1993), including three film families and a camera. In addition, the company spun off its chemical business as "Eastman Chemical Company" by distributing shares to its stockholders. In brief, the year 1992 marked the end of the first phase of Kodak's attempted revitalization transformation and the beginning of Phase II in its transformation, as shown schematically in Figure 6–4.

On October 28, 1993, Kodak's George M. C. Fischer, who had led a revitalization at Motorola Inc., became the new CEO and leader of Eastman Kodak. During 1994, Kodak sold several non-imaging health businesses, including its clinical diagnostic business, the pharmaceutical and consumer health businesses of Sterling Winthrop Inc., and others. The company had finally achieved a coherent, integrated business focus on imaging as its core business and abandoned the "portfolio" approach adopted in the 1980s. This was captured in a statement in the company's 1994 Annual Report: "Our corporate vision is clear—Our heritage has been and our future is to be the world leader in imaging."[10]

Lessons from Kodak's Unsuccessful Transformation

What lessons can we learn from Kodak's attempted revitalization transformation? Although several factors contributed to its lack of success, the most fundamental is that Kodak did not approach its revitalization with a coherent, integrated organizational development strategy. Instead, Kodak approached revitalization in a piecemeal fashion. If we use the framework presented in this book as a lens to assess and evaluate what Kodak did and did not do, the problems encountered and the company's lack of success become clear.

What Kodak actually required was a compound Transformation of the Second and Third Kinds. Specifically, Kodak needed a business vision transformation as well as a revitalization transformation. Kodak did not develop a statement of the vision for its future business—there was no clear integrated concept of what its business would become. As we have observed, this is the foundation for a corporate transformation effort. In addition, in its failure to articulate a sound business definition statement, Kodak did not formulate a true strategic mission.

One of the reasons for Kodak's unsuccessful transformation, and, in turn, a key lesson, is that they used the incorrect "lens" for planning the revitalization. They followed the popular (but limited in usefulness) notion of focusing on "core competencies" in planning their transformation. Unfortunately, this is an inward focus and a smorgasbord approach to divisification rather than a systematic effort. Kodak should have been looking at the market *as well as* their internal capabilities. It should be noted that what is typically viewed as "revitalization" often requires a compound transformation that includes a change in business vision. Kodak simply did not do this and their efforts were *ad hoc*.

Had Kodak used the lens we have proposed in Chapter 2, their mind-set would have been different, and they would have been much more likely to focus on the need for a vision transformation. This is one of the intended benefits of the lens presented here, and, we believe, it would have served Kodak as well.

Another dimension of Kodak's problems with transformation through diversification has been suggested by Robert Hoskisson and Michael Hitt in their book entitled, *Downsizing: How to Tame the Diversified Firm*.[11] Hoskisson and Hitt discuss the effect of diversification on managerial practices. One of the central themes in their book is that when a conglomerate owns businesses that require a great deal of R&D investment to grow, there is a decided tendency to allocate too little capital to these businesses. This might have happened at Kodak. The point, in the context of this book, is that firms take a big risk in diversification if they do not fully understand the nature of the new business they are getting into.

The consequences of Kodak's failed effort at revitalization have been severe. The company, which never had a layoff in its history, has gone through a series of layoffs and early retirement programs. It also sold some of the unprofitable businesses it acquired in its diversification effort. Much of the substantial financial resources the company enjoyed have now been dissipated. Its stock price has been under pressure for years.

As we have seen in the examples of Navistar and Chrysler, the revitalization transformation of a large complex enterprise takes a great deal of time and sometimes must be done in more than one phase. Kodak is now in the process of a second, more successful revitalization under the leadership of George M. C. Fisher. This, in turn, builds upon the decisions made by Kay R. Whitmore, beginning in 1992, to change Kodak's vision. However, it should be noted that the success of this process is still in question. In late 1997, Kodak went through another major lay-off.

The Unsuccessful Business Vision Transformation at Sears

The example of corporate transformation at Sears, Roebuck, & Co. (Sears) is probably one of the most ambitious attempts to transform a company in U.S. history. We will first examine the history and background of Sears, and then discuss its transformation.

The Beginning and Early History

Sears, Roebuck & Co. was founded by Richard Sears and Alvis Curtis Roebuck in the nineteenth century to sell watches through mail order. They soon expanded into offering other products. Sears had spent much of his life in small towns, and he understood the midwestern farmer's needs and wants. Accordingly, this company focused on the rural market.

In 1895, Julius Rosenwald and his brother-in-law, Aaron Nussbaum, bought into the company. They brought with them managerial and organizational systems knowledge and skills that complemented Sears' abilities.

Creating a "New Core Business"

In the 1920s, Sears selected General Robert Wood as his successor. General Wood understood demographics and perceived the population shift from cities and rural areas to the suburbs. Under Wood's leadership, Sears pioneered the strategy of building stores with parking lots along the highways just outside cities. The company went to real estate developers and said: "If you build a shopping center, we will become your anchor tenant." In effect, Wood helped create the uniquely American concept of the shopping mall.

General Wood was a strong visionary leader. In addition to the success of shopping malls, which changed the way the U.S. middle class did their shopping, the General expanded Sears' credit operations to facilitate the sale of appliances. He also created Allstate Insurance Company, a development that foreshadowed a major transformation at Sears later on.

The Seeds of Decline

Unfortunately, there is typically a downside when an organization has a leader as strong as General Wood. Although he had assumed the leadership of Sears in the 1920s, he served until 1954. He did not retire at the mandatory age of sixty-five, and got extensions that lasted nine years. During this period, there was a succession of top executives who might have been able to replace Wood capably. However, as in other companies where the CEO wishes to remain in charge, all these individuals left Sears. After Wood retired, Sears was left with less skilled executives, who had more of a care-taker mentality. Like the situation at Disney after Walt's passing, the Sears executives were in awe of General Wood and tried to make decisions and solve problems "the way the General would do it." This was the seed of a bit-ter harvest for Sears some years later.

Unfortunately, Sears' decades of success had created another problem typ-ical of organizations that experience decline: corporate arrogance. Success led to contempt for competition and a belief that no one could tell Sears, Roebuck & Co. anything about the business it owned. Although revenues continued to grow at Sears during the 1950s and 1960s, the company's sales were not growing in existing stores but in new stores. Sears' market share was decreasing.

The Sears Tower in Chicago, the company's corporate headquarters, was literally and figuratively a symbol of the corporation's majesty and its prob-lem. The building towered over Chicago, but it was a black monolith, almost impenetrable by sunlight. It stood there symbolizing the success, the power, and the remoteness of Sears' management: the twentieth-century equivalent of many European medieval castles—and just as vulnerable to the winds of change.

The Decline and Attempted Transformation

Beginning in the 1970s, Sears began to decline in strength in its core retail merchandise business. The merchandising group developed the wrong strat-egy. It focused on upgrading the image of Sears' stores and ignored the com-petitive threat from discounters. In essence, the group attempted a vision transformation, but failed to consider how this new vision would "fit" in the markets the firm served.

First K-Mart and later Wal★Mart began to eat Sears' lunch. In the 1970s, the buying public became more cost conscious. The natural market for Sears had always been the working class and lower middle class, particularly in rural America. Yet Sears had lost touch with them. This market is cost con-scious and will trade service for quality with low prices. What Wal★Mart and K-Mart offered was a combination of product assortment, price, and convenience (especially in strip malls with lots of parking). In addition, Wal★Mart had a very sophisticated inventory system that kept shelves filled with merchandise that was selling. What the discounters did not offer was lots of salespeople to help you find what you wanted or explain the products. However, this absence of salespeople resulted in lower costs that, in turn, led to lower prices for customers. Sears, on the other hand, had less product variety, with some items out of stock, at higher prices than the discounters, and a number of salespeople who were sometimes of little help. Accordingly, while Sears began to slip, K-Mart and Wal★Mart contin-ued to grow.

Sears' New Vision

Recognizing that they had lost the strategic battle for their core customers to K-Mart and Wal★Mart, Sears developed what might have been a brilliant strategy, if it had been executed properly. It began the process of a major transformation in the nature of Sears and the business it was in. Based on its reading of the future environment in which it would operate, Sears' vision was to transform itself from a consumer goods retailer into a consumer products and services enterprise. The vision was to utilize Sears' name recognition, distribution assets, and customer base as a core focus for distributing other types of "products," particularly financial services products. In a sense (although the company did not explicitly articulate it this way), Sears' vision was to virtually transform itself from a consumer products retailer into a diversified financial services company, which happened to own a retail merchandise division. When the transformation process began, Sears already owned All- State Insurance.

As part of the process of implementing this vision, Sears acquired Coldwell Banker, one of the leading residential and commercial real estate firms. In addition, Sears acquired Dean Witter, a retail stock brokerage company. Sears also introduced the Discover credit card to compete against VISA and MasterCard, and to try to bind Sears' customers to Sears.

The net result of these changes was to create "the Sears Financial Network." These business units of Sears existed alongside the retail merchandising system. Sears had now reached a new stage and created a new vision, as shown schematically in Figure 6–5.

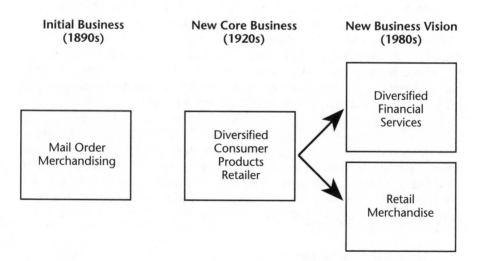

Figure 6–5. Evolution of Sears.

Financial Results of the Transformation

Figure 6–6 indicates some clear trends in the financial results of the components of Sears' business during the period from 1984 through 1991.
Although the revenues of the merchandise group increased every year, net
income from the group's operations began to decline in 1985 from a peak of
$905 million to a low of $257 million in 1990, before rising to $486 million
in 1991. Net income in 1991 was only 54% of what it had been in 1984! In
contrast, net income from the financial services business increased quite
steadily (except for 1990) throughout this period from $701 million in 1984
to more than $1.1. billion in 1991. It must be noted that the lion's share of
net income was attributable to the Allstate Insurance Group. Net Income
from Dean Witter was uneven during this period, and losses were incurred in
three of the seven years. Coldwell Banker was profitable in all seven years,
though net income did fluctuate. Nevertheless, the combined net income of
Dean Witter and Coldwell Banker (excluding Allstate) exceeded that of the
merchandise group in 1990 and was 84% of the net income of the merchandise group in 1991, even though the revenues of the merchandise group
were huge in comparison to these other businesses.

From the data shown in Figure 6–6, it is clear that the core merchandise
business was in trouble. Revenue growth had reached a plateau and even
declined slightly in 1990, and profit had deteriorated for almost a decade.
Allstate insurance was a gem, and both Dean Witter and Coldwell Banker
were significant profit contributors. The combined income from all these
financial service businesses had actually exceeded the profit contribution of
the merchandise business, beginning in 1986 for the entire period through
1991.

If we step back from the details and look at what was happening, it seems
as though Sears had brilliantly transformed itself from a declining merchandise business into a loosely defined consumer products and services business.
Although the merchandising business was in decline, the financial services
businesses were growing and profitable. Nevertheless, Sears was still at its
core a merchant rather than a consumer products and services company, and
merchants were still very much in its leadership positions.

The original transformation had been created under Edward R. Telling,
who was now retired. Edward A. Brennan, who had replaced Telling as
Chairman and CEO, was a traditional "retail store guy." His roots were with
what Sears had been in its glory days, not what it had become. It was also
clear that if current trends continued, the merchandise unit of Sears was des-
tined for a period of long, slow decline. Faced with this situation, the company decided to change its direction and vision of the future.

Problems with the Transformation

The transformation of Sears from a consumer products retailer to a diversified financial services and consumer products business was bold in concept,

	Revenues (billions)									Net Income (millions)							
	1984	1985	1986	1987	1988	1989	1990	1991		1984	1985	1986	1987	1988	1989	1990	1991
Sears	33.8	40.7	44.3	48.4	56.3	55.8	56.0	57.2		1,452	1,894	11,339	1,683	1,454	1,509	902	1,279
Merchandise Group	26.5	26.6	27.1	28.1	30.3	31.6	25.1	24.8		905	786	736	787	524	647	257	486
Financial Services:																	
All State Insurance	9.0	10.4	12.6	15.6	14.9	16.8	18.2	19.4		658	596	738	946	953	815	701	722
Dean Witter	2.5	2.9	3.4	4.0	3.8	4.1	4.6	4.9		(31)	-	(13)	(40)	86	166	233	345
Coldwell Banker	0.8	0.9	1.2	1.2	1.4	1.4	1.4	1.6		74	99	66	129	90	127	26	61
Total Financial Group										701	695	791	1,035	1,125	1,106	960	1,128

Figure 6–6. Sears, Roebuck and Co. Financial Summary (1984–1991).

but its execution left something to be desired. At one level, Sears faced what seems to be the classic problem with corporate transformations: resistance of the original core business to change.

One of the problems with the transformation at Sears was that it was not explicitly recognized as a transformation; rather, it was seen as a strategy of "continuing to pursue other avenues of growth consistent with the company's traditional strengths and experience."[12] In fairness to Sears, the concept of organizational transformations was not used until very recently, and there was not a general understanding that transformations required a different perspective than simply pursuing "strategies for growth." Indeed, that is one of the messages of this book.

The inability to fully appreciate and recognize that Sears was undergoing a transformation led to other problems. For even though the transformation was successful in a financial sense, it was never fully institutionalized in an organizational sense. Specifically, Sears still viewed itself as primarily a merchandising company. Although it has not been widely discussed, some of Sears' major retail players (i.e., some of the store managers in major cities) never bought into the concept of transforming to a diversified financial service business. Their reasons were essentially political.

Financing the transformation was also expensive. Sears did not have sufficient resources to both set up the new financial businesses and simultaneously revitalize the existing retail operations. In addition, the retail operation was being treated (either explicitly or implicitly) as a "cash cow," a business with limited growth potential that would be "milked" to fund new business ventures with (financial) "star" potential.

The Ichabod Crane Approach to Leadership

There also does not appear to have been a single leader of the transformation at Sears, like an Iacocca at Chrysler or even a Chandler at Kodak. It seems that the transformation was a corporate idea that was not championed effectively to get total commitment throughout the Sears organization. Similarly, the ultimate defeat of the business vision transformation does not seem to have been led by any single individual, but was more a product of the organization as a whole. This may suggest that there was something of a leadership vacuum at Sears, which may be one of the critical reasons for the ultimate failure of the transformation. This suggests that Sears can be viewed during this period as something like Ichabod Crane, the headless horseman, a "leaderless" organization that is moving ahead merely by its own momentum.

Lessons from the Sears Transformation

Although the concept of diverting resources from cash cows to fund rising stars is rational from a corporate perspective, it is difficult for people who work in the "cow business" to accept. Given Sears' historical culture of decentralization, the store managers in major metropolitan areas had considerable power. It was their stores that would not be modernized because of insufficient cash. It was their prestige that was being tarnished by the decline in Sears' preeminence as the leading retailer, and some did not support the transformation in a way necessary for ensuring its success. Consequently, a key lesson is that, to be successful, a vision transformation needs the support of key company constituents.

There were other problems with the intended transformation at Sears as well. The Sears financial network was not integrated effectively into the operating structures of the business. Within the financial centers, each operating unit had its own area, staffed with its own people. The financial network was superimposed on the existing Sears' structure, instead of becoming the structure. It was like an "add on" to a house rather than a tear-down amid rebuilding the house.

In addition, the Sears Financial Network never really became an integrated network. It was more a collection of independent financial businesses. The original vision had been to create a true financial supermarket, but that was never actually accomplished.

Dismantling the Transformation

In 1992, Sears underwent, in the words of the company itself, "sweeping changes," with the goal of shaping a stronger company and enhancing shareholder value. Sears announced that it would concentrate on its core retailing business. It planned to sell Dean Witter, its brokerage subsidiary, its Discover Credit Card business, and most of Coldwell Banker, its real estate operation. It also planned to sell a portion of Allstate Insurance, as well as certain other nonretail units.

This decision marked the end of the internal civil war at Sears, which began with the inception of the transformation process. It also marked the end of one of the most ambitious transformation efforts ever undertaken.

A Final Lesson: Crossing the Rubicon

Another lesson of the Sears' transformation for other companies is that crossing the Rubicon is critical. In the days of the Roman Empire, when the armies crossed the Rubicon River there was no turning back. Sears never crossed the Rubicon. It tried to build a new business without dismantling its existing core business. In contrast, when International Harvester decided to emphasize the automotive truck and diesel engine business, it sold off its core agricultural equipment business. For better or worse, it crossed the Rubicon.

Since Sears never totally committed to either revitalizing the retail merchandise business or building a new financial business, it faced a continuing dilemma. It never had the resources it required to do either as well as necessary. What Sears had to do was redesign the entire business enterprise. Specifically, once the new business vision was articulated, Sears needed to design the whole pyramid of organizational development for the new Sears, not just graft changes onto the existing pyramid structure. This is a critical lesson for all companies faced with organizational transformations.

Changing the Game at AT&T

Since the breakup of the Bell System in 1984, AT&T's earnings and future have been unstable. The company embarked upon an ambitious revitalization strategy that was unsuccessful; it is now in the midst of a revised strategy involving a narrowing of its business vision.

Just as with Eastman Kodak and Sears, the transformation at AT&T may be viewed in terms of phases. The first phase was from 1984 to 1994 and was unsuccessful. The second began in 1995 and is not yet complete. Taken together, they illustrate a compound transformation involving both revitalization and business vision changes.

Phase I: Revitalization/Business Vision Transformations

Although AT&T still earns 80 to 90% of its profits from its long distance business, where it controls more than 60% of the market, its initial revitalization strategy was to reposition itself to provide network services for different customers based on features defined by software.

As communications and computers began to merge into a single business, AT&T defined its customer as the "information consumer." The information consumer wants access to many networks, including electronic mail, voice and data networks, and cable television networks, to name just a few. AT&T positioned itself to integrate all these networks. The business vision underlying this change was to transform AT&T from a telephone company to a telecommunications business.

The first phase of AT&T's transformation, begun under James Olson, then the company's CEO, was neither quick nor easy. After the breakup of AT&T in 1984, the company made several false starts into computers and other ventures. Although the long-distance business remained profitable, even that was threatened because AT&T has traditional transmission lines, while its new competitors (Sprint and MCI) installed fiber optic cable that enables the transmission of greater amounts of information less expensively.

Robert Allen assumed the role of CEO after Olson's death in 1988 and reorganized the company into twenty-two individual businesses to increase accountability. Under this structure, AT&T had units such as Business Products, with more than $3 billion in sales of office phone systems and voice mail systems, and AT&T Micro Electronics, which manufactures chips for both AT&T and outside users. The company acquired NCR Corp, which put AT&T into the business of selling computers designed to be connected to networks, such as bank ATMs and retail cash registers. AT&T also acquired McCaw Cellular to get a foothold in cellular communications.

Along with changes in structure and the acquisitions described above,

AT&T also changed certain aspects of its management processes. AT&T used a senior-level planning group to manage the business under Allen's leadership as well as a management development program for hundreds of its middle managers to get them to think more entrepreneurially about their operations. Another aspect of AT&T's transformation was its willingness to abandon the past and adapt to the future. In 1988, Allen had AT&T write off the old wiring for its transmission lines and install fiber optic lines. The write off was $6.7 billion and AT&T reported a loss.

Phase II: A "New" Business Vision Transformation

In September 1995, Allen and AT&T stunned the business community with an announcement that AT&T would "break up" into three independent, publicly traded companies. AT&T created three "new" businesses from the "old" AT&T. These are:
1. AT&T, which will focus on communication services.
2. Lucent Technologies, the equipment unit.
3. NCR, Computer Systems and services.

This decision amounts to a reversal of direction and, in effect, a new business vision for AT&T. In effect, AT&T chose to simplify its business, and then revised its business concept. Specifically, the company has jettisoned its ailing computer unit (largely comprising the NCR business it acquired) as well as its successful equipment business and capital finance business. In theory, before this decision AT&T had achieved a unique business concept in the communication industry. It owned the world's largest and most sophisticated telecommunications network, used and sold equipment from its network systems group, and owned a computer business capable of providing the software and hardware required by the "global information customer." However, the complexity of managing all these different businesses exceeded the advantages of their integration. As Robert Allen has stated,

> Bigger is not always better—particularly in a fast changing world that requires speed and agility. We've reached the point where the advantages of our size and scope, considerable though they may be, are being offset by the time and cost of coordinating and integrating sometimes conflicting business strategies.[13]

Although the second phase of transformation at AT&T involved a reversal of direction and is not yet fully completed, the company has returned to profitability and appears to be on the road to a successful transformation from a regulated telephone monopoly to an unregulated telecommunications business. It must be noted, however, that AT&T is not out of the woods yet.

Epilogue

In 1997, there was continuing turmoil at AT&T but also a significant leadership change. Robert Armstrong, who led one phase of the transformation at

Hughes Electronics, became the new CEO at AT&T. He quickly began to focus the company and divest it of some non-core units.

The Unsuccessful Vision Transformation at Sweet Treats, Inc.[14]

Sweet Treats, Inc. was a manufacturer and distributor of candy products. The company was established in the 1930s and had developed a recognizable brand name throughout the United States. Although it initially developed its own retail stores to distribute its products, beginning in the early 1960s it established a franchise system. In the early 1990s, Sweet Treats, Inc. (or STI as it was called by firm members) had more than 1,000 retail outlets, of which about 10% were company owned and operated.

The STI group of stores sold more than $1 billion of products annually. However, the revenues derived by STI *per se* were approximately $350 million. STI was founded by John and Marsha Sweetert and had been run as a family business until 1982. At that time, the company was purchased by Consume More Foods, a large international food company. Consume More had two divisions based on its manufacturing and retail subsidiaries. Total sales for all Consume More companies were in excess of $5 billion annually.

The Mandate for Growth

After STI was acquired, it was treated as part of the manufacturing group of Consume More. Like other U.S. companies during the 1980s, the management of Consume More was concerned about the possibility of a corporate takeover. Any company that was not rapidly growing and profitable was vulnerable to criticism as well as corporate raiders. Deciding that the best defense was a good offense, the senior management of Consume More issued a "20-20" mandate. This meant that all strategic business units of Consume More were required to grow at a rate of 20% per year and generate profits of 20% before taxes. This 20-20 formula was extremely demanding and put a great deal of pressure on a number of Consume More subsidiary companies, including STI.

Consume More's management approach was to leave companies alone to manage their business, unless they were unsuccessful in meeting their growth and profit targets. From 1982 to 1989, Consume More grew rapidly as a result of overall growth in the U.S. economy. However, in late 1989, sales began to flatten and profits were squeezed as well. Pressure from Consume More began to increase. Questions began to be asked about STI's management strategy. Telephone contact between quarterly review meetings increased (when progress in achieving goals was discussed) and all of STI's management were increasingly aware of a general dissatisfaction from Henry Bellows, the Consume More group executive to whom Stan Fleming, STI's President, reported.

The New Vision: 1990

Informal discussions occurred among STI's executive group about what could be done to meet Consume More's growth requirements. The group included: Thomas S. Jackson, Senior VP of Operations, whose responsibilities included manufacturing, marketing, and human resources; Fred Marshak, Senior VP and CFO, Brenda Hofman, VP Human Resources; Bob Rankin, Senior VP of International Business, who was responsible for developing the company's international franchise network; as well as Stan Fleming, the company's president.

Finally, in July 1990, Stan Fleming decided that the company had to embark on a major transformation if it was going to meet Consume More's growth targets. He concluded that the core business of STI was mature and while there were opportunities in international franchising, the company needed to diversify its new products if it was to grow as aggressively as required by the 20–20 formula. Fleming concluded that diversification would mean not only gaining new markets (internationally) but also getting into new businesses related to STI's core products and not merely adding new product lines. He believed that the growing popularity of frozen yogurt offered expansion opportunities for STI. Accordingly, to facilitate growth, he decided to transform STI from a candy company into a more diversified specialty food products business.

Unfortunately, no consensus existed among all of STI's senior leadership. Tom Jackson, Senior VP of Operations, was not convinced of either the need for diversification or the direction proposed by Stan Fleming.

Implementing the Vision: 1991

The first step taken by STI to implement its new vision was to expand its international operations. This involved having Bob Rankin, Senior VP of International Business, extend the company's network of franchises. Initially, expansion proceeded in Western Europe and Australia. However, within a few years Rankin was traveling to Latin America, parts of Asia, and the former Soviet Union to create deals.

Operational support for the international business came from Tom Jackson's group. The international group was essentially a revenue center and relied on Jackson's group for manufacturing and marketing services and on Corporate for financial and legal services. Problems began to emerge as both Operations and Corporate employees faced conflicting priorities created by the need for these groups to simultaneously meet the demands of the existing business (in the United States) and the ever-increasing demands of the international unit for products and services.

Bob Rankin had no authority over either Corporate staff or Tom Jackson's people. All he and his small group could do was to ask for assistance. Faced with conflicting priorities between their own group and international, the latter's requests were assigned a lower priority. People in international began to grumble that they were seen as "second-class citizens," while those in Jackson's manufacturing and marketing areas felt they were overburdened and were doing their best to do international a favor. In brief, this part of the vision—international expansion—was not smooth.

In implementing the other part of the vision—product diversification—STI hired Stuart McCracken, an experienced corporate acquisition specialist, to lead the charge in finding companies that might be acquired. The company also engaged a management consulting firm to perform a diversification study intended to identify possible new ventures for STI to develop on its own based on its core capabilities. McCracken, who held the title of Senior VP of Corporate Development, was also assigned responsibility for the internal diversification effort. Only broad criteria were established to guide McCracken and avoid putting blinders on his efforts.

The consulting study identified the gourmet chocolate-chip cookie market as a logical extension of STI's existing products: some of STI's products (chocolate) and raw materials (sugar) would serve as inputs for the cookies. The consulting firm recommended that the cookie line be added to the existing retail business, rather than setting up a new franchise system that would be in competition with Mrs. Fields Cookies, as well as smaller stand-alone operators. The concept was that STI could add a complementary line of business with only an incremental cost and without having to build an entire new business infrastructure.

Sweet Treat's senior management liked the idea of diversifying into the gourmet chocolate chip cookie market, but decided to build it as a separate strategic business unit. Tom Jackson argued forcefully that it was not really consistent with STI's candies and would be too complicated for franchises to sell both products. Realizing that he did not have Jackson's support, and also aware that Consume More was in favor of developing new franchises rather than merely expanding existing operations, Stan Fleming supported the notion of a new operation for the cookies. In addition, the STI senior team decided that the growing market for gourmet coffees and related beverages such as espresso and cappuccino made it a good idea to expand the idea of cookies and combine it with coffees.

The executive group decided that the new business would be called "Cookies and Cream." Stuart McCracken was given the responsibility of investigating the feasibility of a start-up or of acquiring an existing small operation that was in difficulty and could be purchased and transformed.

Deal Making: 1992–93

For the next two years, McCracken spent a great deal of time looking for possible acquisitions. The results were that STI acquired two small ventures with growth potential: La Scalla Coffee and Buena Bakeries. Both companies were new ventures with sound products, a small number of stores, and limited infrastructure. The next step was to develop a strategic plan for the scale-up of both businesses.

McCracken developed a business plan for submission to Consume More. The plan was reviewed by the STI Executive Committee. At the review meeting, concern was expressed by the CFO, Fred Marshak, about the length of time required to achieve profitability as well as the capital required to scale up each business. Nevertheless, the group blessed the plan and submitted it to Consume More. Stan Fleming commented that, "The only way we are going to get the capital to grow the business, and, in turn, meet our goals, is through ventures such as Buena Bakeries and La Scalla Coffee."

Unfortunately, Fleming and Marshak were both correct. However, Consume More rejected the business plan for the expansion of Buena and La Scalla. The financial situation at the parent company was now worse and pressure for *current* profits and cash flow were even greater. The message came back to STI to get rid of the new ventures.

The Results: 1994

For the next year, STI faced increasing pressure. Its growth strategy had failed. More than three years of effort were wasted, and people became increasingly demoralized. The two ventures were abandoned. Buena Bakeries was sold back to the original entrepreneur, and La Scalla was simply closed. The pressure for profit improvement at STI led to two layoffs. Finally, Henry Bellows, the group executive who oversaw STI's operations, terminated the entire senior management team at STI. He brought in replacements from another U.S. subsidiary to try their hand at a second phase of revitalization.

Lessons from the Sweet Treats Inc. Transformation

What can we learn from this unsuccessful transformation attempt? The first lesson is that, as we have seen previously, a coherent vision is an essential prerequisite for a successful transformation. The objective of the Sweet Treats transformation was growth and the strategy was diversification. There was no real vision of what Sweet Treats wanted to become; instead, there was merely a series of incremental decisions about specific product diversification opportunities. From its foundation as a candy business, Sweet Treats added bakery products and coffee. The logic chain was: candy plus yogurt plus pastry plus cookies plus coffee. Stated differently, management made a series of incremental product moves designed to increase the company's growth, but without an integrated concept of the business being developed. There never was an attempt to step back and address the fundamental issue of: What business is Sweet Treats in today and what business should it be in the future? Unfortunately, management took a very oversimplified approach to a much more complex problem. They should have viewed the transformation from the perspective of the transformational lens provided in Chapter 2 and with a transfomational plan that will be discussed in Chapter 7.

Another important lesson concerns the lack of effective leadership of the transformation process, which is evident in two areas. First, there was never sufficient commitment or "buy-in" to the diversification strategy by key players, especially Tom Jackson. Stan Fleming needed to ensure that Jackson was on board, but he never did accomplish this. As a result, Jackson resisted the transformation in several large and small ways. Specifically, he never encouraged his people to support the new ventures. Fleming was aware of this, but did not deal with it. In addition, Fleming overestimated his support from the parent company, Consume More—a serious miscalculation. He needed to ensure that Henry Bellows bought in to his strategy.

Another lesson (which again shows that the lens presented in Chapter 2 would have been helpful if it had been used) concerns problems with the extent to which the organization's structure was suitable or supportive of the attempted transformation. A multiproduct business typically requires a divisional rather than a functional structure. Sweet Treats did not change the basic structure of its organization when it added the new businesses. They were grafted onto the existing business, rather than being set up as new independent structures. This was intended to help achieve operational efficiencies, but these intended benefits were more than offset by the problems of coordination and lack of focus upon the new ventures. The consultant used had, in effect, given the wrong advice to management about what structure to use.

Lessons to be Learned

This chapter has examined examples of unsuccessful Transformations of the First, Second, and Third Kinds. After each example, we have identified some of the lessons to be learned. We will now step back from the specifics and distill some lessons from the group of companies as a whole. The first lesson is that organizations must recognize that a transformation is necessary, and that it means more than merely a change in strategy. Adam Osborne did not realize that a transformation was necessary until it was too late to make it successfully. Sweet Treats, Inc. never did recognize the need for a transformation. It simply approached the problem from the perspective of the need to accelerate growth, rather than from the need to reconceptualize their business and, in turn, its key building blocks. In contrast, there was a recognition of the need for transformation at Kodak and Sears. However, in the latter situations, there were problems involved in executing the process.

A second lesson concerns the importance of understanding what needs to be done to make a successful transformation. Although Kodak understood that it needed to revitalize its operations, it lacked an overall vision of what it was trying to become. The lens for building successful organizations would have provided a helpful perspective for management in planning the revitalization transformation at Kodak.

Another lesson concerns the importance of effective leadership in transformations. The lack of such leadership was evident at both Sears and Sweet Treats, Inc., which contributed to their inability to successfully complete their business vision transformations. In both companies, there was insufficient buy-in to the new visions. Sears, at least, had a vision of what it was trying to become, but there was never enough commitment to the vision at the field level (i.e., among the store managers) of the original core business. As you may recall, the same problem occurred at United Airlines in its unsuccessful transformation to a diversified travel company. At Sweet Treats, there was neither a coherent vision nor sufficient buy-in.

A related lesson here is the possibility of the need to cross the Rubicon. Although this is a hypothesis requiring further investigation, it may be that a prerequisite to gaining sufficient commitment to a new vision is the elimination of the possibility of going back to the old vision. Historical evidence supports this idea. For example, on reaching the New World, the explorer Cortéz destroyed his ships. This sent the message that return was impossible and survival depended on the success of their new venture.

Another lesson concerns the nature of planning done as part of the transformation process. Much of the planning by Osborne and Sweet Treats Inc. was operational or product related in nature, rather than the kind that must be done to successfully complete a transformation. The planning at Kodak and Sears seems more strategic than the planning done in the other two companies discussed in this chapter, but it still lacked some critical aspects of true "transformational planning." Specifically, effective transformational planning would have addressed issues such as: What business are we in today and what are we trying to become? What type of structure will our new vision require to facilitate our successful transformation? These and other transformational planning issues are the focus of the next chapter.

Part III

HOW TO CHANGE THE GAME

The Tools of Transformational Management

7

STRATEGIC TRANSFORMATIONAL PLANNING FOR CHANGING THE GAME

First Steps

Previous chapters have presented a lens to use in thinking about transformations as well as a series of examples of actual transformations and their related lessons. Our intent in this chapter, as well as in the next four, is to provide a set of tools that will help executives plan and manage Transformations of the First, Second, and Third Kinds.

The Concept of Strategic Transformational Planning

The present chapter, as the title suggests, deals with the nature and process of what we have termed "strategic transformational planning." This refers to the process of creating a plan for the strategic transformation of either the game an organization is playing or the way it plays the game. In terms of the framework for designing successful organizations presented in Chapter 2, transformational planning involves developing a plan to increase the fit among the four key factors influencing the design of a successful enterprise: (1) the business concept, (2) the six key building blocks of organizational success, (3) the size of the enterprise, and (4) the "environment" (markets, competition, and trends) in which the enterprise will exist.

Defined operationally, strategic transformational planning refers to the planning necessary for transforming an existing organization from what it is today to what it wants to/needs to become in order to maximize the fit between its size, environment, business concept, and organizational design.

This type of planning goes well beyond classic strategic planning. It deals with issues that must be resolved if an organization is to continue to be successful over the long run, adapt to change, and transform itself as required.

For example, it is the kind of planning necessary for transforming Starbucks from a local roaster to a café, from a café to a specialty retailer, and from a specialty retailer to "something else," as described in Chapter 5. It is also the kind of planning required to transform an entrepreneurship such as MediPro Inc. into an entrepreneurially oriented, professionally managed firm, as described in Chapter 3. In effect, this type of planning may be viewed as the next generation of strategic planning, just as WordPerfect 7.0 is the next generation after WordPerfect 6.1. Accordingly, strategic transformational planning builds on the knowledge base of classic strategic planning, but extends it with a different focus and architecture.

Our analysis of the examples presented in Chapters 3 through 6 suggests that when organizations are effective at transformational planning, the probability of a successful transformation is significantly increased. If an organization does not understand or is ineffective at transformational planning, the chances of an unsuccessful transformation also greatly increase. For example, MediPro Industries, American Century Investors, and Compaq Computers (in its first phase of development and later as it began to revitalize its operations) all did a good job of transformational planning and were quite successful. In contrast, Kodak and the company we have called Sweet Treats, Inc. did a poor job of planning and paid the price.

The Strategic Transformational Planning Process: Creating "Solutions" for Different Factor Profiles

The strategic transformational planning process involves assessing the four factors influencing the design of a successful business as "inputs" and "selecting" the appropriate type of transformation process to derive the "output" of a transformed business design. As we noted in Chapter 2, successfully completing different types of transformations involves focusing on one of more of these four factors. Hence, the transformational planning process for each of the three principal types of transformations (i.e., Transformations of the First, Second, and Third Kinds) will be somewhat different.

Planning Entrepreneurial Transformations to Professional Management

A Transformation of the First Kind (a Type I Transformation) involves making adjustments to one or more of the six key building blocks of an organization in order to more effectively "fit" with the size that the company has become. Most typically, this adjustment needs to occur in the areas of operational systems, management systems, and culture. Planning for Transformations of the First Kind involves focusing on what needs to be done to develop the operational systems, management systems (i.e., planning system, organizational structure, management development system, and performance management system) and culture required of an entrepreneurially oriented, professionally managed firm.

The process of planning entrepreneurial transformations to professional management can be illustrated by the example of MediPro Industries, presented in Chapter 3. MediPro began their planning process with a retreat during which they focused on key issues (like clarifying what business they were in) and identifying ways to improve the extent to which the infrastructure of their organization "fit" its size. MediPro did not fundamentally change its business concept, but it did concentrate on clarifying it to make it more customer oriented. It then turned its attention to developing a plan for creating the infrastructure (especially the operational systems, management systems, and culture) needed to support the larger firm that it had become.

Planning Revitalization Transformations

Unlike Transformations of the First Kind, a revitalization transformation can occur at any point in an organization's growth and development. In planning for such a transformation, typically there is a continued focus on existing markets and the identification of possible new markets. An assessment of the environment is also important in evaluating key changes in competition and trends and thus identifying threats and opportunities.

The focus of revitalization transformations is on the entire pyramid of organizational success. A revitalization involves the redesign of the pyramid at all levels to better "fit" with the environment in which the firm finds itself. It may also involve changes in the firm's size. The process of planning revitalization transformations can be illustrated in the example of Miller Brothers, presented in Chapter 4. In that revitalization, the company continued to be in the real estate development and management business. The basic problem facing Miller Brothers was the need to adapt to changes in the environment for real estate development. The company had to redesign all six key building blocks of organizational success to support its revitalization: the company's strategic mission was "to get our house in order."

Business Vision Transformations

The intent of a business vision transformation is to focus on identifying new markets or a new concept for the enterprise's role in existing markets. Markets, competition, and trends are each assessed for new possibilities; a new business concept is then formulated. This, in turn, requires that changes be made in the six key building blocks of organizational success and possibly in the organization's size.

The process of planning business vision transformations can be illustrated by the example of Starbucks, presented in Chapter 5. There the vision transformation began when Howard Schultz identified the concept of transforming Starbucks from a local roaster that sold coffee beans in its retail stores to a "café/specialty retailer." Building on this new business concept, Schultz articulated a loosely defined strategic mission: to establish a national brand as well as a large company by transforming coffee from a commodity to a "truly exquisite product" with brand equity.

At the time of the vision transformation, Starbucks required a significant infusion of financial resources to scale up operations. As noted in Chapter 5, Schultz spent considerable time in convincing potential investors of the viability of his vision. He identified the need to build a company that could become much larger and identified the capabilities required of the larger Starbucks, including people and systems for real estate site selection, store design, and retail operations. He also perceived the need to hire managers with the capabilities to grow with Starbucks as it became a larger enterprise and articulated the kind of culture he wanted for Starbucks (see Figure 5–1). Although Schultz did not explicitly use the pyramid of organizational success framework as a lens in planning for the transformation of Starbucks, his planning was consistent with it.

Transformational Planning as a Tool for Creating the "Solution"

The transformational planning process for each type of transformation which was described above is graphically represented in Figure 7–1. Here we see that the strategic transformational planning process is essentially one of considering the four key drivers of a successful business and creating a business design that is optimal, given the current set of conditions involving each of those four factors. Viewed from this context, we can now see that the strategic transformational planning process is *the* tool for creating the optimal "solution" to the set of problems faced by an enterprise in need of changing its game.

Steps in the Transformational Planning Process

The previous section has provided an overview of the nature of the strategic transformational planning process. This section builds on that overview and offers an approach that operationalizes the strategic transformational planning process into a series of four steps, shown schematically in Figure 7–2.

Those four steps are:
1. Assessing the environment.
2. Reviewing the existing business.
3. Resolving certain core transformational issues.
4. Developing the written strategic transformational plan.

In addition, as suggested by the feedback arrows shown in Figure 7–2 from step 4 to steps 1 and 2, we must note that this type of planning is an iterative process. This means that the process requires periodic monitoring in order to make adjustments in strategy that will help promote a successful transformation.

Environmental Assessment

The first step in the strategic transformational planning process involves assessing the environment in which the organization is operating and will

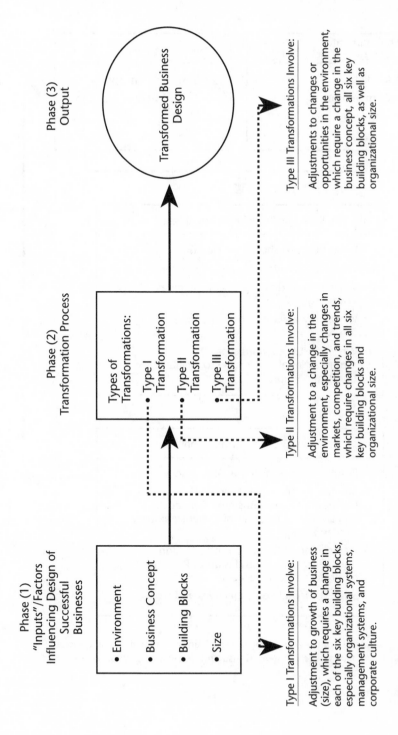

Phase (1)
"Inputs"/Factors
Influencing Design of
Successful
Businesses

• Environment

• Business Concept

• Building Blocks

• Size

Phase (2)
Transformation Process

Types of
Transformations:

• Type I
  Transformation

• Type II
  Transformation

• Type III
  Transformation

Phase (3)
Output

Transformed Business
Design

Type I Transformations Involve:

Adjustment to growth of business
(size), which requires a change in
each of the six key building blocks,
especially organizational systems,
management systems, and
corporate culture.

Type II Transformations Involve:

Adjustment to a change in the
environment, especially changes in
markets, competition, and trends,
which require changes in all six
key building blocks and
organizational size.

Type III Transformations Involve:

Adjustments to changes or
opportunities in the environment,
which require a change in the
business concept, all six key
building blocks, as well as
organizational size.

Figure 7–1. What We Are Doing in the Transformational Planning Process.

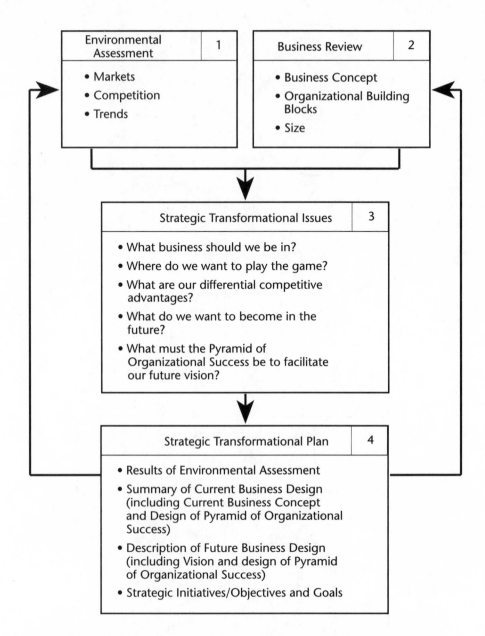

Environmental Assessment	1
• Markets • Competition • Trends	

Business Review	2
• Business Concept • Organizational Building Blocks • Size	

Strategic Transformational Issues	3
• What business should we be in? • Where do we want to play the game? • What are our differential competitive advantages? • What do we want to become in the future? • What must the Pyramid of Organizational Success be to facilitate our future vision?	

Strategic Transformational Plan	4
• Results of Environmental Assessment • Summary of Current Business Design (including Current Business Concept and Design of Pyramid of Organizational Success) • Description of Future Business Design (including Vision and design of Pyramid of Organizational Success) • Strategic Initiatives/Objectives and Goals	

Figure 7–2. Flow Diagram of the Four-Step Strategic Transformational Planning Process.
Source: © *Management Systems* Consulting Corporation, 1996. All rights reserved.

operate in the future. Three key aspects of the environment are critical for assessment. These include the market in which the firm operates, its present and potential competition, and environmental trends. We will examine each of these.

The Firm's Market

All organisms (both biological and human-made) must adapt to their environments to survive. For economic organizations, this means that we need to understand the nature of the market and how it is changing. In performing this analysis, we do not want to get caught up in all of the details of a business; rather, we want to focus only on the most salient features that are critical to the transformation.

As used here, a "market" refers to a defined set of present and/or potential customers for a product or service. For example, there are markets for automobiles, women's apparel, coffee beverages, and computer equipment. Markets vary in terms of their size (i.e., the number of present and potential customers available to be served by the firm), and in analyzing a market, one thing a firm must do is assess its "potential." Each market can also be subdivided into "segments," which are sectors within a market that can be defined or identified in terms of various criteria such as price, quality of product, service level, and product reputation or prestige. Again, if a firm chooses to serve a particular segment, it needs to assess the absolute potential (i.e., size) of that segment.

Wherever feasible, organizations must try to establish niches within markets or market segments. As explained in Chapter 2, a niche is a place within a market where an organization has been able to create or carve out a relatively protected position because of one or more sustainable competitive advantages. A great variety of factors can be a source of competitive advantage. For example, *Architectural Digest* was the first premium magazine of interior design and consequently it established a niche among both affluent readers and the advertisers who wanted to reach them. *Architectural Digest* became so well known that it achieved a high degree of brand equity and status as almost an institution. This helped it greatly when *House and Garden* magazine was reformatted to try and capture more of this market segment. Thus, a niche has important implications for competition in markets.

The Competitive Environment

Except for the relatively rare case of monopolies, all organizations face competition from others who want to capture market share. Accordingly, it is critical in developing an overall business strategy as well as a strategic transformational plan for an organization to assess the competition. This involves identifying the strengths and limitations of key competitors from the standpoint of meeting customer needs.

Whether they are aware of it or not, organizations compete with each other in terms of all six key building blocks of organizational success:

markets, products, resources, operational systems, management systems, and culture. For example, in the early 1960s when Wal★Mart got its start, Sears was the number 1 retailer in the United States, and K-Mart was the number 1 discount retailer. The geographic market focus of both Sears and K-Mart was primarily in the cities and suburbs. Wal★Mart got its start by entering rural markets, where its principal competition was not Sears or K-Mart but the small independent or smaller chain stores. Wal★Mart selected a market in which it did not have to compete with the giants head-on. Wal★Mart was the relatively larger company in its chosen markets, which gave it a competitive advantage. As it gathered strength over the years and developed its capabilities in each of the six key building blocks, it began to compete more directly (and very successfully) with K-Mart and Sears.

Trends
The third dimension of the environmental assessment component of the strategic transformational process concerns trends. A scan of economic, political, cultural, demographic, and technological trends must be done. There are many good sources of secondary research on trends, and much can be learned simply by reading the daily newspaper. However, the real issue is for management to assess the opportunities and implications of the trends before they are fully developed and translate those insights into a transformational strategy. For example, while many people saw the significance of the spread of AIDS for the general population, one entrepreneur, Dan Sandel, saw the implications for health care professionals. His company, Devon Industries, was in the business of designing, manufacturing, and distributing disposable medical products. Recognizing that AIDS represented a significant hazard for health-care professionals, Sandel adapted his products and marketing toward the safety aspects of using Devon's products in a hospital or medical care environment.

The perspective suggested here on spotting trends is the same as that used by many successful investors in business enterprises. For example, as Richard Rainwater, one of the most successful investors of the current generation, has stated, "My objective is to capitalize on major one time transformation in an industry or company."[1] Rainwater also notes that "Most of the time, the critical information that enables me to identify these significant changes is found not on the business pages of the newspaper but on the front page. (In fact, if industry changes are highlighted on the business pages, it is usually too late for my kind of investing)."[2] For example, Rainwater formed Crescent Real Estate Equities in the early 1990s to take advantage of opportunities created by what has come to be known as the "savings and loan crisis." Similarly, he got involved in a company called Mid Ocean Limited, which was created because of the upheaval in the catastrophic reinsurance business after the devastation caused by Hurricane Andrew.[3] The bottom line is that organizations must continuously scan the environment for trends and assess their implications for transformational opportunities.

Comprehensive Business Review

The second step in the strategic transformational planning process involves a comprehensive business review. The objective of this step is to develop a sufficiently deep understanding of "what we are" before we attempt to change or transform it. To help facilitate this analysis, it is necessary to utilize the business model framework previously introduced in Chapter 2. More specifically, we must examine the business concept and the pyramid of organizational success that have evolved for the existing business, as described below.

The Business Concept

The first task in completing the business review is to examine the nature of the business concept. This involves answering the question: What business are we in? Although the answer may seem fairly obvious, many firms (especially entrepreneurships) may have a difficult time reaching consensus on their reply to this deceptively simple question. The obvious answer may not always be the "correct" one, and it may take a firm's management some time to reach agreement.

To identify a firm's current business concept, managers may need to examine its current operations and/or look at the underlying assumptions that govern how it currently operates. Several questions can help identify the business concept:

- Who do we currently target as our customers?
- What needs do our products meet for our current customers?
- What needs do we think they meet?
- What types of customers do we want?
- Who do we consider our biggest competitors? Why?

The outcome of this analysis should be a one- or two-sentence statement that defines the business the firm is currently in. This statement should be something that all the firm's management can agree to. It should also serve as the basis for establishing the firm's strategic direction.

The Building Blocks of Organizational Success

After examining the nature of the current business concept, the next component of the business review involves assessing all six key building blocks that comprise the pyramid of organizational success: the markets in which a firm competes, its products or services, resources, operational systems, management systems, and culture. This assessment includes identifying the firm's key strengths as well as its limitations at each level in the pyramid of organizational success. A strength is anything that helps the firm compete successfully in its chosen market and increases the "fit" between its business concept, size, and environment. A limitation (or area for improvement) is anything that the firm does that detracts from its ability to compete successfully—for example, anything that works against the company having a good fit between its business concept, size, and/or its environment.

Size

The final task of the second step in the strategic transformational planning process concerns the question of organizational size. The basic issue is: What is the current size of the business, and how fast do we anticipate it will/ could/should grow? An answer to this question is necessary for the purpose of planning the appropriate design of the enterprise in order to maximize the fit between size and infrastructure. In a rapidly growing entrepreneurship, the anticipated size and rate of growth are critical to judgments concerning the level of investments in building organizational infrastructure. In a declining business undergoing revitalization, size is also critical to scaling the resources needed for effective and efficient operations. The key point is to plan to manage size by explicitly considering it in the transformational planning process.

A major example of the difference in outcomes when one organization explicitly plans for size and another does not can be seen in the comparison of Compaq and Osborne Computer. From the beginning Compaq planned to become a very large company and articulated a size goal of $1 billion. Although they could not possibly know whether this was realistically attainable or even when it might be attained, it gave them a focus for the kind of enterprise they were building. It should also be recalled that Compaq took eighteen months to plan for what its business was expected to become: a very large, billion-dollar-plus enterprise.

In contrast, Osborne Computer did not explicitly consider the implications of size on its operations, and was therefore constantly playing catch-up in terms of the firm's infrastructure. Ultimately, the building blocks of Osborne Computers were not sufficiently developed to deal with the complexity of running a $100-million business, and the company went bankrupt.

The Core Strategic Transformational Issues

After the first two steps involving the environmental assessment and the comprehensive business review have been completed, the next step in the transformational planning process is to address certain core strategic transformational planning issues. The information needed to address these issues will have been collected as part of the first two steps; the development of a systematic transformational plan requires addressing these issues in a sequential manner.

Although many issues must be resolved in any transformation, there are five key issues that must be resolved by all organizations:

1. What business should we be in in the future (i.e., what game will we play)?
2. Where do we want to play the game?
3. What are our differential competitive advantages and how will we use them to our advantage?
4. What do we want to become in the future?

5. What must the pyramid of organizational success (i.e., the six key building blocks) be to facilitate our future vision (i.e., how will we play the game)?

"What Business Should We Be in?"

The most fundamental issue faced by any organization relates to the nature of its future business concept. All organizations need a focus. If an organization tries to be too many things to too many people, it will not be good in any one particular area, and will be susceptible to being beaten by competitors in many areas. Although this is not well recognized, the most important strategic decision that an organization can make is choosing the business that it is going to compete in (i.e., the game it is going to play).

To answer this question, a firm should first examine the nature of the organization's current business and determine whether or not this is an appropriate focus for the future. Determining whether or not the definition should be changed lies in the analysis of a firm's environment and its current business situation (completed as a result of the business review). Although we have already cited several examples of companies where the proper definition of a business concept was critical to long-term success (including Edison International, Nike, Sears, and Kodak), we will now look at a few additional examples (Xerox, US Surgical, and Ashton-Tate, three very different types of companies) that may be beneficial in clarifying the importance of this issue.

During the 1980s Xerox began to experience the classic symptoms of the need for revitalization or aging pains (see Figure 2–8). The firm had been the darling of growth stock investors for years. However, with maturing product cycles, as well as inroads from foreign competition, Xerox began facing a transformed marketplace. The company's initial response was to diversify away from its core operation without any attempt to define its future business concept—Xerox had set up a number of different businesses in addition to its core photocopying business. It acquired SDS, a scientifically oriented computer company. It established Xerox Learning Systems, and acquired an insurance company. The net result of all of this activity was that there was no coherent focus to the overall business that Xerox had become. In effect, Xerox had (to use a word that has begun to emerge to describe this phenomenon) "diworsified." The firm continued to experience difficulty in the 1980s. In addition to the problems inherent in managing a diverse set of businesses, Xerox also lost significant opportunities related to its core business.

The second phase of Xerox's revitalization transformation began in the late 1980's. One of the first steps involved in this transformation process was for the company to decide what it really was/should be (i.e., to define its future business concept). The new Xerox has defined itself as being in the "document business." The firm provides products and services to help other businesses manage documents. As a result, Xerox has abandoned a number of the other components of its business. It sold SDS, along with the insurance company and Xerox Learning Systems. The net result is that the company has defined a focus for itself and is building on that focus. It uses its focus to determine how resources are to be allocated. Consequently, the firm has been increasingly successful during the last few years and its stock price has risen accordingly.

The issue of defining the future business concept is important not only to companies involving a business (like Xerox) that has declined and needs to be revitalized. Many entrepreneurial companies face the same kind of issue. Specifically, we can find a number of single-product companies that need to build on their initial success and transform themselves from an organization dependent on one product to a true business that has a wide variety of them. This involves clearly defining a future business concept for the organization. One example of this is US Surgical. The company has pioneered a number of different products, including surgical staples and products related to laparoscopy, a surgical procedure for gastrointestinal surgery that is less invasive than traditional surgery. US Surgical has grown to over one billion dollars in annual revenue based on sales of these products. It has solved the problem of defining the concept of the business it should be in, which goes beyond the narrow confines of single products, by stating that it is in the "wound management" business.

Although Xerox and US Surgical have successfully dealt with the issue of "what business should we be in?," other companies have not and they have paid a steep price. For example, Ashton-Tate started with the database management product that was known as dBASE II. Although the firm grew its revenues to more than $100 million and developed subsequent versions of its product, it was never successfully able to develop new products to sustain its growth and make the transformation from a single-product company to a true business, and it never effectively defined what business it should be in. Ultimately it was sold to Borland.

The central theme that underlies each of these examples is that organizations must address the most fundamental issue concerning their business: "What business should we be in in the future?" Each organization must examine what business it is in today and what business it would like to be in the future.

Sometimes it is possible to create a unique business concept that places a company in an advantageous position before others realize what has happened. For example, by combining HFS and CUC into Cendant, Henry Silverman and Walter Forbes have brilliantly created a new type of consumer services company, consisting of recognized brands (AVIS, Coldwell Banker, Ramada) and proprietary marketing systems.

Where Do We Want to Play the Game?
Once the firm has identified the basic game it wants to/needs to play by addressing the question of "What business should we be in?," it next needs to decide *where* this game will or should be played. This involves identifying

Vertical Market Segments					
Horizontal Market Segment	Microcomputers		Mini-computers	Mainframes	Super-computers
	Desktops	Laptops			
I	• Sun Microsystems • Hewlett-Packard				• Silicon Graphics (Cray)
II	• IBM • Apple • Compaq • DEC	• Compaq • Apple • IBM	• DEC • IBM	• IBM	
III	• Packard Bell • AST				

Figure 7–3. The Strategic Board for the Computer Industry.

various market segments and selecting one or more where the firm can compete effectively.

One tool that can be used to answer the question of, "Where do we/should we play the game?" is something we have developed called "The Strategic Board," or more simply "The Board." The strategic board identifies the segments that represent the market for a particular enterprise. For example, Figure 7–3 shows the board for the computer industry.

As we see in this figure, the market can be viewed as composed of vertical and horizontal segments. Vertical segments are those that are defined by different product classes. In the case of computers, there are supercomputers, mainframes, minicomputers, and microcomputers. Within the microcomputer segment are the "subsegments" of desktops and laptops.

In addition to the vertical segments that define a market's structure, there are also horizontal segments that reflect differences in preferences of customer groups concerning price, quality, service, and prestige. These differences are classified in terms of three different market "tiers" or levels. The typical buyer in the Tier I market is affluent enough to afford whatever he or she wishes. Accordingly, their primary concern is for the overall quality, service, and prestige of the product or service received rather than the price *per se*. At the margin there may well be some buyers in the Tier I category who have a significant concern with price. However, buyers in this price category are typically less concerned with price or even price differentials than they are with the other factors. For example, an individual who is purchasing a Tier I luxury automobile may very well not care about a major differential in price between these particular products. Viewed figuratively, the products and services in Tier I can be thought of as ranging from a Cadillac to a Rolls-Royce. This is true not only for automobiles, but for all products and services that fit this particular quality categorization.

The second tier of the marketplace is usually significantly larger than Tier I in terms of the number of customers. The products in this category figuratively range from an Oldsmobile down to a Chevrolet. In Tier II, the buyer is concerned with deriving the "best" (optimal) combination of quality, service, prestige, and price. Typically, the buyer is making trade-offs between two or more of these variables. As before, this marketplace tier is not just applicable to automobiles, but to a full range of products and services.

In Tier III, the typical buyer is concerned primarily with price—quality, service, and prestige are relatively unimportant. This particular segment is generally the largest of all three marketplace tiers. The buyer in this segment is looking for a serviceable product or service; it may well be a commodity or a generic brand. This tier can be symbolically represented by looking from Chevrolet down through Hyundai or Yugo automobiles.

None of the market tiers are necessarily better than another. There are opportunities for success in all three tiers.

To illustrate how the three marketplace tiers do not merely apply to tangible products such as automobiles but to all other products and services as well, consider some examples, such as legal services, medical services, aerospace, and retailing. In Los Angeles, there is a well-known law firm by the name of O'Melveny & Meyers. It operates in the Tier I segment and, to cite a well-known saying, "If you have to ask the price, you probably cannot afford it." In Tier III we have a firm that specializes in being a legal-service supermarket: Jacoby & Meyers. There are certainly many Tier II law firms, and there may even be a "Harry Meyers" in Century City. With respect to medical services, county hospitals and clinics who primarily serve Medicaid patients and the indigent population occupy Tier III of the marketplace. Many HMOs occupy the lower portions of Tier II, while many private physicians are in various levels of Tier II. Tier I tends to be occupied by some of the elite private hospitals as well as by certain private physicians. In the aerospace sector, Hughes Electronics Corporation had traditionally occupied Tier I of the marketplace. It specialized in being able to do whatever was required by its customers, which were subunits of the Department of Defense. Quality, rather than cost, was the primary consideration. Today most aerospace firms occupy Tier II, because the customer is concerned with the trade-off between price, quality, and service. A few aerospace firms occupy Tier III segments. In the retailing sector, Saks Fifth Avenue and Neiman-Marcus occupy Tier I. Stores such as Nordstroms and Macy's occupy Tier II; while Tier III is served by Pic & Save, Ross, and Marshall's.

There are several ways for firms to use this concept of the strategic board to increase the effectiveness of their transformational planning efforts. First, firms must develop a clear understanding of where they are actually competing in terms of the strategic board. It is typically very difficult for firms to simultaneously compete in all three segments of the marketplace. Only some of the largest firms have traditionally been able to accomplish this feat. For example, General Motors begins with its lower-priced Chevrolets and moves its customers all the way through its product ladder to the Tier I version of its

Cadillac. However, in the lower reaches of Tier III, General Motors does not compete with some of the less expensive foreign imports, and it does not compete in the highest levels of Tier I with products offered by Mercedes and Rolls-Royce.

After a firm has identified where it is on the board, it needs to decide which segment or segments of the marketplace it will/should compete in. Ideally, the firm is looking for segments where there is limited competition or none at all. Note that in Figure 7–3 there are a few uncontested segments of the board for computers, such as Tier I minicomputers. It may be that these are open because the potential for any firm to compete in these segments is not great enough to warrant entry (i.e., there are few, if any, customers in that segment). However, if a firm identifies an open segment, it is probably worth some time to find out what the potential actually is and *why* it is open.

Many companies have changed the game in their industries by seeing unserved (i.e., open) or underserved market segments. For example, Southwest Air Lines changed the game by the successful development of its "no frills" yet customer-oriented segment of air travel. Similarly, Bud Knapp, founder of Knapp Communications Corporation, transformed *Architectural Digest* from a trade magazine for architects and designers to the premier consumer magazine of interior design, entering a Tier I segment with no serious competition. Together with Paige Rense, the magazine's editor-in-chief, he did it by changing the vision of the business the magazine was in. As discussed in Chapter 5, Starbucks changed the game in coffee by creating a national brand and chain of cafés, which gave it visibility and equity as a premium brand of coffee. In terms of the strategic board, Howard Schultz saw a segment that had lots of small independent competitors, but no major player.

Whether or not these companies actually used a formal analysis like the strategic board, organizations can gain insights by employing this tool in their strategic transformational planning process.

"What Are Our Differential Competitive Advantages?"
Strengths or core competencies are not the same as "differential competitive advantages," although this is not always recognized. An organization may have a variety of strengths, a variety of things it does well. These may be core competencies. However, they may or may not give the firm a *differential* advantage in the marketplace (i.e., an advantage not possessed by other organizations). This distinction is critical to the mind-set we use to approach strategic transformational planning.

At an annual strategic planning retreat of one *Fortune 100* company, for example, the president of the company was giving a pep talk to the troops. During this talk, he referred to the excellent products that the company had, its state-of-the-art plant and equipment, its strong commitment to research and development, and its deep pockets. All these were true; but were essentially irrelevant to the firm's long-term success. This is because the firm's major competitors all had the same kinds of things. The firm had some significant strengths, but these were canceled or matched by its major competitors. In effect, the firm really had *nothing* that differentiated it from its competition. This is a recipe for long-term disaster, or at least slow decline.

Having core competencies or strengths is not enough. What an organization really needs to do is define those things that will *truly differentiate* it from its present and potential competitors. The appropriate lens for this type of differential competitive analysis is the pyramid of organizational success. In planning a transformation of any kind, management must examine whether it has or it can achieve differential strategic advantages at one or more levels of the pyramid.

The most obvious area where an organization competes with another organization is that of products and markets. Clearly, the products offered by a company are one way in which it differentiates itself from its competitors. However, over the long run, organizations are really competing with each other in terms of their infrastructures and management systems, as well as their products and choice of markets. An effective planning system, a structure that supports the plan, along with an incentive system for motivating employees or managers to achieve the firm's goals can contribute much to the development of new business opportunities, products, and services.

For many organizations, the real opportunities for developing sustainable, differential competitive advantages are at the top of the pyramid of organizational success, rather than in products or services. For example, in the retail sector, a superior level of customer service, built on a culture that emphasizes the role of service, is one of the few areas where sustainable advantage can be established. If we compare Wal★Mart with K-Mart, for instance, there is no product that cannot be offered by both companies. Yet Wal★Mart has come to dominate the discount retail segment and surpass K-Mart, even though the latter was there first and much larger than Wal★Mart for many years. Why? The answer lies in Wal★Mart's advantages in operational systems (especially logistics and information systems), management systems, and an employee-ownership-minded culture based on stock ownership.

Similarly, Cendant Mortgage, under the leadership of CEO Terry Edwards, has developed sustainable advantages in the highly competitive first mortgage industry through a combination of factors, including telemarketing, marketing to affinity groups, and "top block" (outstanding) service.

"What Do We Want to Become?"
The next issue that must be resolved in a corporate transformation process involves what the organization would like to become in the future. We define this as a firm's vision. As indicated in Chapter 2, a vision is essential for giving direction to people and guiding their efforts. It is the overall concept around which a new business is going to be built. A vision includes a statement of the future business concept as well as a "strategic mission" for what the company wants to become as it transforms itself. The business con-

cept defines the game the firm is playing, while the strategic mission is essentially a statement of strategic intent. It represents a statement of broad overall objectives to be achieved. As seen in the case of the Miller Brothers in Chapter 4, their future business concept was to continue operating in the real estate development and management business; their strategic mission was to "get our house in order."

For Starbucks, the vision might consist of "Being a national chain of coffee cafés" (its future business concept) *combined with* "Being recognized as the leading brand of coffee by January 1, 2000" (the company's strategic mission). Similarly, American Century Investors' vision might be "Playing our game in the mutual funds business, while wanting to be recognized as one of the top five mutual fund companies by December 31, 2001."

Since we have already examined several examples of new visions (such as Starbucks, Nike, Edison International, and Disney in Chapter 5), we will not repeat that discussion here. We have also demonstrated (in the examples of Sears and Kodak) that without a guiding concept of what an organization would like to become, an organization can drift from move to move. This can lead to acquisitions of other companies; or the development of a line of businesses that appear to make sense in and of themselves, but really do not have value from the standpoint of long-term strategic development. Another example of this phenomenon can be seen at Whittiker Corporation.

During the 1980s, Whittiker Corporation went on an acquisition binge and bought a very large number of organizations. However, there was no true strategic concept for the business as a whole. There was no vision other than to acquire a number of businesses and diversify. Ultimately, under Joseph Alibrandi, most of these businesses were liquidated and sold to other purchasers—a complete reversal of the diversification process.

What Must the Pyramid of Organizational Success be to Facilitate the Future Vision?
The final key strategic transformational planning issue concerns the six key building blocks of organizations that make up the pyramid of organizational success. Once the vision of the new enterprise has been articulated, the next step is to "mock up" what the organization should look like in terms of these building blocks. For example, after Howard Schultz articulated the vision for Starbucks to transform from a local roaster to a specialty retailer/café, the next step was to articulate what the new business would require in terms of its markets, products, resources, operational systems, management systems, and culture.

An example of a company that did this type of planning well was Compaq Computer, as described in Chapter 3. An example of a company that did it poorly was Osborne Computer, which ultimately failed.

Developing the Transformational Plan

The final step in the transformational planning process involves developing a written transformational plan. There are a variety of reasons for developing a written plan, rather than keeping it "in executives' heads." First, the act of writing itself is an exercise that requires specificity and overcomes any tendency toward vagueness. A written plan can also serve as an effective tool for communicating the firm's direction not only throughout the organization, but to the Board of Directors if there is one.

Figure 7–4 presents a graphic representation of the steps in creating a transformational plan.

At a minimum, a transformational plan must present:

1. The results of the environmental assessment.
2. The results of the comprehensive business review (which systematically identifies what the firm's current organizational design is).
3. A description of what the firm wants to/needs to become as a result of its transformation (what the design of its business will/needs to "look like" after the transformation).
4. Strategic initiatives (or objectives) and goals that detail how the firm will move from its current to its future business design.

Environmental Assessment Results

This section of the plan should provide a brief summary/analysis of key findings from the environmental assessment. This information can be used to address key transformational planning issues in the following ways.

1. The market, competitive, and trend analysis (combined with the results of the firm's analysis of its building blocks of organizational success) can provide valuable information that can help a firm decide *what business it should be in* to compete effectively over the long term.
2. Combining the information collected on the firm's markets and competition can help a firm develop the strategic board for its industry and identify *where it should be playing the game*.
3. The competitive analysis (combined with the results of the firm's analysis of its building blocks of organizational success) should result in the firm's being able to identify its *differential competitive advantages*.
4. The environmental assessment also provides information that can be useful (along with the assessment of the building blocks of organizational success) in helping a firm determine *its vision for the future*.

Although the presentation of this information may vary (depending on the nature of the transformation the firm needs to make), it should be structured so that it is clear to the reader that there has been as comprehensive a look as time permits at key aspects of the firm's environment.

The Firm's Current Business Design

In this section of the plan, the firm should paint a picture of what it currently looks like. This is important because in order to define where it wants to go in the future, it needs to know where it is with respect to the concept of its business (i.e., the game it is playing) and how it is structured (using the building blocks of organizational success) to play this game. This section

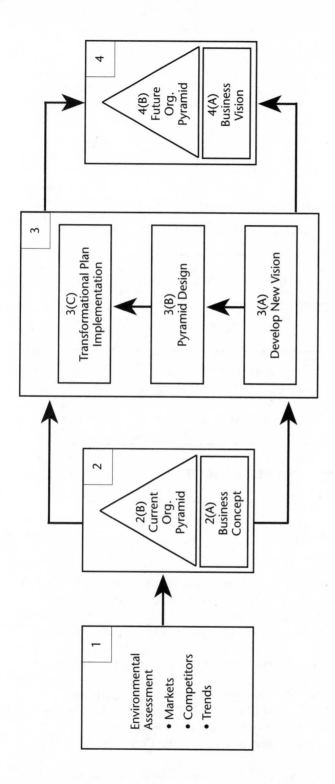

Figure 7–4. The Transformational Planning Process.
Source: © Copyright *Management Systems* Consulting Corporation, 1994, revised 1996. All rights reserved.

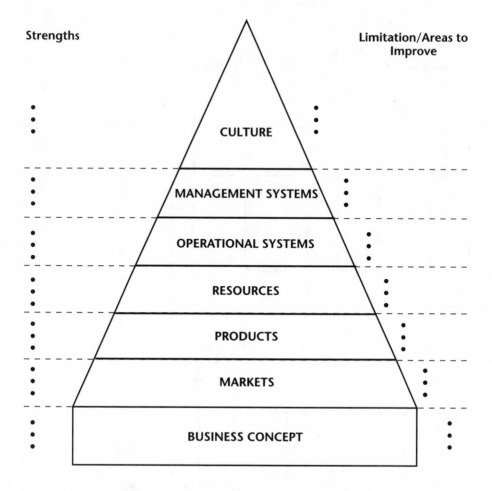

Figure 7–5. Current Business Design.

might be completed in graphic form using the diagram shown in Figure 7–5.

Using this diagram (or whatever format the firm chooses), the firm should first identify (in a non-evaluative fashion):

- Its current business concept (i.e., the nature of the business that the firm is currently in).
- Its current markets (i.e., its customers and the segments in which it currently operates).
- The products and services it currently provides to its customers.
- The resources that it currently has (including human resources, physical and technological resources, and financial resources).
- The list of key operational systems that help the firm manage its business on a day-to-day basis.
- Its current management systems (i.e., how its planning process works,

how it is structured, the process it uses to develop current and future managers, and the nature of the performance management systems that it has in place).
- Key elements of its current culture.

If the firm chooses to use the diagram, this information can be placed inside the pyramid. Once this step has been completed, the firm should then provide a description of the current strengths and limitations of its business design. As suggested earlier, a strength is something that helps the firm compete successfully in its chosen market and increases the "fit" between its business concept, size, and environment.

A limitation (or area of improvement) is anything that the firm does that detracts from its ability to compete successfully (i.e., anything that works against having a good fit between business concept, size, and/or environment). This information can be listed in the relevant space in Figure 7–5 or presented in another format, if desired.

This list of strengths and limitations/areas for future development can provide valuable input into addressing all the transformational planning issues. It also grounds a firm in its own reality as it prepares to outline "where it wants to go and what it wants to become as a result of its transformation."

Describing What the Firm Wants to/Needs to Become
The third section of the transformational plan is where all the transformational planning issues are actually answered through the articulation of the firm's vision and its future business design. The vision represents what the organization would like to become in the future. The business vision is the concept that will drive the development of the future business and serve as the foundation for the development of a pyramid of organizational success.

Again, this step in the transformational planning process can be completed by using a graphic representation of the business design model in which a picture can be painted of what the firm will/should "look like" as a result of the transformation process. This graphic is shown in Figure 7–6. To complete this step, the firm should focus on answering the questions that are inside the future pyramid and the business vision boxes. The answers should be based on an analysis of the current business situation (i.e., the environmental assessment and business review) as well as the manner in which the firm has addressed its key transformational planning issues. The completion of this pyramid provides the picture of what the firm is or needs to become as a result of its transformation. Note that this information can also be presented in another format, if the firm so desires.

Developing Strategic Initiatives and Goals
Once the firm has identified its vision for the future and what the building blocks of organizational success need to be to support this vision, the final step in developing the transformational plan is to identify key strategic initiatives and goals that will help the firm move from where it is today to where it wants to or needs to be in the future.

Figure 7-6. Future Business Design.

Strategic initiatives (or objectives) are broad statements of what the firm must do to change its game. Depending on the nature of the transformation, these strategic initiatives (or objectives) may include retaining certain key strengths that exist within the firm's current infrastructure. They may also include making significant changes in other areas. To maximize the success of the transformation process, however, the firm should set strategic objectives within each of the six building blocks of organizational success: markets, products, resources, operational systems, management systems, and culture. At Navistar, for example, a strategic initiative (or objective) was to increase market share for heavy and medium trucks. After strategic initiatives or objectives have been identified for each building block, the next step is to set goals for each initiative. Goals are specific, measurable, time-dated things that an organization wants to achieve for a given initiative. For example, if one of Starbucks' initiatives is to be present in all major metropolitan areas, a specific goal might be: "To have 2,000 retail locations opened by December 31, 2000."

Specific, measurable, time-dated goals are the mechanism through which an organization can ensure that it is making progress in achieving its vision and changing its game. Without such milestones, the chances of completing the transformation successfully are decreased.

Planning for Different Types of Transformations

As we have seen, the transformational planning process is, at least to some extent, the same for each of the three different types of transformations. However, Transformations of the First, Second, and Third Kinds each require slightly different planning processes as shown in Figure 7–7 and described below.

Planning Entrepreneurial Transformations to Professional Management

As Figure 7–7 indicates, in this type of transformation, there is typically no change in business concept and there is a continued focus on the same markets. Although an environmental assessment is important, a thorough business review is essential, since it is the pyramid of organizational success that must be transformed in Type I Transformations. In Type I Transformations, there is also typically a need to clarify the underlying business concept. As stated earlier, transformations of the First Kind typically focus a great deal of attention on developing the operational systems, management systems, and culture required of an entrepreneurially oriented, professionally managed firm. As seen in Figure 7–7, the rate of growth is also a factor in planning for this type of transformation.

The key transformational planning issue for these types of transformations is: What must the pyramid of organizational success be to facilitate our continued successful growth and development as we transition to an entrepreneurially oriented, professionally managed firm?

Planning Revitalization Transformations

In a revitalization transformation, there is usually a continued focus on existing markets and the identification of possible new markets. The environmental assessment is important in evaluating key changes in competi-

Steps in Strategic Transformational Planning	Type I	Type II	Type III
Environmental Assessment • Markets • Competition • Trends	• Formalize environmental assessment process. • Need to better understand environment.	• Must determine which environmental changes are leading to problems. • Must better adapt infrastructure to environment.	• Use assessment to identify new opportunities and assess threats.
Business Review • Business Concept • Organizational Building Blocks • Size	• Need to clarify Business Concept. • Need to formally assess strengths/ limitations in each level of the Pyramid as they support/don't support size and future growth. • Need to assess fit between size and infrastructure.	• Re-evaluate strengths/ limitations of Pyramid in light of environmental changes.	• Evaluate what changes need to be made in building blocks to support new Vision.
Resolving Transformational Issues	Key Transformational Issue: • What must the Pyramid of Organizational Success be to facilitate our successful growth and development as we transition to an entrepreneurially oriented, professionally managed firm?	Key Transformational Issues: • What are our differential competitive advantages? • What must the Pyramid of Organizational Success (at all levels) be to facilitate our revitalization?	Key Transformational Issues: • What business should we be in in the future? • What do we want to/can we be or become? • What must the Pyramid of Organizational Success be to facilitate the Vision Transformation?
Developing the Transformational Plan	• Develop Vision (clarify the Business Concept and develop the strategic mission). • Develop Strategic Initiatives. • Develop Goals.	• Develop new Vision. • Revise Strategic Initiatives to reflect new organization. • Revise Goals to reflect changes.	• Establish new Vision (new Business Concept and new strategic mission). • Modify Strategic Initiatives (as needed). • Modify Goals (as needed).

Figure 7–7. Planning for Different Types of Transformation.

tion and trends and thus identifying threats and opportunities. The focus of revitalization transformations is on the entire pyramid of organizational success. A revitalization involves the redesign of the pyramid at all levels to better "fit" with the firm's environment.

As seen in Figure 7–7, the key transformational planning issues that must be addressed in a Revitalization Transformation are:

1. What are our differential competitive advantages?
2. What must the pyramid of organizational success be to facilitate our revitalization?

Business Vision Transformations

As Figure 7–7 shows, the intent of the environmental assessment in business vision transformations is to help the firm focus on identifying new markets or a new concept for the enterprise's role in existing markets. Markets, competition, and trends are each assessed for new possibilities. The next step in planning for this type of transformation involves developing the new vision. The key issues in formulating a vision transformation are:

1. What business should we be in in the future?
2. What do we want to become?
3. What must the pyramid of organizational success be to facilitate the vision transformation?

Conclusion

This chapter has focused on the strategic transformational planning process in order to provide a tool for assisting in the process of managing transformations. This process is the next generation beyond classic strategic planning. Transformational planning focuses not just on planning that will help an organization meet the challenges presented by its environment, but also on identifying and meeting the challenges presented by its own growth and how it has managed (or not managed) the building blocks of organizational success. Although transformational planning is not a totally programmable process, we have provided a systematic approach to help facilitate it.

The next step, after transformational planning has been completed, is to execute the plan. A key part of this involves changing the organization's structure (its business units, roles, and reporting relationships). There are many examples of transformational plans that have failed, not because the strategy was poorly conceived but because of an inadequate understanding of the role that structural design plays in implementation. We shall continue our discussion of tools to facilitate the management of transformations in Chapters 8 and 9 by examining the issue of how to transform organizational structure once a company has developed its transformational plan.

8

DESIGNING ORGANIZATIONAL STRUCTURE
Understanding the Fundamentals

Chapter 7 presented a framework and tools for planning organizational transformations. It dealt with the issues involved in creating a plan for the strategic transformation of either the game an organization is playing or the way it plays the game. This chapter and the one that follows take the process of managing transformations to the next step and deal with the issues involved in organizing people to implement the strategic transformation plan.

As we have noted in selected previous chapters, the material presented in the next two chapters is somewhat complex and conceptual in nature. However, we believe that there can be a substantial payoff from an understanding of these concepts and tools. We are reminded of comments made by Alfred P. Sloan in his classic book, *My Years at General Motors*.[1] In discussing an organizational study that he prepared, which has been recognized as a seminal contribution to the foundation of modern management practice in the United States, Sloan stated: "The principles of organization got more attention among us than in the universities. If what follows seems academic, I assure you that we did not think it so."[2]

To effectively manage structure as a tool in the organizational transformation process, one must first understand the role that structure plays in the transformation process and what structure is. We address these topics in the first two sections. In the third section, we introduce some key "fundamentals" of structure design that should be applied in creating a structure that will allow the firm to effectively play its chosen game. Finally, we describe how these fundamentals can be used in designing structure for different types of transformations.

The Role of Structure in Successful Transformations

As we have already seen, especially in Chapters 3 through 6, the way an enterprise is organized (i.e., its organizational structure) is critical for an effective transformation. For example, when Eastman Kodak was engaged in a revitalization transformation, it decided to change its structure and created seventeen autonomous entrepreneurial units. Unfortunately, as the company's CEO Kay R. Whitmore noted, this decentralized structure had costs that became apparent over time. Similarly, the structure used at the company we have called Sweet Treats, Inc. was not effective in facilitating the desired transformation.

To facilitate their planned transformation, organizations must evaluate and sometimes revise their existing structure. The correct structural form for an organization can be a source of sustainable competitive advantage; a suboptimal structure can be a significant competitive weakness. In addition, the success or failure of a transformation can depend, to a very great extent, on the organization's structure. In brief, the key underlying issues a firm must address in successfully completing a transformation are:

1. What structure do we need for playing our chosen game most effectively?
2. How can we effectively create this required structure?

To effectively address the first question, management needs to understand what structure is (i.e., the fundamental concepts behind how to organize and "play" a given game) and the strengths and limitations of the various forms of structure that might be adopted to help the firm win its chosen game. In other words, there is a need for the firm's management to understand some technical aspects of structure design/redesign. Answering the second question involves creating a plan for transforming the organization's structure from what it is today to what it needs to be to support the transformation.

Organizing to Play the Game: Structure Defined

One useful way to think about structure is to view it as how we organize our players to play the game we have chosen to play in the way we have decided to and/or need to play it. There are, in fact, a variety of ways we might organize our team depending on:

- Our overall approach to the game.
- Our own company's strengths and limitations.
- The nature of our competition.

In fact, any structure can work if we understand these three factors and adapt our structure to them. If we think about playing any game such as football or basketball, there are various ways of organizing to play the game. The organization of the team typically reflects the abilities and thinking of the coach and his or her approach to the game. It may also be a reflection of what the coach perceives are the abilities of the team members. In fact, the effective *execution* of any the structure depends (at least to some extent) on the abilities of the players (i.e., their strengths and limitations) and their understanding of the team's overall goals.

Inadequate understanding of the structure and/or the team's strategy (or overall goals) can lead to different executions and different short- or long-term results. A college basketball team, for example, can play the game as if it were a pickup game in a local park, with each individual doing his or her own thing; or it can play as a true team with lots of motion, passing, and coordination among the players. The latter is the type of basketball played by Roy Williams' teams at Kansas, Bobby Knight's teams at Indiana, Pete Carril's teams at Princeton, and the teams coached by the great John Wooden at UCLA. While a pick-up style game can sometimes lead to success —in terms of beating the competition—teams with a true sense of organization will typically be more successful over the long term.

This suggests that understanding how to organize the players on one's team in order to play one's chosen game effectively (and understanding how to communicate this structure to all those involved) can, over the long term, be a source of competitive advantage. This ability to develop and execute new structures effectively is also absolutely critical to the success of any transformation. We turn now to an examination of some fundamental principles associated with designing effective structures to support organizational transformations.

Designing for Success:
Fundamentals of Organizational Structure

In designing organizational structure to support a transformation, one must draw on elements of both science and art. The scientific component of structural design involves developing an understanding of the criteria for successful organizational design and the strengths and limitations of the various structural forms that might be adopted by the organization to play its chosen game. The artistic aspect involves identifying and/or "sculpting" various alternative structures that might effectively support a firm's chosen game and then selecting the structure that will best support the organization's transformation. From a scientific perspective, four important fundamentals of organizational structure design must be understood and effectively managed for a firm to successfully complete its transformation. These are presented and discussed below.

Fundamental 1: There Is No One Best Structure

One fundamental principle that drives the design process is that *there is no one best way of organizing a particular team*. This is because every organization has its own unique personality (or culture), its own set of people, and its own history. Any organizational structure can effectively support a particular transformation if it is designed and managed appropriately.

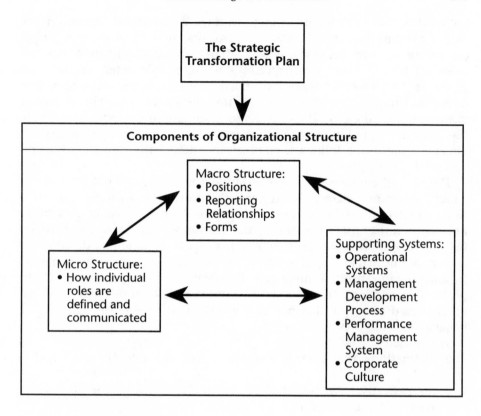

Figure 8–1. The Structure System.

Fundamental 2: There Are Three Components of Structure (Not Just One)

For many people, organizational structure is defined by what is presented on an organizational chart (if one exists). Although this is certainly part of "structure," it is not all there is. Based on our work with organizations, we believe that structure actually consists of three components that need to be designed and managed as a "system" if a structure is to be successfully executed. Figure 8–1 illustrates the three components of the structure system; they are described in more detail below.

The first component is what we call the "macro" structure. This structure consists of the boxes on the organizational chart and how they are connected. The macro structure provides a guide as to how different functions and positions are connected. It helps the players on the team understand what their place is in the larger system.

While this part of structure seems fairly obvious (i.e., that all organizations should have an organization chart), our experience suggests that this is not necessarily the case. We have seen presidents of $50-million companies appear at our offices with handwritten organizational charts that they prepared on the plane before meeting with us. We have also had experience with a $400-million distribution company that refused to create a formal organizational chart because it was too "bureaucratic" and because its entrepreneur (and other senior managers) wanted to be able to tell anyone what to do. In that case, employees complained about never knowing whose directions they should follow, which, in turn, resulted in a certain amount of chaos and wasted effort. There were also more serious consequences: While the company's employees were trying to figure out which senior manager's directives should be followed, competitors entered the firm's market and began taking away share.

The second component of organizational structure is what we call the "micro" structure. Micro structure consists of how the roles and responsibilities of each position-holder on the team are defined. Developing a firm's micro structure consists not only of the technology that is used in developing role descriptions, but also the manner in which these role descriptions are communicated and used within the organization as a guide for behavior. In some organizations, a fundamental problem is that there are no written position descriptions. In others, written position descriptions may exist, but are seldom used by position holders (or their managers) as tools in guiding behavior because they are either:

1. Out-dated.
2. "Something that only Human Resources needs to be concerned with."
3. So ineffectively written that the position-holder finds the information of little or no value.

To be of value, position descriptions must be utilized by position-holders as guides to their behavior.

The third component of organizational structure is what we call "supporting systems." Supporting systems include the operational systems of the organization, its management development process, its performance management systems, and its corporate culture. A structure will not function effectively in the absence of properly designed supporting systems. For example, a firm may decide that it needs to organize in a way that includes general managers and that it should promote these new general managers from within. If this company does not provide management education to those selected in order to help them understand their new role and develop the skills needed to execute the role effectively, the structure will not function properly.

As Figure 8–1 indicates, these three aspects of organizational structure must be designed and managed as a system. If any one is ignored or doesn't fit, the structure will not function properly and the likelihood of the firm's being able to play its chosen game effectively is decreased.

Fundamental 3: There Are Certain Strategic Organizational Design Issues That Must Be Addressed

In designing its structure (including the macro and micro structure as well as the supporting systems), a firm needs to resolve six critical organizational design issues. A firm must address these issues not only for the organization as a whole, but also for its individual subunits (e.g., departments, divisions, or what we call "strategic business units"). The key issues to be resolved in designing an organizational structure are:

1. What is the optimal form required to support the planned transformation?
2. How should the organization be structured in order to have the "best" or most optimal chance of meeting customer needs?
3. What is the simplest structure that will help us achieve the goals in our transformational plan?
4. How can we structure the company so as to promote individual and/or team responsibility and accountability?
5. How can we structure the firm so as to promote entrepreneurship or at least protect the entrepreneurs in the organization?
6. What is the optimal size of the organization?

What Is the Optimal Form?
The most fundamental strategic design issue is identifying the optimal form (i.e., structure) to help the firm achieve the goals it has articulated in its transformational plan. The idea is that "form should follow function" (that the structure should be designed to support the firm's strategy). For example, if an organizational unit is intended to be a profit center, its structure will be inevitably different than if it is intended to be a service center. Similarly, if a business is in several geographical areas, its structure is likely to be different from one that operates from a single location.

A key principle to keep in mind here is that any structure can work if it is properly designed and implemented. This involves ensuring that in choosing a particular form, an organization selects not only an appropriate macro structure (based on a clear understanding of each form's strengths and weaknesses, which we will discuss later in this section), but that it also selects/designs an appropriate micro structure and supporting systems.

How Should We Be Organized to Best Meet Customer Needs?
Another critical issue that must be addressed is how to create an organizational structure that will allow the firm to remain close to its customers. This not only involves increasing the probability of maximizing current sales of existing products, it also has to do with understanding customers' needs so that strategic plans can be based on changes in those needs and perceived trends. It has become increasingly recognized that one of the reasons organizations experience difficulty is that they lose touch with their customers. For

example, IBM lost touch with its customers during the early 1980s when microcomputers were being developed. Accordingly, an organization's structure should be a strategic vehicle for helping the firm focus on customers; this, in turn, ought to be a criterion used in the evaluation of alternative structures during the transformation process.

How Can We Organize in the Simplest Way Possible?

A third issue that must be resolved concerns the benefits of simplicity versus complexity. Unless there are sound reasons for complex structures (and sometimes there are), the ability to organize in the simplest possible way is likely to be best.

How Can We Organize in Order to Maximize Accountability?

A key function of structure is to facilitate the focus of responsibility and accountability in organizations. Specific organizational units are given responsibility for either designated functions or the support of customer groups. This is based on the premise that accountability facilitates motivation. Accordingly, organizational units are sometimes referred to as "responsibility centers." In this context, an issue all firms need to address concerns the extent to which all major customers and functions are the responsibility of someone, either an individual or a team. At times, major organizational functions are "everyone's responsibility" and nobody's. For example, a construction company can be organized according to such functions as land acquisition, engineering, purchasing, sales, marketing, and finance, but with no single person responsible for "profitability." Thus, profit is "everyone's responsibility," but ultimately no one is accountable for profit except the CEO. Similarly, as we will see in the example of a company we call "Growco" (described in Chapter 9), sometimes managers tend to make decisions based on what's best for their functional unit, without considering what is best for the company as a whole, because the latter is not their responsibility.

How Should We Organize to Promote Entrepreneurship?

Another issue for the strategic design of organizational structure concerns the ability of certain structures to foster or facilitate entrepreneurship and other structures to inhibit it. This is particularly relevant in the case of revitalization and business vision transformations, where entrepreneurship and innovative thinking are essential.

Many structures found in organizations simply do not facilitate entrepreneurship. There are a myriad of problems resulting from this, some obvious and some more subtle. The basic problem is that larger organizations tend to drive out some of their most entrepreneurially oriented people because the structure does not adequately support innovation. Most entrepreneurs have some unique characteristics that set them apart from others. They tend to be people who are able to see the possibilities of alternative paradigms. They also often have certain personality traits that others find difficult to deal with. Some entrepreneurs may be described as "off the wall" or "abrasive" and even as people who "don't fit in." As a result, some entrepreneurs have had to leave their own organization during the transformation process. For example, Steven Jobs was forced out of Apple Computers after a power struggle with John Sculley, whom Jobs had himself recruited to help the firm transition to professional management. Similarly, other entrepreneurs such as Jack Tramiel of Commodore Computers, Mitch Kapor of Lotus Corporation, and Loraine Meca from Micro D all left their own companies. Ross Perot was "asked to leave" General Motors after they had acquired Perot's firm, Electronic Data Systems.

In this context it should be noted that Ross Perot described himself this way: "I'm not the oyster, or the pearl in the oyster, I am the irritant which creates the pearl in the oyster." Most entrepreneurs are irritants in this sense. These "irritants" may be difficult to deal with on a daily basis, but they are essential for moving the organization out on the boundaries of the envelope, seeing anomalies in the existing ways of doing things, and helping the organization formulate a new paradigm—all of which are essential in the process of the initial founding of a new venture, in revitalizations, and in business vision transformations.

Entrepreneurs represent an important organizational asset. Indeed, they may be much more valuable than anything on a company's balance sheet.[3] To protect them, and, in turn, preserve a vital corporate asset, the structure must be designed in a way that allows entrepreneurs and innovators to "do their thing" relatively protected from the rest of the organization.

What Is the Optimal Size for Our Company?

For more than thirty years, there has been recognition in the literature on management that size is a fundamental issue or problem in managing organizations.[4] Although economists have long known that there are economies of scale, there are also diseconomies of size in many organizations. The larger an organization becomes, the more complex, and consequently the more difficult it is to manage. This occurs because of the number of interactions between people, the number of people *per se*, and the number of competing interests that develop. From this perspective, "small is (or, at least, can be) beautiful."[5]

There are times when large size represents a necessary or decided advantage, so we are not saying that all organizations ought to be small. Instead, one of the critical long-term strategic decisions an organization must make concerns its optimal size. It is increasingly recognized that certain sizes are optimal for different kinds of operations.[6] For example, it is generally believed that once a professional organization grows beyond one thousand people, it is inherently difficult to manage. The solution for these types of companies and others is sometimes to subdivide the organization into smaller groups.

Unfortunately, subdividing an organization into a set of smaller units is not a panacea since it focuses almost exclusively on the management of the firm's macro structure. Although this will make each of the individual units easier to manage, it will create new challenges related to how the firm can best integrate the several operating units into a whole.

A wide variety of strategies can be used to manage or integrate a series of subunits of a business enterprise. These typically involve how a firm designs and utilizes the micro structure and supporting systems aspects of its structure. Strategies can be viewed on a continuum ranging from the centralized approach used at ITT under Harold Geneen, to the decentralized approach used at Beatrice Foods (when it was a stand-alone entity) under Bill Karnes. Under Geneen, when ITT was an $8-billion corporation, it had a corporate staff of approximately 1,200 people. Although ITT was involved in businesses ranging from telecommunications to hotels to insurance, Geneen and his staff were deeply involved in the operations of every unit. The corporate staff was required to analyze the information and control the operations of the units. This hands-on approach was in dramatic contrast to the "hands-off" approach used by Bill Karnes at Beatrice Foods.

At Beatrice Foods, which was also an $8-billion company, there was a corporate staff of fewer than 100 people. The basic strategy Karnes used was to operate the holding company as a vertical bank. This meant that it was essentially an investment company. Divisions were required to produce a certain rate of return (e.g., 15 % pretax return on investment), and were left free to pursue their own operating policies. If they failed to produce this return, then it "rained advisors." These advisors were intended to help fix up these operations. If the operations could not be fixed up, then the unit would be sold. Teledyne is another organization that has managed itself in this type of decentralized fashion.

Between these two extremes is the strategy used by Bristol Myers-Squibb, which requires each of its subsidiary companies to produce a strategic plan. These plans are reviewed at a corporate or group level depending on the size of the unit. The plan must be consistent with the group's overall strategy, but the evaluation is not done on a line-by-line basis. The process is therefore one that strikes a delicate balance between each business unit's plan and an overall concept for the organization. For example, when Surgitek (a medical engineering) subsidiary at Bristol Myers-Squibb wanted to make two acquisitions in the late 1980s to facilitate its growth, division management allowed both to occur. However, Surgitek was only allowed to keep one of the firms it had acquired while the other was put into a different business group. This is based on a concept of the overall coherence of the set of companies that are a part of Bristol Myers-Squibb. This example also illustrates the role of supporting systems (i.e., shared planning) in implementing a structural approach.

Fundamental 4: To Develop an Appropriate Design, There Is a Need to Understand the Three Pure Macro Structural Forms

With respect to designing and selecting a macro structure that will help a firm achieve its transformational plan, a firm may choose from three basic or

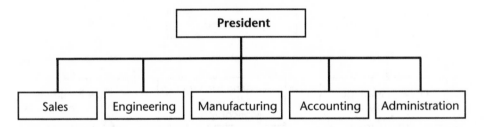

Figure 8–2. Functional Organizational Structure.

pure forms of structure and/or may elect to utilize a "hybrid" or blend of more than one of these forms. Since there is no one best structure (Fundamental 1), understanding the strengths and limitations of each pure structural form can assist a firm in making this important decision. Just as a quarterback must learn to read a defense and understand the various forms of defense to know how to play against them, managers must understand the various macro structural forms in order to effectively design a structure that will support their firm's transformation.

Functional Structure
The most basic form of organization is the so-called "functional structure." In the functional structure, all the key "functions" for operations that must be performed in a business report to a single executive (typically the President or a General Manager) who is responsible for coordinating them. Figure 8–2 depicts this form of structure.

In terms of the metaphor of playing the game, the game being played in a functional structure can best be viewed as a "relay race." For example, in an industrial company, Marketing identifies the need for a product and hands the concept to Engineering, which designs the product and hands the design to Purchasing, which acquires the materials and hands them to Production, which manufacturers the product, and, figuratively at least, hands off responsibility to Sales, which must now sell it. Each function has its own responsibilities; it "runs its lap" and hands the baton to the next area. If something goes wrong, a great deal of finger-pointing can occur, with each area asserting they did "their job." The person responsible for the overall profit of the enterprise is the President or General Manager.

The functional structure of an organization can be used by some of the very smallest of firms and has been found in some of the largest. For example, Kodak was functionally organized when the firm had in excess of $10 billion in annual revenue.

This structure has both strengths and limitations, and is not appropriate in all circumstances. In a functional structure, people tend to be, as implied by the word itself, "functionally focused." They concentrate on such issues as engineering, research and development, marketing, sales, manufacturing,

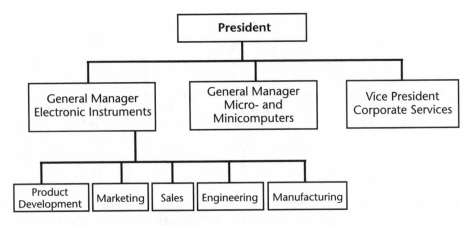

Figure 8–3. Divisional Organizational Structure.

and administration. This is a strength in that people can develop a great deal of functional expertise. The weakness of this approach, however, is that people's perspectives are inevitably influenced by the function to which they report. It is also typically more difficult for the firm to stay in touch with changing customer needs and take steps (including the development of new products) to meet these needs than it is in other types of structures. This is because the organization is designed primarily to focus on developing functional expertise within a stable (e.g., continuing to offer the same product, continuing to serve the same customer, etc.) environment. In this structure, executive time is typically spread thin because the head of the organization must devote a great deal of attention to ensuring that the various functions work effectively together in helping to achieve the firm's goals.

Whenever an organization has more than one set of customers or multiple product lines, a functional structure will be limited in its ability to function as an effective form to meet customer needs. For example, as seen in Chapter 6, Kodak was historically organized in a functional manner, and because the photography business was the company's core business, other potential products did not receive the degree of attention necessary for their growth.

Divisional Structure
The divisional structural form was created to mimic the benefits of relatively small, entrepreneurial businesses. The rationale was to subdivide a larger entity into a set of smaller units, each having their own markets, products, resources, operational systems, management systems, and culture, but with all units sharing certain core resources and a few systems at the corporate level. The intention was for the divisions to simulate being stand-alone (hopefully entrepreneurially oriented) companies, but with the advantages of economies of scale in certain support areas. For example, several divisions

might share corporate resources in the financial, legal, and, perhaps, centralized purchasing areas. Figure 8–3 illustrates divisional structure.

The divisional structure form involves treating every business unit as a separate "profit center," which means that it has responsibility for generating profits as if it were a stand-alone business. This feature is the most powerful aspect of a divisional structure. In contrast, under the functional structure, there is typically only one profit center, which occurs at the corporate level even in very large organizations whose revenues may be in the billions.

Although the divisionalized structure is relatively simple in concept, executing it well is complex. The classic example of an enterprise that has successfully executed the divisional concept is General Electric Company (GE). In 1995, GE's revenues exceeded $70 billion and it earned net income of $6.6 billion. The company's organizational strategy, as described by the three members of GE's Corporate Executive Office, is to create a "new kind of company—one that has, and uses, all of the strengths of a big company, while moving with the speed, hunger and urgency of a small company."[7]

GE is organized into twelve businesses, including aircraft engines, appliances, capital services, lighting, medical systems, NBC, plastics, power systems, and so on. Each of these strategic business units is headed by a President and Chief Executive Officer responsible for the profitability of the business. The role of the GE corporate unit is to: (1) manage the allocation of financial resources among the individual businesses beyond the scope of existing business, (2) focus on R&D and new business development, and (3) provide for development of human resources on a corporate-wide basis. By controlling finance, the corporate office controls the allocation of resources throughout the enterprise and potentially can better achieve optimal investment. By having a corporate center for research and development, GE can potentially achieve synergy across units as well as have the ability to "seed" new businesses. By controlling management development, GE can not only train their managers but also use the educational process as a sophisticated tool for socialization and culture management. We will examine the role of culture management as a tool for managing transformations in Chapter 11.

Although the divisional structure can often be close to ideal from a motivational and management incentive viewpoint, it tends to have limitations as well. From the perspective of the enterprise as a whole, divisional structures lack the cost efficiency of functional structures because they typically require that the same organizational functions are duplicated in each division (e.g., rather than having *one* sales function for the company, all divisions will have their own). Nevertheless, the trade-offs between duplication of personnel versus customer focus and focus on the bottom line are often (but not always) in favor of adopting a divisional approach. Another potential limitation of this structural form is that it can sometimes lead to intense competition between divisions for resources. If this is not controlled through a sophisticated planning process (a supporting system), divisions can waste valuable time fighting among themselves rather than staying focused on meeting customer needs.

A final problem relates to the expertise of managers required to make this structure work. To operate as a divisional structure, an organization needs general managers in charge of each division. These managers require a broad set of skills that enable them to function as the leader of a profit center; they are, in effect, the CEO (Chief Executive Officer) of that division, and this requires a variety of business management skills not all managers possess.

Matrix Structure

In principle, the classic matrix structure tries to achieve the best of both worlds through a mixture of the functional and divisional approaches. Similar to the divisional approach, in a matrix structure there are managers responsible for all aspects of a particular program, project, or client. The matrix structure also includes specific functional areas that are headed by senior managers who typically report directly to the President or General Manager. Figure 8–4 presents an illustration of the matrix form of structure.

In the matrix structure, each program, project, or client manager forms a team of functional specialists (drawn from the various functions) to assist him or her in meeting the needs of the program, project, or client. Functional specialists thus have two or more reporting relationships—to at least one program, project, or client manager and to their functional manager. Functional managers and program/project/client managers must coordinate frequently to ensure that resources (especially people) are allocated in a manner that will allow the company to effectively and efficiently achieve its goals. Individual project/program/client team members may move onto and off teams as needed to support the organization's goals. Thus, one of the primary strengths of a matrix structure is that it increases the flexibility of the organization—an organization is able to invest resources wherever needed to achieve goals and remove them to better maximize overall return. Another strength is that the structure provides for functional specialization, while at the same time permits the organization to focus on meeting customer needs through the development of new products and services.

Unfortunately, although the matrix structure is very powerful in concept, it is extremely difficult to execute in practice. Its main problem is its complexity, along with the need for a very high level of coordination and communication between units and people. In terms of playing the game, a matrix structure requires a great deal of true teamwork.

Both functional and project/program/client managers must work together to ensure that resources (including human resources) are effectively allocated to maximize the firm's overall results. To guarantee that everyone is moving in the same direction and that resources are being effectively invested, a sophisticated planning system is needed. There also needs to be a performance management system that provides an opportunity for both functional and project/client/program managers to have input about an individual team member's performance. Although many organizations talk

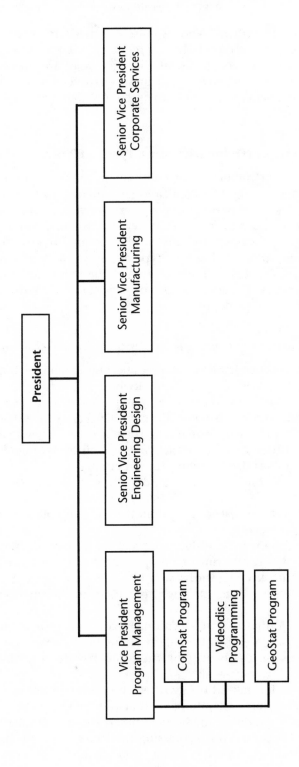

Figure 8–4. Matrix Organizational Structure.

of their "management team" and espouse the need for teamwork, it is achieved relatively rarely, especially in large, complex business enterprises. What makes it work are people who know their roles and responsibilities, can communicate very effectively, adjust when necessary, can trust their teammates, can plan effectively, and can execute. When it works, it is a thing of grace and beauty.

Designing Structure for Different Types of Transformations

The fundamentals of structural design outlined in the last section constitute the science of developing an organizational structure to support a given transformation. The "art" of designing a given structure is comprised of utilizing these fundamentals in creating a variety of structural alternatives from which an organization can choose the "best" structure.[8] In developing these alternatives, organizations facing each type of transformation have different challenges or issues that they must address at the macro, micro, and supporting systems levels. These challenges or issues are summarized in Figure 8–5 and discussed in more depth below.

Key Structural Challenges or Issues to be Addressed in Type I Transformations

A Transformation of the First Kind involves becoming a professionally managed organization and does not typically include a structural *change* per se. Instead, changing the game to that of a more professional firm requires that all three aspects of structure become more formalized. At the same time, the firm needs to ensure that in formalizing their structure, they maintain the positive aspects of their entrepreneurial culture. This involves addressing (in a more formal manner) the following key structural issues:
- What form will our organization adopt to ensure success over the long term?
- How can we ensure that we are promoting accountability at an individual and unit level?
- How can we retain the positive aspects of the entrepreneurial firm— including fostering a culture of entrepreneurship, staying close to our customers, and "keeping things simple"—within our new structure?

To address these issues, firms making this type of transformation typically need to:
- Create more formalized organizational charts that provide position-holders and units with information about how they relate to one another (thus clearly identifying the form that the organization is adopting to achieve its goals).
- Develop more formalized (i.e., written) position descriptions and/or update existing job descriptions so that they reflect what position-holders should be doing in the now much larger organization that the firm has become (thus addressing the issues of how to promote individual and/or team responsibility and accountability).

Structure Component	Type I Transformation	Type II Transformation	Type III Transformation
Macro Structure	• Formalize structure through creation of organizational charts. • Evaluate extent to which structure is consistent with strategy (as articulated in transformational plan).	• Re-evaluate structure for extent to which it meets current customer needs, promotes entrepreneurship and minimizes complexity. • May need to look for opportunities to "down-size" or "right-size" structure.	• Create new structure to support new vision.
Micro Structure	• Formalize (i.e. prepare written) job/position descriptions that clarify accountabilities and responsibilities.	• Re-write/revise job descriptions in order to promote better focus on the customer, accountability for meeting needs of new market/environment, and promote entrepreneurship.	• Revise job descriptions in order to focus position-holders on doing what needs to be done to achieve new vision.
Supporting Systems	• Create more sophisticated operational systems to support structure. • Create a more formal approach to management development and performance management and a more formal approach to corporate culture management in order to support the new structure.	• Review/revise existing operational systems in order to minimize bureaucracy and better support the company's structure and goals. • May need to revise management development and performance management processes to better support the new structure. • Redefine the corporate culture so as to promote accountability within the new organization, entrepreneurship, and staying close to the customer.	• Review/revise operational systems, management development and performance management processes, and the corporate culture in order to better support the new vision and structure.

Figure 7–7. Planning for Different Types of Transformation.

- Establish more sophisticated operational systems, create a more formalized approach to management development and performance
  management, and examine how the firm's culture should be managed to best support the structure that the firm has adopted (which
  also helps address the issue of holding people and units accountable
  for results).

One of the key challenges these organizations face is overcoming the feeling that creating a more formalized structure will lead to "bureaucracy." This
can be accomplished by ensuring that entrepreneurs and the entrepreneurial
spirit of the organization are somehow retained (through how the culture is
managed) and through ensuring that the organization has been structured in
a way that maintains a focus on keeping it as simple and "small" as possible.

Another aspect of structural change that may accompany a transformation to professional management is the creation of the Chief Operating
Officer or COO position. As a company grows in size, the management of the
enterprise becomes more complex. The founder or entrepreneur may require
someone to assist him or her in building the infrastructure required to run
the much larger organization effectively and efficiently. The hiring of a COO
can provide the entrepreneur with the time to focus on developing and
implementing the firm's long-term vision and building key relationships
with those outside the company (e.g., shareholders, potential investors,
boards of directors, etc.) In terms of revenues, there is a great deal of varia-
tion among companies as to when this tends to occur. Sometimes it occurs as
early as $100 million in annual revenues or sooner.

Key Structural Issues/Challenges to be Addressed in Type II Transformations

Transformations of the Second Kind can involve major changes in organizational structure. Since revitalization transformations entail making adjustments to environmental changes, there is usually some corresponding
change in organizational structure. Key structural issues that must be
addressed in completing this type of transformation include:

- Should we change our organizational form in order to revitalize the
  firm and better meet the needs of our current markets/customers?
- What is the optimal size for the company as a whole and for individual business units for us to compete effectively in the new environment and promote entrepreneurship?
- How should accountabilities and responsibilities of individuals and
  units change to better support the revitalization process and achievement of our transformational plan?

The first thing the organization needs to do is evaluate its structure in
terms of its ability to support the revitalization process. Most firms making
this type of transformation typically find that a key element to be considered
in evaluating the organizational form is the size the organization should
adopt to better fit with its environment. Sometimes this is euphemistically

termed "downsizing" or "right sizing," but it usually involves a reduction in staff size.

Downsizing or right-sizing should not merely involve shrinking the organization; instead, the structure should be re-conceptualized and redesigned as appropriate for the revitalized enterprise. This can involve not only redefining the macro structure, but also redefining individual or unit roles and responsibilities to be more consistent with the environment in which the firm is operating. For example, as we noted in Chapter 5, Navistar did not merely shrink its organization and retain the same structure; rather, it reconceptualized its structure from a functional to a divisional matrix form. It also eliminated its planning department and redefined managers' roles to include responsibility (and accountability) for developing, implementing, and monitoring plans that would help the larger organization accomplish its goals. Finally, it offered training to managers in how to develop and utilize an effective approach to planning as well as training in other management skills needed for effectively implementing these plans.

No single structural form is ideal or optimal for revitalization transformations. When a transformation of the Second Kind involves expansion of an enterprise into several businesses, there will typically be a change from a functional structure to either a divisional or matrix structure. For example, when Kodak began the first stage of its revitalization, it changed its structure from a functional to a divisional one. If a business focus narrows, there can be a change from a divisional to a functional structure. For example, when Allegis (a diversified travel company created by UAL Inc.) reversed its transformation back to United Airlines and divested Hertz and Hilton International Hotels (as we will examine further in Chapter 10), it reverted to a functional structure from a divisionalized structure.

Key Structural Challenges or Issues to be Addressed in Type III Transformations

Since Transformations of the Third Kind involve a change in business vision, they are often accompanied by changes in organizational structure as well. Key structural issues that must be addressed in this type of transformation include:

- What structural form should we adopt to enable us to achieve our new vision and stay close to our customers?
- How will we define individual and unit responsibilities within the new structure to maximize our ability to achieve our mission?
- What is the optimal size of the company and its various business units that will allow us to effectively and efficiently achieve our vision?
- How can we ensure that we are fostering entrepreneurship within our structure and keeping that structure as simple as possible?

When a firm embarks on a business vision transformation, it typically needs to be prepared to make some major changes in all three components of its structure—macro, micro, and supporting systems. Structure, in fact, should be a major topic of discussion during the firm's transformational planning process. As is true in the other types of transformations, in the absence of an appropriate, well-thought-out, and communicated structure, the vision transformation will fail.

The business vision transformation from SCE Corp to Edison International involved a major structural change, as described in Chapter 5. The company transformed its structure from a functional structure to a divisionalized concept, with the new "Mission Businesses" comprising a separate entrepreneurial strategic unit. Similarly, the transformation of Disney from a motion picture company to a diversified entertainment business has led to the creation of a set of autonomous but strategically related business units.

Organization Structure: The Next Step

This chapter has begun our examination of how to design an organizational structure that will support a firm's transformation. We have examined what structure is and introduced some of the key fundamentals of structure design that are required in order for a firm to effectively play its chosen game. We continue our discussion of structure and the role it plays in changing the game in Chapter 9 by presenting a step-by-step approach for managing the structural transformation process as well as a detailed example of how one company utilized this process in changing its game.

9

DESIGNING ORGANIZATIONAL STRUCTURE

Tailoring It to the New Game

This chapter builds on Chapter 8, which introduced some of the fundamentals of organization structure, and discusses the steps a firm needs to take in designing a structure to support a successful transformation. The chapter also includes a comprehensive example of how one company used this process to change its structure and, in turn, its game.

Managing the Structural Transformation Process

Figure 9–1 presents the steps of a systematic approach that a firm can use in designing organizational structure to support its transformation.

Step 1: Review of Strategic Transformational Plan and Identification of Key Elements

The process of designing organizational structure to support the transformation begins with a review of the strategic transformational plan that has been developed. The goal of this review is to identify the firm's strategy (and its key elements) so that the structure can be designed to support it (i.e., so that "form follows function").

Step 2: Identification of Structural "Requirements" to Support the Transformational Plan

Once the review of the strategic transformational plan has been completed and the elements of the firm's strategy defined, the next step is to identify what the structure needs to do to support the plan. We refer to this as identifying the "structural requirements." If a firm is transforming from an

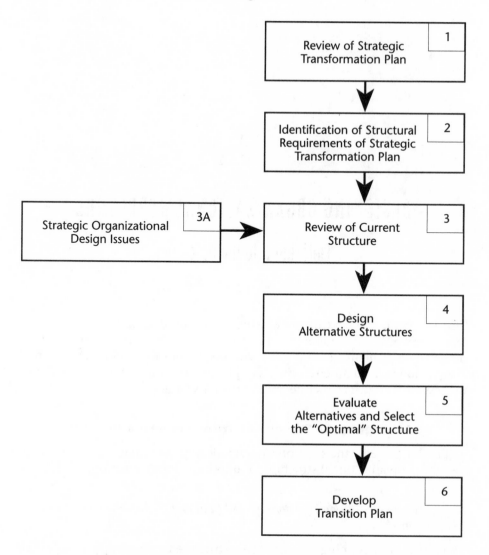

Figure 9–1. Process for Designing Organizational Structure Transformations.

entrepreneurial organization to a professionally managed firm (as at Medi-pro Industries) and its business concept will remain the same after the transformation, then the structure requirements will typically include formalizing the existing structure (which will most typically be functional in nature). In contrast, if a firm is facing a revitalization transformation, structural requirements will identify what the new structure will need to do to assist the firm in better meeting the demands of its new environment. As stated earlier, organizations that are involved in vision transformations will have structural requirements that explicitly identify the structural implications of their change in vision. At Starbucks, for example, the firm identified four related strategic components of its future business—retail, speciality sales to other corporations, a mail-order business, and international expansion. These four key strategic elements have implications for the company's structure and serve as the foundation for developing the requirements for "what the structure should do."

Given this strategic vision, Starbucks in fact has transformed its organizational structure from a functional structure to a divisionalized-matrix hybrid. In 1995, the company created four business units: retail, specialty sales, direct response, and international. The retail unit is responsible for the development and management of more than 1,000 stores. The specialty sales unit oversees corporate sales and joint ventures. For example, it has responsibility for sales to United Airlines, Barnes and Noble, and Sheraton Hotels; for the joint venture with Pepsico for coffee-based drinks such as Frappuccino©; and for the joint venture with Dreyer's Ice Cream. The direct response unit has responsibility for Starbucks' mail-order business as well as the "America Online Cafe Starbucks." The international unit is responsible for joint ventures with companies that will jointly own and manage Starbucks stores around the world. Starbucks' first international joint venture was with SAZ-ABY, Inc. in Japan. Their first stores opened in Tokyo during the summer of 1996. In 1997, Starbucks opened stores in Singapore and Manila.

Step 3: Review of Current Structure

In this step, the current structure is examined from two perspectives:
1. The extent to which it meets the structural "requirements" that were identified during the review of the transformational plan.
2. The extent to which it helps the firm address the key strategic organizational design issues previously discussed in Chapter 8.

This review is intended to help the company answer the question: "Do we have the 'right' structure already in place to help us achieve the goals outlined in our transformational plan?"

For many firms facing a Type I Transformation, there may not be a very formal (i.e., written) definition of the firm's structure (including an organization chart, job descriptions, and formalized systems to support the structure) or the structure that the firm has "on paper" may no longer reflect how the firm really works. For firms attempting to change their game from that of an entrepreneurship to a professionally managed firm, Step 3 may begin with having the firm's management prepare:
1. A current organizational chart.
2. Updated role descriptions for at least all management positions within the company.

Once the current organization chart and role descriptions have been completed, they should be assessed for the extent to which they meet the structural requirements defined in Step 2 and how they help the firm address key structural issues. During Step 3, firms facing a Type I Transformation should also assess the extent to which supporting systems currently support the structure that the firm has adopted. Firms facing a Type II or Type III Transformation will typically have more formalized (i.e., written) organization charts and job descriptions that can serve as a starting point for reviewing the structure. The task facing these firms is to assess the extent to which these components of structure are consistent with the objectives and goals that have been articulated in the transformational plan (i.e., the extent to which they meet the structural requirements previously identified). Firms facing such transformations also need to assess the extent to which current supporting systems (which may be quite formalized) adequately meet the structural requirements identified and help the firm effectively address the structural issues previously discussed in Chapter 8.

Step 3 helps the company identify the greatest opportunities for change, as well as where the structure is already effectively supporting the firm's strategy. For example, it was clear to Kay R. Whitmore in 1993 that Eastman Kodak's decentralized structure was no longer appropriate for the company. As part of the decision to transform Kodak from a conglomerate to a company focused on imaging, Whitmore made the decision to change the structure, as described in Chapter 6.

Step 4: Design Alternative Structures

This step involves formulating alternative structures to support the transformation. While it is important that those involved in designing various alternative structures understand the structural fundamentals discussed in Chapter 8 (i.e., the science of structural design), this is the step where "art" also plays a critical role. During this step, any number of structural configurations may be generated.

Here is a step-by-step approach for generating alternative structures:

1. Using the structural requirements generated in Step 2 and the key structural issues discussed in Chapter 8 as input, identify the key "functions" that the organization must have in place to adequately meet these requirements and address these issues. For example, a firm facing a revitalization transformation might have identified a need to "get closer to the customer." This might lead to the firm identifying marketing, market research, customer service, and sales, as key functions that in some way need to be included in their structure.

2. Once the list of key functions has been identified, determine whether any functions should be combined to minimize the extent to which the firm becomes overly functionalized at the expense of working together to meet customer needs. For example, some firms combine sales and marketing into a single unit. Some firms, having identified that planning is a key function, opt to give responsibility for planning to individual managers rather than create a separate planning function.

3. Develop a final list of key functions to be included in the structure.
4. Using the list of key functions as input, "craft" or design various alternative macro structures. The key functions will become (in some shape or form) the boxes within the organization charts that are developed. Instead of focusing on creating only one structure, we suggest that a firm develop *at least* three alternative structures that meet the structural requirements and address the strategic organizational design issues. Since there is no one best structure, all structures developed will have some weaknesses (i.e., they will not meet all the structural requirements and/or will not adequately address key structural issues). The goal of this step, however, is to come up with at least three of the "best" structures for the organization.
5. Determine how the organization's operational systems, management development and performance management systems, and culture need to be designed to support each structural alternative. In Step 4, this does not need to be a very in-depth analysis. However, key systems issues should be identified because (as we will see in Step 5), they will have an impact on the costs of implementing each alternative. For example, if one alternative structure is a matrix, supporting systems will need to include:
   - Helping managers develop the capabilities to manage effectively within a matrix environment.
   - Providing training to all possible team members on how to work as a team and manage meetings effectively.
   - Developing a performance management process in which individuals are evaluated not only by their functional manager, but also by the project/program/client manager on whose team they serve.
   - Developing operational systems that provide the information needed for managers to effectively monitor performance against goals within a matrix environment.

Firms facing a Type I Transformation may not need to go through Step 4 in the structural transformation process because their greatest challenge is typically to "formalize" rather than redesign their structures. However, even for these firms, it is sometimes useful to at least think about possible alternative structures *before* they "lock in" on their current structure as "the best."

Step 5: Evaluate Alternatives and Select the "Best" Structure

The next step is to evaluate the extent to which the structural alternatives generated in Step 4 meet the structural requirements (identified in Step 2) and address the strategic organizational design issues discussed in Chapter 8. Then, based on this evaluation, the firm should select the structure that will "best" fit with the strategy outlined in its transformational plan.

This evaluation of alternatives results in a list of strengths and limitations of the various structures and allows the firm to assess the overall costs and benefits of adopting each structure. During this step, a firm should also assess the extent to which it has the resources needed for adopting a particular structure. This involves assessing:

- The number of people the organization currently has that are available to fill key positions.
- The extent to which current managers and employees possess the skills needed to occupy key positions and whether the firm can make (grow from existing personnel) or needs to buy personnel to fill key positions.
- The systems the firm has in place to support the structure.
- The impact (either positive or negative) that adopting the structure will have on the firm's culture and whether the culture of the organization needs to change to support this new structure.

Strengths and limitations should be identified in writing. Then, based on an analysis of these strengths and limitations, a firm should determine which structure will "best" help the firm change its game and/or play its chosen game most effectively.

Although their main challenge is formalizing their structure, even firms facing a Type I Transformation should spend some time analyzing the extent to which the formal organization chart, role descriptions, and supporting systems they have identified in Step 3 meet structural requirements and address key issues. If significant "gaps" are identified, the firm's management may want to make some adjustments in one or more components of its structure.

Step 6: Develop a Transition Plan

The final step in the structural transformation process is to identify how a firm will move from its current to its new (or optimal) structure. In brief, this step involves developing a structural transformation plan (which should be included as a part of the firm's overall transformational plan). Although it may be feasible to move directly from the current structure to the desired future structure, it is often necessary to move first to an intermediate structure. When an organization defines what its "optimal" structure ought to be, it is not uncommon for that to be quite different from how it is currently organized (especially for firms facing a Type II or Type III Transformation). To fully implement a very different structure may require some time as both people and systems are acquired and/or developed to support it.

For example, when organizations transform themselves from functional structures to divisional structures, they will need people with general management capabilities to run the new strategic business units. Often an organization may have a significant number of high-level technical or functional specialists (e.g., VP's of Marketing, Sales, R&D, Engineering, Manufacturing, etc.), but not true profit-center managers. Thus, the organization may require some time to develop general managers and make the change from the current to the proposed ideal structure in a series of transitional steps. This was the case at a medical engineering company that had two product lines, used

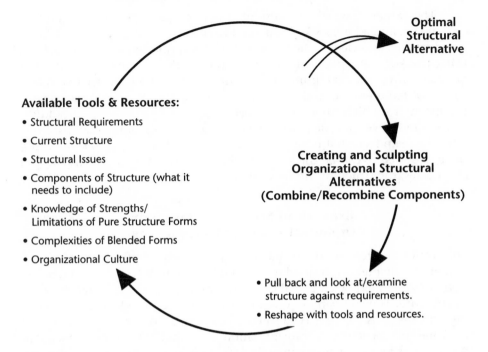

Optimal Structural Alternative

Available Tools & Resources:

- Structural Requirements
- Current Structure
- Structural Issues
- Components of Structure (what it needs to include)
- Knowledge of Strengths/ Limitations of Pure Structure Forms
- Complexities of Blended Forms
- Organizational Culture

Creating and Sculpting Organizational Structural Alternatives (Combine/Recombine Components)

- Pull back and look at/examine structure against requirements.
- Reshape with tools and resources.

Figure 9–2. Designing and Redesigning Organizational Structure.

a functional structure, and planned to expand through acquisition. In the process of helping management develop a strategic transformational plan, the authors, who served as consultants to the firm, pointed out that the company did not have a sufficient number of general managers to immediately move to a divisionalized structure. Accordingly, the company planned to move to the desired divisional structure in two stages, with the first stage focused on developing both people and systems to support this structure.

The Process as a Whole

Although the process shown in Figure 9–1 is linear in nature, in reality it is less "step-by-step" than it appears. As Figure 9–2 illustrates, the structural transformation process is really more circular in nature—i.e., a firm may actually go through several cycles of design and/or redesign before the "optimal" structure emerges from the process.

As shown in this figure, the process begins with having those involved develop a clear understanding of:

1. The fundamentals of structural design (including the process just discussed).
2. The key elements of the firm's structure (based on an assessment of the firm's strategy).

3. The extent to which the current structure meets structural requirements and addresses key structural issues.

Based on this knowledge, the team then crafts various alternative structures using the key elements/components of the firm's structure as inputs. The next step involves examining the extent to which each alternative meets structural requirements and addresses key issues. If there are problems with the extent to which alternatives meet structural requirements or address issues, alternatives may be redesigned or recrafted. This process will continue until the team feels that it has arrived at the "best" structure. In some cases, the best structure can be the structure that the firm already has in place. In other cases, the structure will need to be quite different.

Example of Structural Design in Organizational Transformations

This section is intended to illustrate how the process described in the last section of this chapter can be used to help a firm design its structure. In this section, we describe how an actual company used this process in transforming its structure. The company in question was a medical products manufacturing firm that was facing a Type III (i.e., Business Vision Transformation). At the time they began their transformation, they had been in business about twelve years and were approximately $500 million in revenues. For the purposes of this illustration, we will call the company "Growco."[1]

We have selected this example to illustrate the process of structural design in organizational transformations for a variety of reasons. However, the most important reason is that it operationalizes all the steps in of the process of structural redesign. In addition, the company had grown very rapidly (at a rate of approximately 50% per year) in the years preceding the initiation of the structural design process, and it had experienced most of the classic symptoms of growing pains identified in Chapter 2 (See Figure 2–7). Accordingly, the structural change had some aspects of a transformation to professional management as well as a vision transformation.

Company Background

Growco began as a small start-up, building on a unique product idea that was generated during a cocktail party conversation. The product the company developed (a medical device) was extremely innovative and, almost overnight, the firm had become a dominant player in its market. In fact, the firm rose so quickly in its dominance of the market that when a much larger company came calling, a decision was made to sell Growco and become part of the larger organization. However, for the most part, those who had started the company remained to help take it into the future.

Signs and Signals of the Need for a Transformation

Although Growco had been extremely successful with its single product (and had developed different versions of this same product to appeal to different tiers of the market), the firm also recognized that its environment was changing and the opportunity to sustain the very high level of growth it had experienced in the past was diminishing. Competitors were releasing less expensive products that appealed to many of the company's traditional customers. In addition, since the product was somewhat specialized (designed to meet the needs of a limited target audience), Growco determined that it needed to diversify its product line and begin serving new markets. In other words, the company decided to diversify and embarked on a business vision transformation.

Elements of Growco's Transformational Plan

Based on an assessment of its current environment, along with an assessment of its current internal capabilities, Growco's management developed a plan for taking the company into the future. In developing its transformational plan, the firm utilized the pyramid of organizational success (discussed in Chapter 2) as a tool. Some of the strategic initiatives identified in this plan included the following:

- To become a global enterprise. Traditionally, the firm had sold its existing product primarily in the United States. Although the company's external assessment indicated that there were significant competitors in Europe and Asia, the firm felt that their product would appeal to customers in these markets and saw this as a source of continued growth.
- To diversify beyond the single product currently offered. As stated earlier, while management knew that there were opportunities to increase sales of its current product through expanding internationally, it also believed that at some point in the not too distant future, the market for this product would become saturated.
- To become a "world-class" competitor, leading the industry in low-cost manufacturing, product quality, and customer satisfaction. The goal of this strategic objective was to focus the company on being the best in its industry and help it develop a sustainable competitive advantage.
- To position the company for continued growth. Whatever products or markets the firm entered, continued growth was viewed as essential to the firm's long-term success. Growco's parent expected growth in its subsidiary companies and whenever growth had slowed, the parent had come in to "help." Growco's management wanted to sustain its growth in order to keep its parent from interfering in the firm's operations.

- To continue to promote the positive elements of the firm's culture (including teamwork). Teamwork had been an extremely important and very real part of the firm's culture since the very beginning. In fact, the firm had been utilizing teams of employees to help develop new products, as well as to tackle organizational issues.

Designing an Organization to Support the Transformation

In late 1993, Growco's president retained a management consulting firm to assist him and his senior management team in designing a structure to help take his firm into the future. The consulting firm was to serve as a resource to the senior management team and partner with them in the design of their new structure. Using the structural design process presented in Figure 9–1, the steps that this organization went through in designing its new structure are outlined below.

Step 1: Review of Strategic Transformational Plan

A team of consultants worked with the firm's senior management team to identify the key strategic initiatives (listed above) of the firm's transformational plan. These became the basis for Step 2 of the process.

Step 2: Identify Structural Requirements

Since Growco's senior management team and the consulting firm were acting as partners in the design of the firm's new structure, some initial training needed to be provided to Growco's management on the fundamentals of structure and structure design. This occurred during an afternoon session in which the senior management team was also asked to identify, based on their knowledge of the firm's transformational plan, the list of structural requirements (i.e., what their new structure needed to do). Senior management indicated that Growco's new structure should:

- Integrate international and U.S. operations. As the firm moved into international markets, it wanted to ensure that silos were not created between markets.
- Promote a "life of product" approach to product development and management. It was important that both existing and new products be managed from "cradle to grave" in order to best meet customer needs.
- Support growth of the existing product line while at the same time promote effective diversification.
- Promote effective and efficient decision-making. Timely decisions, made at the right level, using the best information available, would greatly aid the firm in achieving its long-term goals.
- Minimize redundancy of effort and maximize focus on valued-added activities. There was concern that as the firm continued to grow, some functions or people might not always be focused on what was most important to the firm's success.

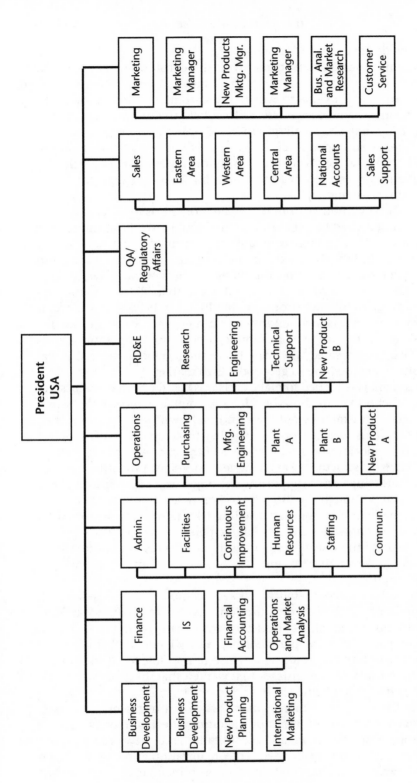

Figure 9–3. Growco's "Current" Structure.

Step 3: Evaluation of Current Structure

Growco's senior management team asked the consulting team to evaluate the extent to which its current structure met the requirements outlined above as well as the extent to which the current structure addressed key strategic organizational design issues. To collect the information needed to complete this analysis, small group-based interviews with a sample of employees representing all levels and all functions within the organization were used. The analysis focused not only on an assessment of the firm's macro structure (presented in Figure 9–3), but also on the micro structure and supporting systems.

Some of the key findings from this evaluation are as follows:

- The company had become overly "functionalized." Even though the firm was a $500-million company, it continued to be functionally organized. In fact, there were so many unique functions (some with very interesting titles) that the company had become overly compartmentalized. Further, it was not clear that all these functions added value to the firm (from the standpoint of helping it achieve its goals). In many cases, functions had been created as a way of solving problems as they arose. For example, a new product planning function had been created when the firm's management felt that it was simply taking too long to get products to market.

- Senior managers tended to make decisions based on what was best for their function versus those best for the company as a whole. Senior managers, for example, only saw and had input to budgets for their own functions (versus working together to determine how resources should be allocated to meet the needs of the company as a whole).

- The current structure was designed to focus primarily on U.S. sales/marketing versus supporting the objective of becoming a global enterprise. Although the firm was trying to develop a presence in the global market, it was primarily selling its products through its sister companies. Growco had created a one-person function that served as the liaison to these sister companies in order to help promote sales. It was felt, however, that this function was not enough to promote adequate international sales.

- Profit and loss accountability and key decision-making resided with the president of the U.S. organization. Given that the firm was functionally organized, all key decisions were made by the president of the company. Since the president had a very large number of people reporting to him and since he was also responsible for serving as the liaison to the parent organization, it was felt that this structure would not be effective and efficient over the long term.

- While the company's management promoted teamwork, the team management "system" was not operating effectively or efficiently. The roles, responsibilities, and accountabilities of new product teams had not been formally clarified. The organization also had not determined what would happen to project team members once a product was developed and released to the market. This created a certain amount of anxiety for team members. Another problem was that new product development teams did not have a single champion who represented them on the senior management team. Some teams reported to Manufacturing; others to R&D. Beyond the more formal product development teams, there were also problems with other teams and committees that had been created to resolve certain organizational issues. One problem was that the culture of the company caused certain people to believe that teams should be formed for *every* purpose. One story told in the company was that there had been a cross-functional team of managers formed to choose the brand of coffee to put in the firm's coffee makers. While this may be an important issue, it probably is not the best use of a manager's time. Further, there were also instances where multiple teams were working on the same project, resulting in duplication of effort.

- The current structure was fairly inflexible. The functional structure of the organization did not provide the firm with the flexibility needed to focus both on its existing product as well as on developing totally new products to meet new customer needs.

- The division of roles and responsibilities between units was not always defined. Given the organization's very rapid growth, it was not always clear who should be responsible or accountable for what. This sometimes led to multiple people/units working on the same things and certain things not getting done because they were "no one's responsibility."

- There was no single unit managing the ongoing product development process from the idea stage through the sale. The company was operating in a relay-race fashion that sometimes resulted in "dropped batons" or the feeling that there were excessive delays in getting new products to market.

In brief, Growco's structure did not adequately support the strategic initiatives that had been outlined in its transformational plan. The company needed to develop a structure more consistent with the requirements identified in Step 2.

Step 4 and Step 5: Design the Desired Structure, Evaluate Alternatives, and Select the "Best" Alternative

Using the evaluation of Growco's current structure as input, the consultants facilitated a workshop session during which Growco's forty most senior managers (consisting of the president, the vice presidents, and all of the vice presidents' direct reports) were:

- Trained in structure management concepts.
- Presented with information about the requirements for Growco's future structure.
- Given the opportunity to utilize the skills presented during the training session in developing various alternative structures.

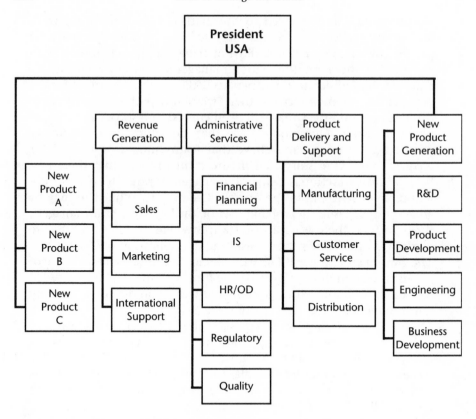

Figure 9–4. Structural Alternative 1.

The forty managers who participated in this session worked in small teams to generate six different organizational structures; and assess the strengths and limitations of each structure from the standpoint of meeting the firm's long-term goals. These structures provided Growco's managers with the opportunity to have significant input into the design of their structure, while at the same time supplying the consulting team with information about how willing Growco's management was to change its current structure. It also gave Growco's top managers the opportunity to "see" that the current structure would not be the "best" structure as the company moved forward in its transformation process.

Based on the output of the workshop session, as well as additional analysis completed by the consultant team, three different alternative structures (two of which were generated during the workshop) were created, analyzed, and presented to Growco's president and vice presidents for their consideration. These three alternative structures are briefly explained below, followed by a chart summarizing the extent to which each structure meets the structural requirements defined in Step 2.

Structural Alternative 1: Consolidation of Major Functions and Development of Stand Alone Product Teams

In this structure (shown in Figure 9–4), a true matrix is created in which the managers of various new product development teams report directly to the president. These product teams consist of functional specialists who are "matrixed in" from the four functional units—Revenue Generation (Sales/Marketing), Administrative Services (Finance, Accounting, Regulatory, and HR), Product Delivery (Manufacturing, Customer Service, and Distribution) and New Product Generation (R&D, Product Development, and Engineering).

A major strength of this structure is that the new product development teams are consolidated and report directly to the president. A major limitation is that the president is still very much responsible for the company's overall management and has a very wide span of control. Further, those in charge of the new product teams need to be very skilled managers to function effectively with existing senior managers who occupy functional roles. Another problem is that this structure may not adequately address how the firm will enter and support totally new product lines. What happens, for example, when the new product has been launched? Does it become a new

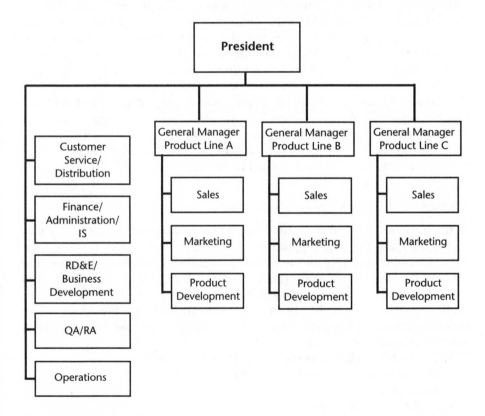

Figure 9–5. Structural Alternative 2.

division? If so, how will this occur? The final problem with this structure is that it does not explicitly support entrance into a global marketplace. The International function is buried within the organization and, therefore may not receive all the attention that it deserves.

Alternative 2: Diversification Through Addition of Two New Products

In this alternative, "pseudo-divisions" are created in which general managers become directly responsible for the sales, marketing, and product development of their particular product lines within the overall business. These general managers draw on the resources of the various functions (shown on the left side of the structure chart in Figure 9–5) to assist them in meeting the goals of maximizing sales within their divisions.

A strength of this structure is that all general managers are responsible for supporting their businesses on a global basis and ensuring that they are maximizing the effectiveness of their *product lines*. A potential problem, however, is that no single position has responsibility for identifying and meeting *customer needs* within a particular market. Another problem is that the structure may increase duplication of effort since each product line has its own marketing, sales, customer service, and product development units. If these product lines are being sold to the same customer, the organization may be needlessly wasting resources. Although the structure reduces the span of control for the president, to operate effectively all general managers must develop the ability to be CEOs of their divisions. At Growco, it was not clear that there were individuals with these skills and capabilities.

Both alternatives 1 and 2 require very effective planning, control, and culture management processes to ensure that all pieces of the organization are moving in the same (and correct) direction toward maximizing results and achieving goals. At the time that the study was conducted, these systems were not as developed as they needed to be.

Alternative 3: Divisionalized Matrix Structure

In this structure (shown in Figure 9–6), a pseudo-division is created to focus on the company's current product line. The person who heads this division, although not controlling all the resources (e.g., manufacturing, engineering, etc.) needed to achieve appropriate results within this product line, does have profit and loss responsibility. In other words, the profit and loss responsibility for this division has been pushed down from the president to the general manager of the product division. This structure also has individual senior managers focused on:

- Specific markets/customers (i.e., SVPs of markets).
- R&D and new business development.
- Operations.
- Administrative activities.

Product diversification outside the existing product line is the responsibility of the SVP of New Business/R&D (with all new product teams reporting to

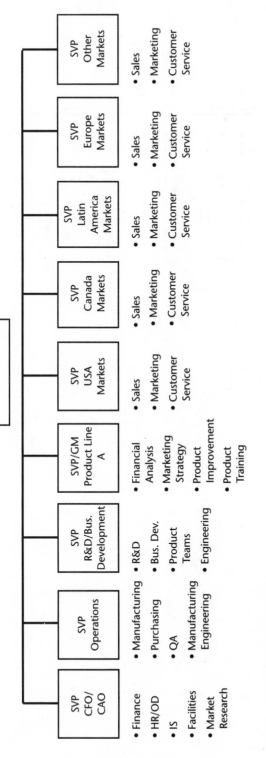

Figure 9–6. Structural Alternative 3.

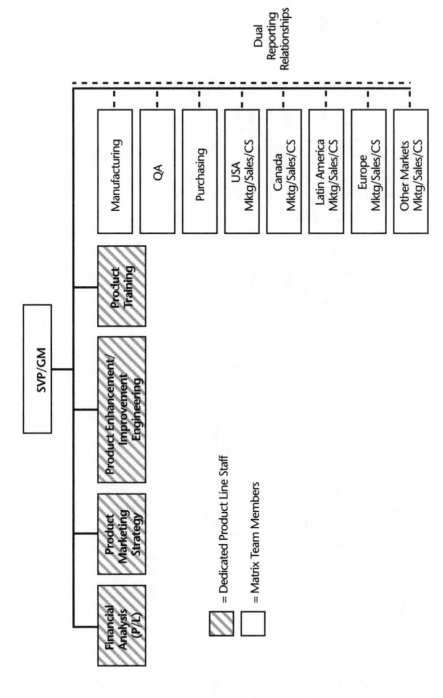

Figure 9–7. Matrix Structure of Product Division.

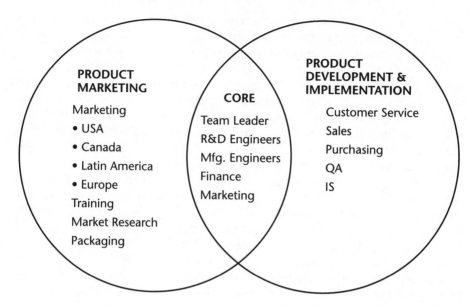

Figure 9–8. Matrix Structure for New Product Development Teams.

this individual). The SVP of Operations is responsible for ensuring that the firm is focused on becoming a world-class producer. Since the company had decided that whatever new products it developed would involve very similar manufacturing techniques, it was felt that creating divisionalized manufacturing units would increase costs and decrease the production unit's ability to continuously improve its operations. The firm also felt that whatever products it developed would be sold to similar (if not the same) customers.

Hence, they felt it did not make sense to assign each division its own sales force. The SVP/General Manager of the Product Line Division therefore oversees a cross-functional team, including members who are matrixed in from other relevant functions (see Figure 9–7). The small staff that reports to the SVP/General Manager focuses on financial analysis, product strategy, product improvement, and product-specific training. The various market units, headed by the SVP Markets, are responsible in this structure for working with product line general managers to establish sales and product improvement goals, and for working with R&D/Business Development in the development of new products.

Within R&D, there are new product teams headed by product managers. As shown in Figure 9–8, these teams include members who matrix in from various functions, depending on the phase of product development. (This was fairly similar to what had been occurring at Growco, although the process of matrixing in and out of the teams had never been formalized.)

Although this structure is the most complex of the three alternatives presented to and analyzed by Growco's senior management team, it has a number of strengths. The most significant strength is that this structure creates units to focus on each of the key strategic initiatives (within the firm's transformational plan). The general manager concentrates on growing the existing product sales through his or her team, while new Business Development/R&D focuses on developing new products (while at the same time having resources available to support the existing product line). The SVP of Operations is responsible for helping the company develop as a world-class manufacturer, while the SVPs of Markets are responsible for ensuring that customer needs in their particular market are understood, utilized in developing new products and services, and are adequately met.

In this structure, the president has responsibility for ensuring that there is adequate focus on the firm's long-term strategic development and has the time required to perform this task since this position is no longer responsible for the profit and loss of the existing product line. Another significant strength of this alternative is that it provides flexibility for future expansion into new markets and diversification of product lines. If, for example, the firm were to develop a completely new product line (through the efforts of its new product teams), this could eventually evolve into another "division" headed by a general manager.

The major limitation of this structure is that it requires a great deal of coordination between units. Although this is certainly an issue, since Growco's managers and employees had become accustomed to functioning within a structure that promoted a high level of teamwork, this did not seem to be a major problem. Another potential problem in implementing this structure was that all senior managers needed to develop very effective general management skills, which not all of them possessed.

Based on the evaluation of alternatives (summarized in Figure 9–9), Growco's senior management determined that Alternative 3 would best meet their long-term needs and help them achieve the goals outlined in their transformational plan.

Step 6: Identify Transitional Steps
While Growco determined that Alternative 3 would best meet their needs, they did not immediately evolve into this structure. Instead, they moved to a transitional state in which the president served as the general manager of the existing product line and in which it was felt that a SVP of the Latin American Market was not yet needed. The remainder of the structure was adopted, with plans to move forward in completing the structural transformation within two years.

Follow-Up

Growco has continued to be successful in its current market. While it struggles with making the complete transition to its new structure, it has become acutely aware of the impact structure can have on its long-term effectiveness.[2]

Structure Requirements	Alternative 1	Alternative 2	Alternative 3
Integrates international to support global strategy.	◑	●	●
Promotes "life of the product" approach to product management.	◑	◑	●
Supports diversification through product development and acquisition.	◑	◑	●
Fosters a strong customer service orientation.	○	◑	●
Promotes effective and efficient decision making.	◑	◑	◑
Builds in a strategic focus with clear individual and unit roles.	◑	◑	●
Promotes effective communication and coordination throughout firm.	◑	◑	◑
Maintains concern for employees while promoting accountability.	◑	●	●
Has effective spans of control without adding unnecessary levels and unnecessary functions.	○	◑	●
Supports positive aspects of existing culture and promotes desired culture.	◑	◑	●

Meets requirements: ●
Partially meets requirements: ◑
Does not meet requirements: ○

Figure 9–9. Summary Evaluation of Growco's Three Alternative Structures.

Conclusion

This chapter, together with Chapter 8, has examined the issues involved in transforming an organization's structure after a strategic transformational plan has been developed. We have shown that the choice of the form of organization to help implement a transformational plan is a strategic issue in itself.

Many organizations approach the issue of structural design independently from questions of strategic vision. When that strategy fails, they tend to blame the problems on imperfections in the strategy itself rather than appreciate the role of structure and the need for structural transformations to support their organizational transformations. Other organizations recognize the need for structural transformation as a component of overall organizational transformation. The concepts and process described in Chapters 8 and 9 are intended to assist managers in accomplishing the structural changes required as part of the transformation process.

Throughout these two chapters we have noted the role of management development, culture, and performance management systems as key aspects (i.e., supporting systems) for changing organizational structure. For example, unless we have people who possess general management capabilities, we cannot use a divisional structure effectively. Unless we have a true team culture, it will be difficult to implement a matrix structure. Similarly, unless we have the correct type of performance management system, people will not be motivated effectively under any of the structural forms. Taken together, these elements are a part of the process of transforming behavior needed to support an organizational transformation. In brief, unless behavior is changed, a corporate transformation will not be successful, as we saw in the examples of Sears and Sweet Treats Inc. We next deal with the critical issue of how to transform behavior to support organizational transformations in the next two chapters.

10

TRANSFORMING BEHAVIOR TO PLAY THE NEW GAME

Leadership and Management Development

One of the greatest challenges facing an organization that is attempting to change its game is that of helping to transform the behavior of its employees (i.e., its players and coaches). The very success of every type of transformation depends, to a great extent, on the ability of the company's team to support it through changes in their own behavior. For example, the successful transformation at Starbucks Coffee (described in Chapter 5) involved people behaving in ways more consistent with a professionally managed firm. In contrast, the unsuccessful transformation of UAL to Allegis (described later in this chapter) was caused, at least in part, by the lack of behavioral change on the part of employees within this company.

This process of behavioral transformation begins with the firm's most senior managers. These individuals must possess and be able to effectively utilize what we will refer to as "transformational leadership" skills. We, therefore, begin our look at behavioral change by examining the role that leadership plays in transforming the behavior of employees throughout the organization.

Transforming behavior frequently involves helping individuals develop new or revised ways of approaching their roles, new ways of thinking, and frequently new and different skills. With this understanding, we examine the nature of the changes in behavior that are required to support each of the three different types of transformations. This is followed by a discussion of how the process of management development can be used to facilitate behavioral change.

Throughout, we draw on examples of companies that have successfully and unsuccessfully utilized leadership and management development as tools in transforming behavior.

Transformational Leadership:
The Foundation of Behavioral Change

As we have seen in the examples presented throughout, leadership plays a significant (if not *the* most significant) role in determining whether a transformation will ultimately succeed or fail. Leadership, in this case, is defined as the process of influencing the members of an organization to increase the probability that they will support the transformation and help the organization effectively play its new game. In fact, an effective transformational leader is someone who can create through his or her own words and actions a contagious enthusiasm for the firm's business concept and transformational plan so that others will understand and behave in ways that will support it.

To illustrate the impact that leadership can have on a transformation, consider the example of the attempted, but ultimately unsuccessful, business vision transformation at UAL, Inc. In the mid 1980s, under the leadership of Richard Ferris, UAL, Inc. had the vision of making the transformation from an airline to a diversified travel company (and even changed its name from UAL to Allegis Corp.). Consistent with this vision, the company acquired Hilton International Hotels and Hertz car rental. It also acquired the company that came to be known as Mileage Plus and set up Apollo Travel Services, which was later called Covia, and United Vacations. It already owned Westin Hotels.

Ferris's vision, which was brilliant and put UAL at the forefront of this type of business concept for his industry, was unsuccessful because he was not able to get one of the key groups of employees to buy into his vision. Specifically, the pilots at UAL never supported the vision and spearheaded a potential buyout of the company that led to a great deal of internal turmoil at UAL and ultimately to Ferris's resignation. Clearly, the behavior of people was a critical determinant in the outcome of this attempted transformation. Ferris had not effectively executed his role as a transformational leader and, as a result, was unsuccessful at influencing the behavior of people to work in ways consistent with the new vision he was trying to promote.

We should not infer that Ferris' vision for UAL was unsound, or even that the vision *per se* was unsuccessful in terms of the company's performance and stock price. Ferris was simply unsuccessful in getting people to buy into the vision. In fact, reviewing the financial performance of the components of UAL-Allegis for the period from 1985 to 1987, it is clear that Ferris's strategy was successful in financial terms. As seen in Figure 10–1, UAL Inc. was unprofitable in both 1985 and 1986, while both subsidiaries (Hertz and the hotel chains) were profitable both years.[1] The UAL, Inc. 1987 annual report does not break out the profitability of Hertz Corporation and the hotels because it lumps them together as "discontinued operations." However, the report does indicate the earnings from discontinued operations amounted to $68.8 million in 1987, while the company showed a loss from continuing operations of $4.2 million.[2] Clearly, at least for the period when the transfor-

	1986[a]	1985[a]
Airline	(80,634)	(88,223)
Hertz Rental & Leasing	49,223	3,808[b]
Hotels	75,212	25,142
Consolidated	11,600	(48,683)

[a] In millions of dollars.
[b] For a period of 4 months.

Figure 10–1. UAL Incorporated—Allegis Corporation Financial Performance (1985–1986).

mation occurred, the financial performance of the travel services company concept was superior to the performance of UAL, Inc. as an airline business.

In reviewing the company's stock price during the period of transformation, however, the picture of the market's reaction is mixed. More specifically, in April 1986, the company's stock price was approximately $10 per share. From that date (when the name Allegis was announced) until March 1987, the stock price was flat. From March 1987 until October 1987, when the stock market crashed, Allegis's stock price increased to a peak of about $16. After the crash it declined to approximately $12, and then stayed in a trading range with a gradual increase to about $14 by May 1988, when the company announced its decision to change its name back to UAL, Inc. From May 1988, the stock price steadily increased to a peak of about $48 in the period of August to September 1989, after which it began a decline that is probably attributable to the economic recession of 1989 to 1991. The performance of the company's stock price was mildly positive during the period after the concept of the transformation was announced, despite Wall Street's lukewarm reception of the strategy.

This example suggests a key lesson: No matter how viable a vision may seem, there must be commitment by the organization's key constituents to that vision if the transformation is to be successful. This, in turn, requires effective leadership. Unfortunately, in the example of the transformation from UAL to Allegis, the vision worked in financial terms, but it never was accepted by one of the core groups in the company—the airline pilots. This led to a series of events that caused this transformation to be reversed. In brief, Ferris's failure as a transformational leader was caused by the inability to manage the organizational dynamics required to support the transformation, not by a failure of vision.

The foundation of any successful organizational transformation lies in the ability of its most senior managers to understand and effectively employ what we call "transformational leadership skills." The five key transformational leadership skills are:

1. *Transformational Planning*: developing, implementing, and monitoring a transformational plan.
2. *Organizational Structure Management*: designing a structure consistent with the game that the company wants to or needs to play.
3. *Management Development*: helping to develop other managers' skills and capabilities (through management development programs and processes) so that they can effectively support the organization's transformation.
4. *Performance Management System Design and Management*: designing and implementing effective performance management systems that will influence all of the organization's members to behave in ways consistent with the new game.
5. *Corporate Culture Management*: effectively creating and managing a corporate culture that is consistent with the new game the company is playing.

The first two skills (i.e., transformational planning and organization structure design) were discussed earlier. Management development will be discussed later in this chapter; and the remaining two skills are the subject of Chapter 11.

Developing and being able to effectively utilize these five skills may require some significant changes in senior management's roles, their skills, and their mind-sets. In some situations, senior managers may need to redefine their *roles* so that they view themselves as the champions of the transformation process. They may also need to free up time to devote to the transformation process (i.e., devoting time to transformational planning, organization design, management development, designing and implementing new performance management systems, and developing strategies to more effectively manage the corporate culture).

In other situations, senior managers may not possess the necessary transformational leadership skills. In these instances, they may need to seek training in whatever skill area they are lacking. We will discuss some strategies for developing transformational leadership (and other management) skills later in this chapter. In still other cases, senior managers may not have developed the mind-set (or what we call the "inner game of management"[3]) that is consistent with the changes they need to make in their own behavior and in their organizations. Although we will explain this concept in detail later in this chapter, there are a variety of ways that the inner game can affect a leader's ability to effectively fulfill his or her role. In many entrepreneurial firms, for example, the CEO may find it difficult to "let go" of the details and free up the time needed to devote to transformational planning issues (i.e., the CEO's need for control is too high). In companies that are experiencing decline, sometimes senior managers take such pride in what their *own* functional team does that they have a difficult time working as a team with other senior managers to develop and implement a transformational plan (since their self-esteem is linked to their functional area's performance versus the performance of the company as a whole). In an organization's attempt at a vision transformation, the CEO and/or other members of senior management may feel that certain required structural changes will result in "too much conflict" or "hurt feelings," so they do not make the required changes at all (i.e., their need to be liked may be interfering with what they need to do in their roles as transformational leaders).

Senior management's (and especially the CEO's) willingness to make the required changes in their own behavior (including developing and being able to effectively employ the five key transformational leadership skills listed above) is one of the prerequisites for successful organizational and behavioral change. In the absence of such support from the top, the likelihood that a transformation will be successful is dramatically decreased.

The Key Components of Behavioral Transformations

Attempting to influence people to behave in ways that support the needed transformation is not an easy task. In fact, the first challenge is to simply understand what leads people to behave as they do. We believe that people's behavior in organizations results from the interaction of three factors:

1. Their understanding (or lack of understanding) of their organizational role.
2. The skills that they possess to effectively execute their role.
3. How they manage their mind-set.

The manner in which these three components come together to influence behavior is illustrated in the following equation:

$$\text{Behavior} = \begin{array}{c}\text{Understanding} \\ \text{of role}\end{array} + \text{Skills} + \begin{array}{c}\text{Mind-set that supports} \\ \text{effective implementation} \\ \text{of role and skills}\end{array}$$

This equation suggests that behavioral transformations are dependent on finding the right combination of these three factors that will, in turn, support the organization's transformation. We will now explain each component of this equation.

Role Understanding

One of the first challenges in transforming behavior is helping people understand what is involved in their role. A role is simply a set of expectations about how an individual player or coach will utilize his or her time to help the company achieve its goals. In many organizations, the implicit philosophy seems to be that people will simply *know* what they need to do. Unfortunately, this is not often the case, especially for firms embarking on a transformation. It is at these times in an organization's life that both managers and other employees find that their roles are most unclear. Employees and managers might understand what they were supposed to do in the past, but the expectations that the organization has of them for the future are vague at best. In the absence of clear role definitions, many people continue to do what they are good at and what they like to do, rather than what they need to do to support the transformation. If people do not understand that they need to focus on different tasks and spend their time differently in order to support the transformation, there will be problems in playing the chosen game effectively.

Skills

Skills are defined as the technical knowledge or ability an individual possesses in some area. In the player's role, these skills tend to be technical in nature. In the management role, the skills that need to be focused on tend to be more interpersonal and administrative (versus the skills needed to perform some technical task). In either case, transformations will typically involve changes in the skills that individuals must possess to effectively play the new game. This means that an organization will need to invest not only in technical training, but also in management development if it wants to be successful at the transformation process.

Mind-set

The mind-set component of the equation focuses on how individuals attempt to satisfy basic underlying needs through the work they perform. When an individual's needs are out of alignment with what the organization requires him or her to do, the person may be unable to effectively utilize the skills that may have been developed through either technical or management education. For managers, we call this mindset component the "inner game of management."[4] This inner game consists of the following three subfactors:
  1. How the individual manages his or her need for control.
  2. The source of the individual's self esteem.
  3. How the individual manages his or her need to be liked.
Effective managers understand that they need to:
  • Feel comfortable having indirect versus direct control over results (i.e., they can't micromanage everything).
  • Learn how to derive their sense of self-worth from the accomplishments of their team (versus their own personal efforts) and from their ability to be the "best" manager versus being the best at a technical job.
  • Learn how to manage their need to be liked in a way that does not interfere with the ability to effectively execute their roles as coaches (e.g., by asking people to do things that they may not want to do; by dealing effectively with conflict; by learning how to say "No," etc.).
     To transform the behavior of people involves understanding and managing these three components *at all levels of the organization.* However, as stated previously, *all* other behavioral change is contingent on senior management's ability to transform their own behavior and effectively utilize transformational leadership skills.

Behavioral Change to Support Different Types of Transformations

Assuming that the most senior managers are committed to changing their behavior in order to facilitate the successful completion of the transformation process, the next challenge is to focus on transforming the behavior of others within the organization. Both managers (i.e., the coaches) and other employees (i.e., the players) will typically need to change their own behavior (sometimes in only minor ways, and sometimes in major ones) so that it will more effectively support the new game that the company has chosen to play.

For organizations changing their game to that of a more professionalized firm (i.e., making a Type I Transformation), both players and coaches need to support the implementation of, and learn how to effectively utilize more formalized systems for managing the business. This can be a far cry from a situation in which people have been allowed to do "whatever they feel is appropriate," or in which the entrepreneur or founder has made a practice of telling everyone (even down to the shop floor) what to do. It can also be very difficult to move from a situation in which organizational systems and processes have been very people dependent and informal to one in which there needs to be a greater reliance on more sophisticated and sometimes automated systems.

Firms attempting to make a revitalization transformation (i.e., a Type II Transformation) face a different situation. In these firms, the challenge is to help people increase their abilities to operate in an environment where there will be less bureaucracy and more accountability. If a firm has been in decline for even a few years, both players and coaches may suffer from a certain amount of insecurity that makes them suspicious of proposed changes in "how we do things." In other cases, employees have been through so many "programs of the month" as the firm has tried unsuccessfully to change that they may be in a "wait-and-see" mode with respect to proposed changes. The first step in helping individuals transform their behavior in these organizations is to eliminate the barriers created by "too much red tape" and find ways of promoting innovation and creativity. In addition, players and coaches must both develop the skills needed to operate in a somewhat less structured environment and learn how to recognize and reward each other for innovation.

The behavior needed to support a vision transformation (i.e., a Type III Transformation) can be similar to that required to play the old game effectively or it can be dramatically different. In this type of transformation, possibly the most important behavior is flexibility and a willingness to change.

Although there is no cookbook for the exact nature of the behavior needed to support each type of transformation, Figure 10–2 presents some aspects of what players and coaches should do differently to effectively support each type of transformation.

Transformation	Behavior Before Transformation	Behavior to Support Transformation
Type I	**Coaches:** • Utilize "shoot from the hip" decision-making. • Invest little time in the long-term management of the firm (including strategic planning, organizational development, etc.). • Do a great deal of technical work versus manage the work of others. • Utilize informal systems as a key management tool.	**Coaches:** • Have developed effective decision-making skills and utilize the best information available in making decisions in a timely manner. • Spend adequate time on managing the long-term aspects of the firm's business. • Spend adequate time managing others versus doing all the technical work themselves. • Understand and utilize formal operational and management systems to most effectively and efficiently achieve results.
	Players: • Follow coaches' orders (especially the entrepreneur's) *or* "do whatever they want to do" (since coaches are too busy doing work to provide adequate direction). • May not have the skills needed to effectively perform their roles, but are rewarded for being there. • May not spend time on value-added activities because they may not know what to do.	**Players:** • Have a clear understanding of what is expected of them and work to achieve these goals. • Through training, have developed the skills needed to effectively perform their roles. • Spend time on value-added activities that they and/or others have identified.

Figure 10–2. Behavior Changes to Support Each Type of Transformation.

Some of these changes can be fairly dramatic. It is therefore important for a firm to consider the behavioral changes that need to be made to support its new game as a key element of its transformational plan.

Three Tools to Facilitate Behavioral Transformations

Three separate, but related tools can be used to help an organization transform the behavior of its coaches and players so that it effectively supports the new game that the firm is playing. These three tools are:

1. Management development.
2. Performance management.
3. Corporate culture management.

Management development is a system that can be used to help coaches develop leadership and other key skills needed to support the transformation

Transformation	Behavior Before Transformation	Behavior to Support Transformation
Type II	**Coaches:** • Utilize overly complicated or bureaucratic methods to accomplish many tasks. • Communicate either verbally or nonverbally that, "This is my area of responsibility ... Stay out." • May lack adequate skills to manage a company of the firm's current size, but will not admit it. • May sometimes look for others to blame when things go wrong. • May do too much technical work or may delegate *everything* to others. • May focus on the long-term management of the firm, but the processes for doing so may be too complex to function effectively and/or these processes may change from month to month or year to year. • May spend an inordinate amount of time covering their vested interests. **Players:** • May not understand what they should be focused on because it keeps changing. • May spend an inordinate amount of time covering their vested interests. • May compete with others to show how valuable they are in order to avoid being laid off during the next downsizing or rightsizing.	**Coaches:** • Utilize the most effective and efficient methods to complete key tasks. • Have developed the ability to work effectively with others to achieve key goals. • Have developed and utilize effective management skills that help players increase their productivity. • Work to solve problems jointly versus looking for someone to blame. • Focus the right amount of attention on management activities and effectively delegate technical work to players. • Work with other managers to redesign and implement key management systems that will support the organization's transformation. • Devote time to value-added activities including identifying and working to resolve problems within and outside of their areas of responsibility. **Players:** • Have a clear understanding of what needs to be focused on and understand the goals related to their performance. • Spend time working with other team members to surface and resolve problems, versus competing with others for attention. • Have developed the skills needed to effectively perform their roles.

Figure 10–2. (cont.) Behavior Changes to Support Each Type of Transformation.

(including skills needed to influence the behavior of others). Through management development, managers can learn how to design and effectively utilize performance management systems and a corporate culture that enables the organization to help focus all employees on accomplishing the firm's goals. Performance management systems and corporate culture management are discussed in the next chapter.

Transformation	Behavior Before Transformation	Behavior to Support Transformation
Type III	**Coaches:** • Can exhibit any or all of the behaviors present in a pre-Type 1 or pre-Type II Transformation.	**Coaches:** • Promote, through words and actions, innovation and entrepreneurship. • Understand the firm's new vision and behave in ways consistent with it. • Devote time to thinking about and implementing the systems, processes, and structures needed to support the new vision. • Devote time to communicating the new vision to employees and reinforcing behavior that is consistent with the new vision. • Have developed the skills needed to be an effective manager in the new environment.
	Players: • Can exhibit any or all of the behaviors present in a pre-Type I or pre-Type II Transformation.	**Players:** • Make suggestions about changes that need to be made to better support the firm's vision and may participate in making these changes. • Have developed the skills to effectively participate as effective team members in the new environment.

Figure 10–2. (cont.) Behavior Changes to Support Each Type of Transformation.

Transforming Coaches' Behavior Through Management Development

Management development consists of the process a firm uses to develop the coaching capabilities needed to support the effective playing of its chosen game. In our view, the goal of any management development program *should be* to facilitate behavioral change. To accomplish this goal, the program needs to focus on helping individuals:

- understand their roles (i.e., understand what an "effective" manager/coach does).
- develop new skills.
- develop a mind-set consistent with the requirements of their role (i.e., help them learn how to manage their inner game of management).

Most people do not naturally think, act, or behave in ways consistent with being an effective manager. As organizations change their games, the capabilities of their management teams also need to be transformed. Transformations may require that managers change their role, develop new skills, and/or develop different mind-sets so as to better support the new game.

A role change involves learning how to spend one's time in new and different ways with the overall goal being to maximize the productivity of the team in playing the new game. Role changes can be communicated formally (through job descriptions) and informally (through discussions with more senior managers). During each transformation, an organization should step back and analyze how best to utilize its management team—for example, what the role of each team member will and should be.

Skill changes typically occur in the context of training programs or courses and so traditional management development most typically focuses on this area. Few, if any, traditional training programs devote time to discussing and helping managers understand the mind-set (i.e., the inner game) dimension of their roles. This can lead to problems with managers effectively implementing what they have learned and represents a flaw in traditional management education. It is even more of a problem when an organization is faced with making a transformation since managers need to understand not only what to do, but how to think in ways consistent with being effective at coaching the new game.

Based on our work with managers and organizations undergoing transformations, we have developed a "Management Development Grid" that identifies some of the key capabilities managers facing each type of transformation need to develop. These capabilities are presented in Figure 10–3 and discussed briefly below.

As shown in this grid, all three types of transformations require that managers throughout the organization develop an appreciation for, and the ability to support (if not use), effective transformational leadership skills. This is a prerequisite for a successful transformation of any type. All three types of transformations also require that the management development process devote some attention to helping each level of management understand what their roles will be as coaches in the new game. These roles should, in fact, be defined as a part of the organizational design process that was the subject of Chapters 8 and 9.

Management Development Programs to Help Facilitate Type I Transformations

Firms facing a Type I Transformation frequently have not provided any type of systematic management education in the past. The first challenge these firms face is implementing and finding ways to hold their managers accountable for participating in these programs. In these firms, those in management roles may not completely understand what managers need to do since many of them have been promoted up through the ranks. Further, these individuals may not be aware of the need for developing new skills. Instead, individuals in management roles may simply work harder and faster, continuing to do the same things they did when the firm was much

Transformation	Understanding the Management Role	Management Skills To Be Developed	The Inner Game of Management
All	• Clearly define roles and responsibilities. • Determine what percentage of time each level of management should devote to managing others versus doing technical work.	• All senior managers—transformational leadership skills (including transformational planning, organizational design, management development, performance management systems development and management, and corporate culture management). • All other managers—understand the role they play in helping senior managers implement transformational leadership skills.	
Type I	• Need to focus more time on managing others versus doing technical work. • Need to spend more time on planning and people development.	• Time management and delegation skills. • Day-to-day leadership skills that will help them influence people to achieve the firm's goals. • Decision-making (individual and team-based). • Systematic recruiting, selection, and training of employees. • Meeting management. • Planning and project management. • Effective goal-setting.	• Learn to manage the need for control (e.g., learn how to "let go"). • Learn how to derive one's sense of self-worth from the accomplishments of one's team versus doing everything one's self. • Learn to manage the need to be liked so that one is comfortable dealing with conflict, providing negative feedback, and directing others in order to accomplish goals.

Figure 10–3. The Management Development Grid.

Transformation	Understanding the Management Role	Management Skills To Be Developed	The Inner Game of Management
Type II	• Senior managers need to view their role as corporate versus functional managers (e.g., they can no longer fight for what's best for their own areas at the expense of what is best for the company as a whole). • Other managers need to devote time to streamlining systems and processes; identifying ways to "get work out."	• Facilitating entrepreneurship. • Innovation creation and management. • Organizational structure design (to help increase efficiency). • Change management. • Corporate culture management (at all levels). • Effective problem-solving and decision-making. • Effective communication.	• Strike the right balance between having too little and too much control over results. • Senior managers: learn to derive one's sense of self-worth from the achievements of the company versus just one's functional area. • Don't compete with other areas for attention. • Focus on providing both positive feedback and constructive criticism (i.e., learn to manage one's need to be liked).
Type III	• Promote the new vision through words and actions. • Devote time to communicating the new vision and recognizing those who support it.	• Change management. • Creating an entrepreneurial environment. • Strategic thinking. • Communication. • Organizational design. • Culture management.	• "Let go" of the old ways of doing things in order to support the new vision. • Learn to derive one's sense of self-worth from helping to make the new vision a reality. • Manage the need to be liked so that it does not interfere with the sometimes difficult changes that need to be made to help realize the new vision.

Figure 10–3. (cont.) The Management Development Grid.

smaller. They may have come to believe that this behavior represents effective management and, since the firm has been successful, may not understand the need to change.

Management development for firms facing Type I Transformations needs to focus on helping those in management roles:

- Accept that, no matter how successful they have been in the past, they will need to make changes in their own behavior to help their organization continue its success.

- Understand what is involved in being a manager within a firm that is now professionally managed (including spending less time "fighting fires" and more time working on and implementing plans for promoting the firm's long-term development).
- Develop and/or refine certain core management skills (e.g., time management, delegation, decision-making, day-to-day leadership, etc.).
- Play an inner game of management consistent with managing people within a more professionalized firm.

With respect to the inner game of management, firms facing a Type I Transformation must help their managers learn how to "let go" of the technical work and derive satisfaction from managing the work of others. In many of these firms, the corporate culture has been supportive of managers exercising a great deal of control over results and doing a great deal of the work themselves. This must change if the firm is to successfully complete its transformation. Managers also need to learn how to more effectively manage their need to be liked so that it is consistent with what they must do in their new roles. In a firm attempting to make the transformation to professional management, people have often been promoted to management roles from within the company. As a result, they may be supervising people that they have literally grown up with in the firm. In these situations, some managers have a difficult time understanding that they must now ask their associates to do certain things that the associates may not want to do (but may need to do to support the transformation process). They may also have to provide constructive criticism to these individuals on their performance. For managers who have not yet learned how to manage their need to be liked, these types of responsibilities are difficult to perform.

Management Development to Help Facilitate Type II Transformations

Managers in many organizations that are attempting to revitalize have typically (but not always) been exposed to one or more management development programs during their tenure with the organization (unless they have been with the organization only a short time). Because companies facing these types of transformations tend to be large, well-established firms, they typically have a Human Resource Management or Organizational Development function that has been focused on designing and implementing management education programs for a number of years. The problem in this case is not that these managers lack basic training. Instead, the type of training being provided may not adequately support the behavioral changes required for successfully completing the revitalization transformation. Managers' abilities to effectively implement what they have learned may also have been hindered by a lack of support from an organization that is "mired in bureaucracy."

In brief, along with all the other systems within the organization, the management development program for these firms also needs to be revitalized. In some situations, this may mean that management development must become more of an ongoing *process* versus a series of one-shot events. A curriculum needs to be designed that will help individuals at all levels of management make the appropriate transformations in their own behavior. Further, all managers need to be held accountable for developing, using, and continuously improving their coaching skills in order to support the transformation process.

To illustrate the difference between what needs to be done and what is typically done in organizations facing a revitalization transformation, let's take a look at one large company's management development process before embarking on a revitalization. In this multibillion-dollar organization, there was a very extensive training catalogue from which managers could choose the courses they thought would best meet their needs. Unfortunately, managers didn't always *know* what their needs were and/or simply didn't have time to go to training sessions. Further, although the organization said that it valued training, it did not hold its managers accountable for attending management education courses to improve their skills. Hence, the programs being offered did little to influence behavior.

Another problem with the "course catalogue" approach to management development that this and some other large firms use is that there is sometimes no true curriculum of courses that individuals must complete that will help qualify them to effectively perform their roles. The assumption seems to be that if managers are taking any courses at all, they must be learning something of value. Unfortunately, this is not always the case.

The first step for an organization undergoing a Type II Transformation is to carefully examine its management development program and process to determine what changes need to be made to adequately support the transformation. In terms of content, these programs should focus on helping those in management roles learn how to:

- Best implement their roles as managers in an environment in which there is less red tape and bureaucracy.
- Identify ways of streamlining processes and, working alone or with others, developing and implementing strategies for increasing the organization's efficiency.
- Refine and/or develop skills in the areas of change management, organizational innovation, and problem-solving/decision-making (among other things).
- Manage their inner games of management so that through their own behavior they will support the revitalization process.

With the inner game, the main challenge for managers in an organization facing revitalization is to learn how to feel comfortable "letting go" of the old (and sometimes bureaucratic) ways of doing things. Since in many of these organizations there has been a tendency for managers to focus almost exclusively on their own areas of responsibility, they also need to learn how to derive their sense of self-worth from being a part of a team that is working together to revitalize the organization (e.g., they need to give up the old way of competing with others). Finally, they need to focus a great deal of attention on providing adequate positive reinforcement and feedback to those who support (through words and actions) the sometimes very painful changes the organization must make.

Management Development to Support Type III Transformations

Organizations facing a Type III Transformation may or may not have previously conducted or supported management education efforts. If they are small, entrepreneurial firms, they will typically be faced with building a management development program from the ground up and should consider including some of the elements that would be part of a program for firms facing a Type I Transformation. If these firms are large and well established, they will typically need to reexamine the process they use for developing managers, as is the case for firms facing a Type II Transformation. For organizations undergoing a Type III Transformation, the key challenge is to develop managers with the capabilities to articulate, communicate, and support (through words and actions) the new vision. Since organizations undergoing a vision transformation are attempting to change the very foundation of their business, they must ensure that their managers behave in ways consistent with this new vision.

Programs to assist organizations in making this type of transformation should focus on helping managers:

- Understand the very important role they play in modeling behavior consistent with the new vision.
- Create strategies for carving out the time needed to focus on articulating the new vision and making it a reality.
- Develop strategic thinking, strategic planning, organizational design, and corporate culture management skills.
- Obtain the skills needed to promote entrepreneurship and innovation.
- Manage their inner game in ways that support the new vision.

Managers in organizations facing a Type III Transformation must be encouraged to devote sufficient time not only to articulating the firm's vision, but also ensuring that it is effectively communicated. This may involve spending time one on one or in group meetings with direct reports discussing what the new vision means and how to effectively support it. In managing the inner game, these managers must learn to feel comfortable deriving their sense of self-worth from the steps they take to make the new vision a reality. They also need to feel comfortable asking people within the organization to focus on new and different types of activities and/or do new and different types of tasks (which they may not always want to do).

Developing and Implementing Management Development Programs That Help Transform Behavior

As stated previously, the success of any management development program should be measured in terms of its ability to transform the behavior of participants. Because true behavioral change does not tend to happen overnight, participants must view management development as a continuous process of:

- Examining and developing a clear understanding of their roles, given the current game the organization is playing.
- Learning new concepts and skills.
- Applying these concepts in their daily work.
- Monitoring and reporting on results.
- Making adjustments, as needed, to become more effective managers and better support the organization's game.

Developing appropriate management capabilities can be facilitated through in-house, group-based management development programs; through outside management development courses; through one-on-one coaching; through self-initiated development (e.g., reading books, completing self-development modules, etc.); or through some combination of these various methods. Although all these methods are certainly effective at developing skills, our work with managers in organizations facing transformations suggests that the greatest amount of behavioral change tends to occur when the program:

1. Has been designed to meet the unique needs of the organization, given the transformation that it wants to accomplish.
2. Contains a series of courses that build upon each other, rather than a series of stand alone courses.
3. Allocates time to having participants set and report on progress against goals related to improving their performance in ways that support the organizational transformation.
4. Provides participants with the opportunity to discuss and frequently work to resolve key issues related to the organization's transformation process.
5. Offers the same training to all levels of management (from the CEO to first line supervisors).

Organizations embarking on transformations face a unique set of challenges that cannot always be addressed through standardized (i.e., "off-the-shelf") courses. Although these types of courses can certainly become a part of a management education process that is intended to transform behavior, they frequently must be tailored to meet the unique needs of a firm facing a transformation.

To have the greatest impact on behavior, management development also should be viewed as a process, rather than as a series of events. This means that the program is carefully designed so that each course builds on the learning of the previous course. In addition, participants need to be encouraged to apply what they have learned to their daily activities. To promote this, participants should be asked to commit to doing something differently as a result of what they learn in each session. At subsequent sessions, participants should be asked to report on their progress in achieving the goals they have set. This helps build in accountability for individual learning and behavioral change.

To help promote the organization's transformation, sessions should also include some time during which participants can discuss *relevant* issues related to the organization's transformation process. This can occur through a discussion of how changes are being perceived and/or barriers that individuals are encountering in applying what they have learned. To have the greatest impact on organizational transformations, management development must be provided to all levels of management. Every level needs to develop an understanding of what changes are required in their own and other coaches' behavior in order to support the organization's transformation. This is why the program an organization utilizes to influence the behavior of its coaches should be consistent throughout the organization. All managers must be able to speak the same language when it comes to management development so that they can recognize "what's working" and "what's not" with respect to achieving appropriate behavioral change.

We have found that programs that include at least some in-house training tend to achieve the best results. Conducting at least some of the training in house provides the organization with a greater ability to hold participants accountable for making needed changes in their behavior. In addition, these programs provide participants with more opportunities to discuss and resolve specific organizational issues with their peers, versus with those who represent other organizations.

Developing and implementing an appropriate management development program is important because if managers have not made the appropriate transformations in their own behavior, they will be ineffective in helping the organization complete its transformation. Individuals throughout the organization (including, but not limited to managers) will not be as productive as they could be, and certain key tasks required to complete the transformation will remain undone because managers do not view them as important (as a result of how they view their role), or don't understand how to do them (as a result of ineffective skills), and/or are prevented from effectively employing the skills they possess in completing these tasks because they have not mastered an appropriate inner game of management.

Conclusion

This chapter focused on introducing the reader to the behavioral aspects of organizational transformations and has described the important role leadership plays in not only helping to transform the behavior of individuals within an organization, but in changing the overall game that the organization is playing. This chapter also discussed one of the tools for changing behavior: i.e., management development. Management development focuses on changing the behavior of coaches.

In the next chapter, we discuss two additional, powerful tools that can be used to transform the behavior of people within an organization that is changing its game. These two tools—performance management systems and corporate culture management—are intended to help transform the behavior of *all* employees.

11

TRANSFORMING BEHAVIOR TO PLAY THE NEW GAME

Utilizing Performance Management Systems and Corporate Culture Management

Building on the concepts in Chapter 10, this chapter presents two additional tools that organizations can use to help transform the behavior of their employees and more effectively play the new game. In the last chapter, the focus was primarily on how to transform the behavior of coaches through helping them understand their roles as transformational leaders and utilizing management development as a tool to help develop the skills, mind-set, and roles needed to effectively coach the new game. The two tools discussed here—performance management systems and corporate culture management—while driven by the coaches on the team, can be used to help transform the behavior of *all* employees on the firm's team.

The Nature and Importance of Performance Management Systems[1]

Broadly defined, a performance management system consists of a set of mechanisms designed to increase the probability that people will behave in ways that lead to the attainment of an organization's goals. In the context of organizational transformations, performance management systems need to be designed so that they motivate people to behave in ways consistent with the new game the organization is going to play. To maximize this probability, performance management systems must be designed and managed at the company, "functional unit" (e.g., department, division, etc.), and individual levels of the organization.

Components of an Effective Performance Management System

There are five key components of an effective performance management system:
   1. Strategic initiatives (or objectives) and goals.
   2. Measurement system.
   3. Progress review/feedback.
   4. Performance appraisal.
   5. Rewards.
We turn now to a discussion of these five components and how they interact to form a system.

Strategic Initiatives (or Objectives) and Goals

As described in Chapter 7, once a firm has identified where it wants to be with respect to its transformation, it must then identify the key strategic initiatives (or objectives) and goals that will help it move from where it is today to where it wants or needs to be in the future. Strategic initiatives (or objectives) are broad statements of what the firm needs to do to change its game. Objectives help to further define what is expected at the organizational, functional unit, and/or individual levels of the organization. To maximize the success of the transformation process, strategic objectives at the corporate level should be set within each of the six building blocks of organizational success. At the organizational and functional unit levels, objectives are most typically presented in the context of transformational plans. Objectives define how the organization and/or the functional unit plans to play the new game. For example, an objective within the organizational building block of management systems for a firm that is making a Type II (i.e., revitalization) Transformation might be: "To develop a structure that will allow us to compete more effectively in our current market."

Goals define the level of performance expected for a specific accountability or objective. Goals should be specific, measurable, and time dated. To maximize the effectiveness of utilizing goals as a tool for influencing behavior, each goal should be assigned to a particular individual. This means that, even at the corporate level, individual names are attached to goals. Goals also need to be stated in terms of *results* to be achieved versus actions to be taken. Finally, goals need to be set so that they are realistic. Realistic, in this context, means that there is a fairly high (e.g., 80 to 90%), but not certain, probability that the goal will be achieved if the person responsible for it exerts an appropriate amount of effort. Goals should stretch people, but not to the point where they break them. If there is no probability of failing, the goal will not serve as an effective motivational device since the person responsible for the goal will discount its importance—it simply isn't challenging. Conversely, if there is only a 20 to 30% chance of being successful at achieving a goal, most people won't even try or will give up since the probability of success is too low.

At the organizational and functional unit levels of the company, goals are usually set for each objective. At an individual level, goals are typically set in the context of the position-holder's role and linked both to what the corporation as a whole and the functional unit the position reports to wants to accomplish. The skills and experience of the individual occupying the position should also be considered in setting individual goals. An example of a goal under the corporate objective presented above might be:

Objective: "To develop a structure that will allow us to compete more effectively in our current market."

Goal: To eliminate 20% of our workforce through attrition by FYE 20xx. (President)

The Measurement System

Measurement consists of assigning numbers to objects according to rules.[2] In designing an effective performance management system, the organization must determine *what* is going to be measured and *how* these measurements will be completed. It also needs to develop appropriate measurement *systems* to track progress against goals. The appropriateness of a measurement system depends, to a great extent, on the nature of the goals that have been set. Even if a goal appears measurable on the surface, it will be ineffective at influencing behavior if there is no system to measure performance against it. In one $10-million organization, for example, a goal had been set that "All products and services we offer will be profitable." On the surface this seems like a reasonable and measurable goal, yet the organization had failed to develop the operational systems needed to determine whether each product was in fact profitable. The organization may very well have been losing money on certain products or services because there was no way to measure product profitability.

Another problem that organizations face is measuring the wrong things. Sometimes, companies focus on measuring what is easiest to measure (or those things for which they have already created systems to measure performance) versus measuring what they ought to be measuring. This is particularly true as organizations begin to change their games. They may not have the systems in place to tell them how they are performing relative to the new game. In these cases, a key goal ought to be to develop these needed systems that will allow the firm to play its chosen game more effectively and assess how it is performing relative to the goals that it has set in its transformational plan.

Progress Review and Feedback

Even if a firm has developed effective measurement systems, its performance management system will not function effectively unless the information from the act of measuring performance is "fed back" to the organization, functional unit or individual.

At the organizational and functional unit levels, this means that periodically (usually quarterly) throughout the year, the company or functional unit needs to review its progress against goals using the measurements obtained. This will allow the company and/or functional unit to make needed adjustments to increase the probability of achieving the goals (or, in some cases, the firm may need to change a goal because the measurement process indicates it is no longer realistic). Measurement alone does not ensure that change will be made—decision-makers need to *use* the information provided by the measurement process. This is particularly important as a firm attempts to transform itself from one type of organization to another. During this process, continuous adjustments are required to ensure that the goals outlined in the transformational plan are being met or adjusted, as needed.

At an individual level, managers must ensure that they are continually (at least every month and sometimes more frequently) providing feedback to individual team members on the extent to which they are meeting goals. This can occur through holding regularly scheduled one-on-one meetings with each team member during which performance against goals is reviewed and discussed. The more measurable individual goals are, the easier it will be for the manager to provide feedback as well as for the receiver of this feedback to understand "where he or she stands." Again, it is essential for the manager to have an effective measurement system that will supply the information needed in order to provide this type of feedback.

Performance Appraisal

The difference between progress review and performance appraisal is that the latter is an evaluation of performance, while the former is an assessment of progress in achieving goals for the purpose of facilitating corrective action (if needed). The performance appraisal process is intended to provide the organization, functional unit, and/or individual performer with a chance to evaluate what has been achieved during the entire planning period (which, in many cases, is a year in length). The performance appraisal process is usually much more formal than the performance review process (especially at the individual level).

At the company and functional unit levels, the performance appraisal process will typically occur in the context of the firm's or department's annual planning meeting. During this meeting, the team (whether the senior management team focused on the company's performance or the department's management team focused on the unit's performance) should review what has been achieved in the previous year relative to the goals that were set. This review serves as the foundation for building the following year's plan.

At the individual level, the performance evaluation process typically involves having the manager prepare a formal written appraisal of each individual team member's performance against goals. In some organizations, each member is also asked to evaluate his or her own performance. Once the written appraisal has been prepared, the manager will meet one on one with each team member to review the evaluation. If the manager has effectively carried out the other steps in the performance management process (including conducting periodic reviews of performance), the formal performance evaluation should come as no surprise to the individual in question. It will generally be more of a formality.

Rewards

Rewards are intended to recognize behavior consistent with the goals of the organization. Although the flip side of rewards is punishment, most organizations rely on the absence of rewards as the major form of punishment for employees. Rewards can consist of financial incentives for performance against goals, awards for outstanding performance, "pats on the back," and other tangible signs that an employee has performed effectively. There are, however, other types of rewards that should be considered by organizations (especially those attempting to change their games). These rewards—known as "intrinsic rewards"—are those employees receive simply by performing the job they are asked to do. "Intrinsic rewards" can be quite motivating and long-lasting. Therefore, as organizations begin to change the game they are playing, they should consider how they might create jobs or roles that would be (in and of themselves) rewarding to the employees who occupy them.

A further consideration involved in designing and administering reward systems is that something is not a reward unless it is valued by the employee receiving it. Research suggests that managers are not always effective at understanding what types of rewards their employees really want. [3] Therefore, managers need to consciously consider what each team member might find of value when they are designing this component of the performance management system.

The System as a Whole

The five key components described above must be carefully designed so as to effectively influence people in the organization to be concerned with achieving the goals that will help the firm transform itself. These components also need to be organized into a system, as shown in Figure 11–1.

Although this diagram may seem somewhat complex, it is really fairly simple to use and extremely important in promoting the behavior needed for successfully completing a transformation. All the components must be designed and appropriately "hooked up" for the system to function effectively. We will describe how this system works in a little more detail.

As shown in this figure, the process of influencing behavior using a performance management system begins with establishing *Strategic Initiatives (Objectives) and Goals* (Step 1). These initiatives and goals (which are developed as a part of the transformational planning process) influence how the organization, its departments or divisions, and/or individual contributors

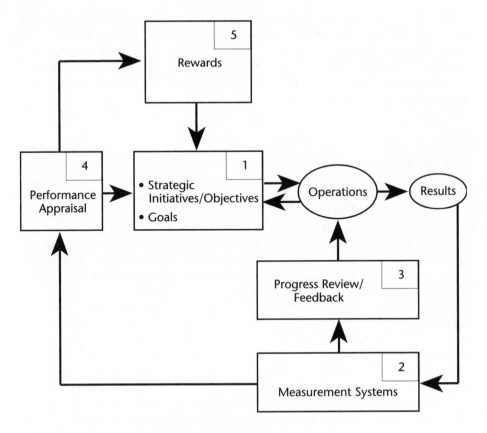

Figure 11–1. The Performance Management System.

will *Operate or Behave*. This behavior and how the firm or its major functions operate, in turn, will lead to *Results*. Assuming that the firm has designed appropriate *Measurement Systems* (Step 2), these results can be measured. Measurements can be compared with the goals established in Step 1 to determine whether the firm is making progress in successfully completing its transformation. The results of this comparison should be fed back to the organization as a whole, its major functions, and/or individual contributors. This *Progress Review/Feedback* (Step 3) should include identifying where the organization, its functional units, and/or individual performers are "on track," and where they need to take corrective action to increase the probability of achieving the goals. Measurement and review of progress against goals should be conducted on a regular basis throughout the planning period to maximize the probability that the needed transformations in behavior (to support the organization's transformation) will occur. The intent of these first three steps is to help people (and the entire organization) adjust their behavior so that they will be in better alignment with their goals.

At the end of the planning period, the organization as a whole, its functional units, and the individuals within the company should conduct a formal *Performance Appraisal* (Step 4) of the extent to which they have successfully met their goals. This evaluation should then be linked to the *Rewards* (Step 5) that are received: Those who successfully achieve their goals should receive higher rewards than those who don't. This will help motivate successful performers to continue working toward the achievement of desired results and should help motivate those who have been unsuccessful to change their behavior. Based on this evaluation, new goals (Step 1) should be set to help the firm continue its progress toward a successful transformation.

Using a Performance Management System to Help Change the Game

Each type of transformation brings with it a unique set of challenges concerned with effectively designing and utilizing a performance management system. These are shown in Figure 11–2 and discussed below.

Designing Performance Management Systems to Support Type I Transformations

The basic challenge faced by an organization making this type of transformation is that entrepreneurial firms have not usually taken or had the time to design effective performance management systems.

Since these organizations frequently do not even have a basic planning process in place (in which they have developed objectives and measurable goals), the first challenge they will face is creating this part of the performance management system. Next, they will need to develop systems that will allow them to measure performance against key goals. In particular, these systems will need to be designed to measure performance with respect to designing needed operational systems, management systems, and corporate culture. To ensure that this type of transformation is successfully completed, the firm's management will also need to implement at least quarterly review meetings during which they can assess performance at a corporate level. Along with this, they will need to train their managers in how to effectively provide feedback to direct reports and encourage them to do so on a regular basis. Finally, the firm will need to review and possibly revise its reward system so that rewards are given to those individuals who support the changes the firm needs to make—including the transition to being planners versus firefighters.

Designing Performance Management Systems to Support Type II Transformations

To successfully complete these types of transformations, performance management systems need to help the firm increase its fit with its environment. This may involve making some adjustments to existing performance management systems. In some cases, firms that need to revitalize their operations have performance management systems that are no longer functioning

Performance Management Component	Type I Transformations	Type II Transformations	Type III Transformations
Strategic Initiatives/Objectives and Goals	Need to define at all levels (since there has typically been no formal planning process in the past).	Need to change at all levels. Must focus on rebuilding the organization to better fit with the environment. New goals are needed to support changes in the organization's infrastructure in order to better fit with the environment. Specific, measurable goals are needed in order to hold people accountable for supporting required changes.	Need to redefine at all levels to fit with the new vision and hold people accountable for behaving in ways consistent with the new vision.
Measurement System	Need to create and/or refine in order to measure goals being set at all levels.	May need to get the red-tape out of the system and develop strategies for more effectively utilizing information produced by measurement systems. May need to design new measurement systems.	May need to design new measurement systems and/or refine existing systems to support the new vision.

Figure 11–2. Designing an Effective Performance Management System for Different Types of Transformations.

Performance Management Component	Type I Transformations	Type II Transformations	Type III Transformations
Performance Review/Feedback	Need to create a formalized system for providing feedback to the organization as a whole, functional units, and individuals. Managers may need to be trained in how to effectively utilize information provided by measurement systems in providing feedback.	Need to start utilizing the information provided by measurement systems more effectively in making decisions, providing feedback, and working to adjust behavior at the individual, functional unit, and organizational levels.	Performance review and feedback should be focused on the extent to which the firm and its major functions are making progress in achieving the new vision. At the individual level, the focus should be on providing feedback on the extent to which behavior is consistent with the new vision.
Performance Appraisal	Need to create a formalized system that is focused on performance against goals. Need to build in an annual process at the organizational, departmental, and individual levels to review performance.	Need to review and/or revise system so that it focuses people, departments, and the organization as a whole on achieving goals related to operating in ways more consistent with the existing environment.	Need to ensure that performance against achieving the new vision is reviewed annually at the company, departmental, and individual levels.
Rewards	Rewards should be given to the planners, versus the firefighters. The firm needs to ensure that rewards are linked to behavior consistent with becoming a more professionalized firm.	Rewards need to be given to those who change their behavior in ways consistent with the new environment in which the firm is operating.	Rewards should promote the new vision.

Figure 11-2. (cont.) Designing an Effective Performance Management System for Different Types of Transformations.

effectively. This might be the result of having a poor design in the first place. It might also be the result of the firm's creating such bureaucratic systems for assessing performance that they are no longer functioning effectively.

To successfully make a Type II Transformation, a firm must typically refine how it sets goals at the organizational, functional unit, and individual levels of the organization. For example, are all goals specific, measurable, and time dated? Or are individuals held accountable for achieving only vague goals? Are goals set in the "right" areas to help the firm change its game? If not, goals may need to be revised and managers (and other employees) educated on what is most important to the firm's success in the new environment (which may be very different from what was important in the past).

Firms that need to make a Type II Transformation also must examine their measurement systems to ensure that they are measuring the right things versus measuring those that are easiest to measure. In some companies, for example, employees are held accountable for, and their performance is measured on, factors like "judgment," "organizational skills," "attitude," and so on. While these may be important to the organization, they communicate little in terms of the specific, measurable things that the organization wants the employee to *achieve*. Further, the goals can only be measured in a fairly subjective manner, which can result in conflict and/or managers who provide very positive feedback (even if it is not deserved) in order to avoid the problems associated with unhappy employees.

In the performance appraisal process, a firm facing a Type II Transformation typically needs to redesign the system so that it focuses the company, its departments or functions, and individual employees on those things that will help the firm be successful in its new environment. Firms in need of revitalization have sometimes created performance appraisal systems that reward individuals simply for "showing up" at the job or for the hours worked versus for achieving specific, measurable goals. Some firms involved in this type of transformation have also evolved into a situation in which performance appraisals are not used as motivational tools. Instead, they have become something managers dread and may not even do. Some employees in firms requiring revitalization can't even remember the last time they had a formal review. The lack of an effective performance appraisal process, in fact, may be one factor that contributed to the firm's decline in the first place: people have been doing whatever they felt they should be doing versus doing what would provide the greatest value to the organization over the long term.

The reward system for firms making a Type II Transformation typically needs a major overhaul. In many cases, the firm can no longer recognize and reward people in the same way or for the same behavior as it has in the past. Changing this part of the performance management system can be the most difficult and have the greatest impact on employee morale (not always in a positive manner). Altering the reward system may mean, for example, that while employees received bonuses in the past (sometimes representing 50% or more of their base pay), there may no longer be bonuses calculated in the same way and/or they may be contingent on both individual achievement of goals versus simply the firm's performance. This may mean that certain people who have come to view bonuses as an entitlement may become disenchanted with the "new system" and leave the organization. While this is not necessarily negative, the organization must be aware of the possible costs associated with such changes and find ways (through how they manage their culture) to minimize the impact such employee response can have on overall organizational productivity and performance.

Designing Performance Management Systems to Support Type III Transformations

Because Type III Transformations involve a change in the firm's vision, they will typically entail significant changes in the design and implementation of the performance management system. The first two elements of the overall company's performance management system—strategic initiatives or objectives, and goals—will probably need to be redefined to support the achievement of the new vision. In turn, the firm may need to create new measurement systems or redesign existing systems so that its management can better track performance against new goals.

The performance review and feedback system should be designed and managed in a way that the firm as a whole, its departments or functions, and individual employees are receiving feedback on the extent to which their behavior is consistent with the new vision. On an annual basis, the company, its departments, and individual employees need to receive a formal appraisal of the extent to which they have met the goals that are consistent with achieving the new vision. Finally, rewards need to be given to those who actively support the achievement of the new vision. In brief, the entire system may need to be designed or redesigned to support people behaving in ways that are very different from the ways they have behaved in the past.

Implications of Performance Management System Design for Organizational Transformations

Successfully completing any organizational transformation depends, to a great extent, on the design and implementation of effective performance management systems. As a firm's management begins to plan for its transformation, they need to ensure that they have effectively designed every element in the firm's performance management system, along with each department's and each individual's. Further, all the pieces of each system need to be properly "hooked up" if the system is to function effectively in promoting behavior consistent with the firm's new game. In the absence of well-designed performance management systems, even the best transformational plan will not succeed because people will not be motivated to support it.

Transforming Behavior Through Culture Management: An Overview[4]

Effectively utilizing corporate culture as a tool in transforming behavior involves:

- Developing an understanding of what culture is.
- Understanding the differences between an organization's "stated" and "real" cultures.
- Knowing how to analyze and identify a firm's real culture.
- Developing a clear statement of what the culture needs to be in order to support the transformation process.
- Being able to utilize certain tools and techniques to transform the culture from what it is to what it needs to be to support the transformation process.

We discuss each of these topics below.

What Is Corporate Culture?

Corporate culture consists of the values, beliefs, and norms present in an organization. Values are what the firm holds to be important with respect to activities, such as how it treats its employees and customers, and the standards of performance that it believes are important to achieve. Beliefs are assumptions that are made about a firm's employees (who they are, how they behave, etc.), its customers, and its performance standards. Norms are unwritten rules of behavior (e.g., how people of different status are referred to, dress codes, etc.).

Corporate culture can be thought of as the firm's personality, and it can have a powerful effect on the behavior of individuals within an organization. Most typically, a culture develops as an outgrowth of the founder's personality, but is changed over time as the company grows. New employees bring with them their own needs and values that help to shape the culture. Sometimes this is positive. In other cases, a culture changes in ways that no longer support the company's goals. This is, in fact, the situation faced by firms in need of making a transformation. In many cases, the culture no longer fits with what the company has become or wants to be in the future.

Culture is one aspect of infrastructure that firms of all sizes can fail to properly manage. Culture is viewed as something so "fuzzy" that it is difficult to understand and therefore the tendency is to ignore it or treat it as something that is a given. Unfortunately, corporate culture can have a significant impact on individual employee behavior and, if it is not understood and managed, it can undermine the firm's ability to make a successful transformation.

There are three dimensions of culture that all firms must consider in preparing for and making a successful transformation:

1. *Treatment of employees*:   The values, beliefs, and norms related to how employees are treated. Included in this area are also issues related to teams and teamwork.
2. *Treatment of customers*:   How the firm will treat those who purchase its products and/or services. For example, how should employees talk about their customers/clients?
3. *Performance standards/employee accountability*:   The performance standards that employees should be held accountable for in helping the company play its new game.

The Difference Between "Real" and "Stated" Culture

The first challenge a firm making a transformation faces is developing a clear understanding of what its current culture actually is. When asked, "What is your corporate culture?," many managers will proudly point to the written values statement displayed on walls or on the back of their business cards. Although this is certainly a starting point for understanding what is important to a company and what the culture of the firm *might be*, there are many examples of firms with well-developed values statements that in no way reflect the reality of what their employees actually experience. In one firm, for example, their stated values included the following:

Commitment to our customers.

Respect and support for our employees.

Trust.

Recognition for good performance.

Quality products. We will only produce those products that we would purchase ourselves.

The company's real culture consisted of the following elements:
- The firm's management had no idea who its customers really were and had taken few steps over the years to understand and listen to them.
- Employees were respected and supported so long as they remained loyal to the organization. It was seen as an act of disloyalty for an individual to leave the firm.
- Although you could trust the people within your area, senior management was not to be trusted. It was better to tell them what they wanted to hear, rather than what they should hear to avoid trouble.
- People were recognized and rewarded more for who they knew and what areas of the company they worked in than for their actual performance.

- Very few members of senior management would actually purchase any products that the company produced. In addition, when those who sold these products encountered a quality problem, they were told: "Find a way to sell it anyway."

Methods for Identifying a Firm's "Real" Culture

If a firm's true culture can be so different from what its *stated* culture is, how does a firm's management go about understanding it? Although this is not an easy task, a firm can use a variety of ways to identify its *real* culture. One is to interview employees about what they believe the key aspects of the firm's current culture are. Since identifying culture is like understanding an individual's personality, it involves some skill on the part of the interviewer to uncover key elements of the culture that affect employee behavior. Questions should be constructed around each of the key cultural elements—treatment of employees, treatment of customers, and performance standards/accountability. These questions should be as open-ended as possible to assist the interviewer in understanding what the culture is and its impact on employee behavior.

Another technique that has proven valuable in understanding a firm's current culture is to have employees write or tell stories about what it is like to work for the company. These stories can be about the individual personally or accounts that form the foundation of the organization's folklore. For example, one story told at a very large company undergoing a revitalization transformation went something like this:

> A senior manager took a proposal to our president that asked for $200,000 to fund a particular project. The proposal was made verbally. There was no written information or background as to why the funds were needed or what the return on this investment might be. The president basically told the senior manager that he had not done his 'homework' and had not utilized the new planning tools and techniques that the organization had committed to using about six months before. In brief, the senior manager was told to go back and redo the proposal in the appropriate form and resubmit it. Until then, there would be no funding.

When the president of this company was asked whether this story was true, he said that no such incident had happened, but that he was glad such a story existed. The reason was that the story helped to reinforce changes in the firm's culture—in this case from a situation in which any senior manager could request resources and would probably receive them to one in which decisions for funding would be based on solid analysis and information about the return on investment to the company (very important in an organization that had experienced decline and was trying to revitalize).

A final tool for collecting information about an organization's current culture is to design and administer a "corporate culture survey." This is *not* the same as an attitude survey and a firm should avoid using "off-the-shelf" products to collect information on its culture. Instead, a firm should develop a series of questions about the firm's current culture to which employees can respond in writing. This survey might include open-ended questions (e.g., "How would you describe the manner in which employees are treated?") or be designed using a scale on which employees can indicate the extent to which they believe certain elements are part of the firm's current culture. In this case, the firm's management must carefully construct survey items (usually using elements of their "desired" culture that we discuss below). Whatever method is used in constructing these surveys, employees should be asked to respond anonymously to increase their willingness to be honest and to maximize the return rate.

Developing a Clear Statement of the Firm's Desired Culture

Once a firm understands what its culture is and the impact it has on its employees, the next step is to develop a clear understanding and statement of what the culture needs to be to help the firm change the game. For each type of transformation, certain key elements are essential to achieving success.

Key Cultural Elements That Support Type I Transformations

The key challenge for a firm embarking on a Type I Transformation involves creating and formalizing systems, structure, and processes to support the much larger company that it has become. The culture, in turn, must change to support this "formalization" process. In creating a desired culture that will support a Type I Transformation, managers should consider the following:

- *Treatment of employees*: The culture of the organization needs to continue to emphasize that employees are a firm's most valuable resource and that, even in the face of change, the positive aspects of the firm's culture (most typically things like people feeling that they are a part of a family, that the company cares about them, etc.) will not be lost. However, because the firm is now much larger, certain aspects of its culture involving treatment of employees may need to be adjusted. For example, it may no longer be practical to emphasize that "we are a family" when that family now includes upwards of 500 people. Instead, the firm may decide to adjust this element of its culture to focus on teamwork—"we are all one team."
- *Treatment of customers*: Firms making a Type I Transformation have typically been successful because they have remained close to their customers (although certain ways of operating may have become outdated and no longer meet customer or employee needs). An organization changing its game to that of a professional firm will usually retain its focus on customers while at the same time ensure that more formal systems and processes are in place that can be utilized to most

effectively and efficiently meet customer needs as the firm continues to grow.

- *Performance standards/accountability*:   Employees should be rewarded based on performance instead of other more subjective criteria like tenure with the firm (or no criteria at all). This is probably the area where employees will feel the most change in the firm's culture as it moves toward playing the game of professional management. As a result of rewarding individuals based on performance (using a more sophisticated performance management system), some employees may come to feel that their service to the company is no longer appreciated. The firm must guard against this by ensuring that these employees are recognized for their tenure, but clarifying that tenure will not be the only criteria on which they are rewarded.

Key Cultural Elements That Support Type II Transformations

Revitalization transformations typically involve a fairly major overhaul of a firm's culture. In part, this is because many of the systems (including culture) have either become very bureaucratic or have been allowed to drift to the point where "everyone is doing his or her own thing." In creating a desired culture which will support a Type II Transformation, managers need to consider the following:

- *Treatment of employees*:   Employees of firms that have been in decline typically (but not always) suffer from low morale as a result of their firm's performance. There are also sometimes pockets of employees in these firms who have hidden and survived previous attempts to help the firm improve its performance (including downsizing) and don't necessarily contribute significantly to the firm's achievement of its goals. Finally, there are still other employees in these firms whom individuals can point to as the "favored few" who continue to survive even though nearly everyone in the firm believes that they are incompetent. Why do they survive? Because they have learned how to play the political games that are so prevalent in firms requiring a revitalization transformation.

  Firms making this type of transformation need to construct their desired culture so that it reenergizes their employee base. The culture should not promote the idea that there will be no further downsizing or right-sizing (as this may be needed). Instead, it should emphasize that employees who work hard and support the changes that the firm needs to make (as painful as they may be) will be recognized for their efforts. Those who continue to play the old game will not be as valued as those who learn to play the new game and support the changes the firm needs to make.

- *Treatment of customers*:   Firms in need of revitalizing their operations have typically lost touch with their customer base. In some cases, customers have come to be viewed as a "nuisance." In one firm, this was conveyed to customers through their inability to reach a real person—most of the time they received an individual's voice mail—and through the reluctance of the firm to adjust its products to meet their needs. This firm jokingly referred to its Manufacturing and R&D departments as "Field of Dreams." The belief was, "If we build it, they will buy it. We don't need to listen to our customers." The problem was that this firm was operating in a very competitive marketplace and when it began to lose significant share and see its stock price decline, it recognized that it needed to revitalize. Firms making a revitalization transformation need to adjust their culture so that customers are, again, truly valued.

- *Performance standards/accountability*: Firms making a Type II Transformation also need to ensure that they are holding departments and individuals accountable for personal transformations and for achieving the types of goals consistent with this type of transformation. In some cases, organizations in decline have individuals who are held accountable for little more than "coming to work." In other cases, the goal-setting and performance management processes have become so distorted that they are no longer functioning effectively in focusing people on what needs to be done to accomplish the firm's goals. In other words, changes in this area of culture typically will also involve a major redesign of the performance management process.

Key Cultural Elements That Support Type III Transformations

Because a Type III Transformation involves changing the firm's vision, usually there will also be some significant changes in each of the three dimensions of the firm's culture. A firm making this type of transformation faces the challenge of maintaining the positive aspects of its old culture while at the same time promoting a culture more consistent with what the company wants to become. Some of the key aspects of a desired culture that will support this type of transformation are discussed below.

- *Treatment of employees*: Although employees must be encouraged to embrace the change in vision, there will also need to be a recognition that some employees will mourn for the "way we used to do things" or "what we used to be." In designing and managing the desired culture, firms facing a Type III Transformation need to strike a balance between wholeheartedly embracing the new vision and letting employees mourn the past. Firms facing this type of transformation need to create a culture that recognizes the successes of the past while at the same time promotes new ways of operating. In focusing on employees, the new culture should promote entrepreneurship and valuing people who promote innovation and/or who are innovators themselves.
- *Treatment of customers*: As a result of the vision transformation, the firm may or may not continue to service the same customers and

therefore may need to develop different approaches to customer service. For example, Starbucks, which began as a local roaster and sold coffee beans, had to change its entire concept of customer service when it transformed to a specialty retailer/café. As a local roaster, with retail distribution outlets, customers picked their bags of coffee beans. Customer service was minimal. Occasionally, the person behind the counter would brew up a pot of coffee and serve it as free samples. Today, Starbucks expends a great deal of effort in selecting and training its "baristas" (the people who serve coffee) in not only proper brewing technique but also dealing with its affluent customer base.

In other cases, a firm making a vision transformation will continue to service existing customers, but in different ways. For example, with deregulation of the telephone industry, AT&T (and its various subsidiary companies) continued to service basically the same customer base, but was literally forced to improve the extent to which the company anticipated and met customer needs. Although in the past, customers would tolerate certain inconveniences because they had no alternative, competition from other carriers (e.g., Sprint, MCI, etc.) has helped push AT&T toward improved customer service and to providing customers with what they want (including lower-priced long-distance service).

- *Performance standards and accountability*:   Recognizing and rewarding individuals for their contributions to innovation plays a significant role in helping a firm successfully complete a Type III Transformation. Without innovation, the vision transformation is doomed to failure. Employees also must be held accountable for embracing and supporting the company's new vision.

Strategies for Transforming an Organization's Culture

Once a firm has determined what its current culture is and what it needs to be to support its transformation, the next step is to develop a culture management plan that will assist the firm in moving from where it is to where it wants to or needs to be. The steps in developing this corporate culture management plan are outlined below:

1. Identify the firm's current culture. This can be done through interviews, the telling of stories, and/or a culture survey.
2. Define the firm's desired culture (i.e., the culture that will support the firm's transformation). Typically, it is senior management's role to define the desired culture, although they may want to solicit input from others within the organization. The desired culture should be defined in the context of developing the firm's transformational plan (which was the subject of Chapter 7).
3. Identify "gaps" between the current and desired cultures. The firm's management must determine areas where there is an inconsistency

between the current and desired culture. The idea behind developing a culture management plan is to close these gaps. In some cases, management may decide that they can "live with" a particular aspect of the current culture that is not completely consistent with what they envision their culture needs to be since it will not be detrimental to successfully completing the transformation. In other cases, they may need to dramatically redefine a value, belief, or norm to increase the probability of successfully completing their firm's transformation.

4. Identify the highest priority areas where the current culture is inconsistent with the desired culture. These should be areas in which the firm's management feels that if the culture is not changed, it will have a significant negative impact on the firm's ability to complete its transformation.

5. Focusing on these highest priority areas, develop a plan to create a culture that is more consistent with the new game that the firm is playing and/or how it has chosen to play the game. Creating such a culture will usually involve making changes in other areas of the pyramid of organizational success (discussed in Chapter 2). Some specific areas that might be focused on and changed include:

   • *Recruiting and selection:* The firm will want to ensure that it is recruiting and selecting people who have values consistent with the desired culture. Although there is generally no method that will guarantee that the firm hires people who will embrace its culture, it is worth evaluating the extent to which existing selection practices enable the firm to identify these types of individuals.

   • *Training and development:* A firm should also evaluate the extent to which its training processes support its new culture. If, for example, a firm is making a Type I Transformation in which it now wants to hold people more accountable for behavior consistent with its goals, it must be sure that it has educated people about what these goals are and provided training in the skills necessary for achieving them.

   • *Marketing and sales:* Although all three types of transformations may require some changes in this area, it is particularly important for firms facing Type II and Type III transformations to examine how their marketing and sales processes support the values that they want to have concerning treatment of customers.

   • *Communication systems:* Regardless of the type of transformation that the firm is making, it will be important that senior management both explicitly and implicitly communicate the desired culture to all employees. Explicit communication can occur in memos, meetings in which the new culture is discussed, phone conferences, and so on. Implicit communication occurs through the actions of senior managers and others within the organization. Senior managers, in particular, need to ensure that their behavior is consistent with the values, beliefs, and norms that constitute the desired culture.

- *Performance management systems*: These systems should be designed in a way that promotes behavior consistent with the new culture. Each component of the system (discussed earlier in this chapter) needs to be designed to increase the likelihood that individuals will behave in ways consistent with the firm's "new" culture. This includes rewarding and recognizing those who exemplify the new culture and finding ways to "correct" those who continue to operate in inconsistent ways.
- *Management development*: All managers within the company must be trained in what corporate culture is and how to manage it effectively. In addition, they need to understand how to influence others to adopt and behave in ways consistent with this culture.
- *Structure*: In some cases, an organization needs to change its structure to better support the new culture. This can include formalizing role descriptions (discussed in Chapter 8) as well as changing roles and reporting relationships. Changes in structure sometimes go hand-in-hand with changes in corporate culture.

6. Implement the culture management plan and monitor performance against the plan. Once a firm has determined which aspects of its culture it wants to focus on and *how* it will work to make its desired culture real through adjusting other aspects of its infrastructure, it needs to implement this plan. This is typically done in the context of the overall transformational plan and monitored during quarterly review meetings to ensure that progress is occurring in making the desired culture "real." Since culture typically takes no less than two years to change, it is at this point that the firm might want to readminister a culture survey to see how its efforts in this area have paid off.

Conclusion

This chapter discussed two tools for facilitating the behavioral transformations that are an essential ingredient in the success of any organizational transformation. With the concepts and tools presented in this and the previous chapter, we have now examined all the key ingredients necessary to manage organizational transformations successfully, including transformational planning, organizational structure design, and the set of tools to facilitate behavioral change.

The next chapter presents a capstone example of how the management of one firm, the Bell-Carter Olive Company, utilized all these ingredients to successfully transform itself.

Part IV

HOW TO CHANGE THE GAME

Some Overall Lessons

12

CHANGING THE GAME IN ACTION

The Bell-Carter Olive Company[1]

The first eleven chapters of this book were devoted to providing a framework for understanding transformations and their impact on long-term organizational success as well as describing tools that can be used for managing these transformations. In this chapter, we present a comprehensive example of a company that has completed several transformations during its sixty-seven-year history and that is currently facing the challenges of completing a compound transformation—from an entrepreneurship to a professionally managed firm as well as a vision transformation. This example is comprehensive in a dual sense. First, because Bell-Carter has been in business since 1912, the company has experienced all the transformations described in this book: (1) entrepreneurial transformations to professional management, including the special case of family business transformations, (2) revitalization transformations, (3) business vision transformations, and even (4) compound transformations. Although our principal interest is in the most recent period of the company's development (from 1992 through 1997), we also briefly review the earlier periods to both describe the historical development of the firm and illustrate some transformations made at previous points. Figure 12–1 offers a brief overview of the transformations Bell-Carter Olive Company has made during its history.

This example is also comprehensive in the sense that, in the process of making its most recent transformations, the company is utilizing and applying most (if not all) the concepts, ideas, overall approach, and specific tools for managing transformations that we have presented throughout this book.

Since both authors have served as consultants to this company at various points in this process, we have a great deal of first-hand knowledge about its transformation process and the results achieved. This, in turn, provides a

Dates	Type of Transformation
1912	Company founded as olive grower.
1930s	Business Vision Transformation: From company growing olives to one that both grew and *processed* olives (transformation brought on by the need to revitalize existing growing business).
1970s	Business Vision Transformation: From a branded olive company to a "private-label" business concept. The company begins to hire professional managers and sets in motion the seeds of transformation to professional management.
1973	Family Business Transformation: Tim and Jud Carter assume leadership of the firm.
1992	Business Vision Transformation: From a private-label business to a private-label and branded business with the acquisition of Lindsay Olives.
1994	The transformation from Entrepreneurship to Professional Management. The Revitalization of the Lindsay Olive business unit.

Figure 12–1. Bell-Carter Olive Company's Transformation Chronology.

special opportunity to illustrate how the concepts, framework, and tools we have discussed can have practical value.

Since Bell-Carter has been in business almost a century, we have organized the discussion of its transformations into three different historical periods. First, we describe the development of and transformations made by the company during the period from 1912, when the company was founded, through 1973, when the third generation of family members took over the firm's leadership. During this period the company made two key types of transformations, including a business vision transformation and the transformation from one generation of managers to another. Next, we analyze the transformations made during the period from 1973, when Tim and Jud Carter (the company's current leaders) took over from their father, to 1992, which marked the beginning of the third and current phase of the company's transformation process. The company made another business vision transformation during this period and began the process of transforming to a more professionally managed firm. Finally, we examine the most recent period in the company's development (from 1992 to 1997) to illustrate a compound transformation involving the change from entrepreneurship to professional management, a business vision transformation, and the revitalization of a business unit resulting from the vision transformation.

Bell-Carter Olive Company's Early History

Bell-Carter Olive Company (Bell-Carter), currently the largest canner of table olives in the world, had its beginning (as did many of today's olive processors) in *growing* rather than canning olives. Brothers Arthur and Henry Bell, the original founders of the company, purchased a small olive grove in Reedley, California, just south of Fresno, in 1912 and began harvesting and selling olives to various processors in central California.

The First Transformation: Changing the Business Vision

At the start of the Depression in 1930, the brothers found that they no longer had anyone to sell their olives to. In brief, the environment had changed and they were facing the need to change their game. Arthur began searching for someplace that had a boiler (required for processing the olives) and located a dry cleaning company in Berkeley, California. In 1930, the brothers began packing, distributing, and marketing their own olives under the "Bell's brand." This, in essence, represented the company's first transformation: a vision transformation from a firm that grew olives to one that *both* grew and processed olives.

The California olive industry of those early years was dominated by families who had low expectations of profits yet high hopes of living well. According to Tim Carter (grandson of the founders and the company's current CEO), many companies were operating with a "fly by the seat of your pants" mentality and a belief that each year would simply "take care of itself." Long-range planning focused on "what could be achieved in the next 20 minutes." The reason behind this, according to Tim, was that the management of most companies viewed themselves as growers. They ran their business from crop to crop instead of taking a future-oriented perspective of their business. They were operating as small entrepreneurships who did not yet see the need to change their game.

The olive market expanded throughout the 1950s and 1960s into grocery stores, delicatessens, and supermarkets. Most olive companies continued to operate with very informal systems. According to Tim, many companies assumed that, "As long as my bank account is growing, everything must be OK."

In the mid-1960s, the third generation of the family joined the business with the entry of Tim (in 1964) and Jud (in 1965) Carter. When Tim and Jud entered the company, sales were only $1 million, but the olive market was continuing to expand. The company had several growth opportunities, but its culture did not necessarily support taking advantage of these opportunities. Tim and Jud found a number of employees asking: "Wouldn't it be nice to keep the company small?" Even though some employees were anxious about what growth might mean to them and to the company, the two brothers decided they wanted to grow the firm. To do so, however, they knew that they had to focus some attention on building the infrastructure needed to support a larger company. In particular, according to Tim, they realized that they needed to invest in those things that would make the company "the most efficient and low-cost producer that we could be." As a result, nearly all the profits earned were reinvested in the plant. In brief, the brothers recognized that there was a need to change the game to that of a more professionalized firm. However, their major focus in the early years was mainly on resources and operational systems versus the higher levels of the pyramid of organizational success.

1973: The Third Generation Takes Over and Completes Another Transformation

By the time Tim and Jud Carter took over the day-to-day management of the company from their father in 1973 (with Tim managing the sales and administrative side of the business and Jud focusing on production and developing/maintaining grower relationships), the company's sales had grown to $6 million and the firm had achieved a record profit of $208,000. While the Carters recognized that they had to continue focusing on building production capabilities, they also identified a new opportunity within their market and initiated the first vision transformation that they would manage during their tenure as the firms' leaders.

Changing the Business Concept: Creating a New Vision

The 1970s brought what Tim Carter describes as "some tough times," as the olive industry began to consolidate (i.e., as the environment changed). In 1958, there had been twenty-seven U.S. olive companies, but by the early 1970s, only a few large players remained. One was Bell-Carter. It had survived, in part, because of the company's focus on developing the resources and operational systems needed to support its growth. However, as the environment changed, even this was not enough to ensure continued success.

Although Bell-Carter had been founded as a branded olive company (with the Bell's label) and had continued to offer the Bell's brand throughout its history, it also produced private label olives that were purchased by others and sold under another firm's own brand or house name (like Townhouse, Sysco, etc.). In analyzing their business, the Carter brothers determined that the margins in branded olives were so thin that the best they could do under the environmental conditions of the 1970s was to break even. They decided to change the firm's game to that of a "private label" company, a concept that, at the time, was fairly unique. They would leave the branded business to others like Lindsay Olives and Early California. Primary customers for Bell-Carter became major grocery store chains who wanted to offer their customers a lower cost olive under their own house label. Other customers included food service companies like Sysco who also wanted to supply olives to restaurants and industrial customers with their own brand. As stated previously, the Bell's brand was not abandoned. Instead, it was simply given less focus as Bell-Carter began to build its private label dominance.

Creating an Infrastructure to Support the New Vision

The Carters also recognized that the company would require additional resources and would need to focus on constantly improving its operational systems if it was going to effectively and efficiently meet the needs of the customers/market the firm had chosen to serve and, at the same time, continue to grow. Efforts focused on acquiring not only the people, but also the facilities, equipment, and technology to take the firm into the future.

New people were hired, including more professional managers. In 1978, the company purchased an olive-packing plant in Corning, California, that was renovated and made fully operational in 1980. In 1979, new administrative offices were acquired in Lafayette, California, where they remain today. In 1990, Bell-Carter acquired the operating assets of Olives, Inc. This acquisition enabled the company to increase its annual production capacity by 10,000 tons. In addition, the firm continued focusing on acquiring state-of-the art equipment and developing state-of-the-art processes within its plant to continue its movement toward low-cost production—a key to success in a highly competitive market.

Results of the Transformation

As a result of the efforts of the Carters and their management team, the firm had acquired a 75% market share in the private label olive business by 1993. In other words, the vision transformation that the Carters had begun in the 1970s appeared to have been a success. This, however, was not the end of the transformations this firm would face. Another was on the horizon that would be brought about partly by the need to acquire additional raw product to support the firm's growth and partly by an opportunity created by the failure of a major competitor.

1992: The Trigger for the Compound Transformation at Bell-Carter

In September 1992, Tim and Jud Carter were presented with an opportunity for further growth. Lindsay Olive Company, one of the most recognized brands of olives in the United States, came up for sale. At one time, Lindsay had a 40% share of the branded olive market. However, since the early 1980s, that share had been dropping, partly due to a lack of advertising. This drop had produced significant problems for the company, which was, by 1992, essentially bankrupt. Lindsay was in negotiations with one of Bell-Carter's competitors, but, at the last minute, these negotiations fell through. The processing facility owned by Lindsay was not what interested the Carters because they had capacity at their existing plant; they wanted Lindsay's olive inventory and grower base to help meet market demands. The Carters made an offer and within a week became the owners of not only additional inventory, but also the Lindsay brand. (Unfortunately, the firm was unable to acquire all the growers). The game for Bell-Carter, almost by accident, seemed to need to change again: Now the company was faced with the challenge of maintaining its focus on its private label while at the same time having the opportunity to rebuild the Lindsay brand. In Tim Carter's words, the Lindsay purchase led to the creation of "a whole new company."

Although Bell-Carter Olive Company had, during its history, changed its game twice before—from an olive-growing company in 1912 to an olive processor/canner in 1930 and then from primarily a branded company to primarily a private label company in the 1970s—the transformation it faced in the 1990s presented significantly greater challenges than the previous two. The environment in which the company operated in the 1990s was much more competitive than what it had faced in its early years. No longer was the industry made up of small companies content with just making a living. Now, the black olive industry consisted of only four major competitors, each intent on growing market share within a fairly constrained environment (i.e., there were only so many olive consumers in the United States), which meant that market share gained by one competitor came at the expense of another.

Bell-Carter also encountered the challenges of rapid internal growth. According to Tim Carter, the firm's revenues, at the time of the Lindsay acquisition in 1992, were $53 million. A year later (in part because of the Lindsay acquisition), they had grown to $85 million. According to Tim, while Bell-Carter was successful, its resources and operational systems were stretched by growth. Bell-Carter was in need of making another transformation.

Changing the Game: The Transformation Process at Bell-Carter

With the almost overnight doubling of their company's size, the Carter brothers recognized that their company could no longer continue operating as it had. They began to take the steps needed to transform from an entrepreneurship to a professionally managed firm. A decision was also made to focus more attention on the branded side of the business and rebuild the Lindsay brand. In other words, the firm embarked on a compound transformation—to continue the process it had begun in the 1970s of becoming a professionally managed firm, while at the same time change its business concept to that of a "private label company that is rebuilding a brand."

Transformational Planning: Developing a Plan to Change the Game

Although Bell-Carter's management team had been doing planning for several years, the Carter brothers realized in 1994 that they needed to develop a more sophisticated approach to this process. Planning at the company in the past had typically focused more on what the firm wanted to achieve in the coming year than on what it needed to become in the long term and how it was going to get there. So, in the face of both external and internal pressures, the Carters and their senior management team embarked on a process of *strategically* planning for the firm's future and its transformation. The steps the firm's management took in creating Bell-Carter's transformational plan are outlined below.

1994: Completing the Environmental Assessment and Reviewing the Existing Business

A consulting firm was brought in to assist Bell-Carter in designing and implementing its transformational planning process. According to Tim, this step was taken because, "Once we determined what we needed to do, we realized we needed someone to help. The process [of changing the game to professional management] is a lot more complex than meets the eye and you can't afford to make mistakes."

The transformational planning process began with the administration of a "planning survey" to all members of the firm's senior management team. This survey was designed to collect information on Bell-Carter's environment and internal capabilities. Survey results were summarized in a report that, along with competitive and industry studies the firm had already conducted/collected, served as input to completing the firm's Environmental Assessment and Business Review. This information was also used to help the firm's management identify key strategic issues that had to be addressed to align Bell-Carter's pyramid of organizational success with both its environment and its size.

Environmental Assessment

As noted previously, Bell-Carter was facing (and continues to face today) a saturated and highly competitive market. However, no single competitor in 1994 dominated or controlled the *entire* olive category (which includes not only private label and branded ripe black olives, but also green olives). This represented a potential opportunity for Bell-Carter.

The company's primary customers included not only those who purchased olives in grocery stores; but also the grocery stores themselves, brokers, restaurants, and restaurant/industrial suppliers (like Sysco). Customers wanted a good price as well as good service (including having olives available in the size and quantity they wanted when they wanted them). Bell-Carter traditionally had a reputation for good service that the company felt could be built on as it moved into the future.

Olive consumers (i.e., end users) of the 1990's presented certain challenges for all olive producers. The consumer market for black ripe olives (about 90,000 tons a year) was not expected to grow dramatically; it was difficult to influence consumer taste preferences (for or against olives) and since olives are high in fat (although nutritious), the trend toward low fat foods made olives somewhat unattractive to certain customer groups. Olive growers, in a sense, were also customers of, or at least partners with, the firm. Not only did Bell-Carter compete for customers, but it also competed for raw product (since there were only so many olives produced in the United States each year). A key to any olive company's success is its ability to develop and maintain strong relationships with growers. Since all domestic growers receive the same price for their olives (all olive packers purchase olives at market prices that are set by the industry leader), there is little or no monetary incentive for a grower to switch from one olive packer to another. Therefore, developing good relationships with the grower community can greatly contribute to a company's success.

In 1994, there were four major competitors (one a subsidiary of Campbell's) in the black olive market vying for market share. Some competitors had certain vulnerabilities (including poor customer relations and poor management). Two of Bell-Carter's competitors offered not only black olives, but also a variety of other products to their customers, which gave them a potential advantage in terms of keeping their shipping costs low (since they could ship black olives with these other products). Such diversification also helped these companies minimize the impact on their business of lower black olive sales (resulting from a lack of raw product and/or changing customer preferences). There was, however, a potential disadvantage: since black olives represented only one of several products, these companies did not necessarily focus as much attention on their olive product line (including developing an understanding of customer and grower needs) as Bell-Carter did.

Based on an analysis of the information collected in the environmental assessment, the firm's management team identified several key issues to address in its transformation plan. These included:

- What can be done to better understand and "beat" the competition?
- What steps might be taken to influence consumers to purchase more olives?
- What can be done to maintain strong relationships with growers?

Business Review
The company's business review revealed that there were a number of areas on which the firm might focus to achieve better results within its market. The outcome of this review is graphically presented in Figure 12–2 and discussed below.

Defining the Firm's Business Concept. It was clear that even though Bell-Carter had acquired the Lindsay brand, the business concept that employees "lived by" was still very much that of a private-label olive company. As stated previously, the decision to become a private label firm (made in the 1970s) had contributed greatly to the firm's success. However, the Carters and their management team knew that opportunities existed within the branded business and that their business concept was going to need to change.

The Building Blocks of Organizational Success. Information collected through the administration of the planning survey suggested that while the firm had

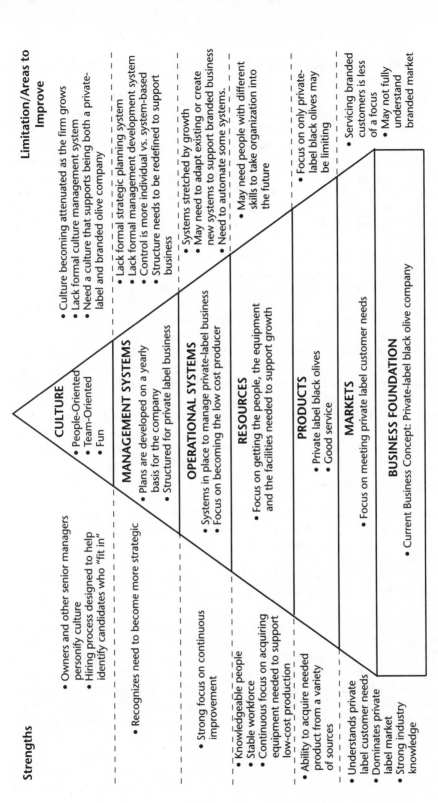

Strengths

Limitation/Areas to Improve

CULTURE
- People-Oriented
- Team-Oriented
- Fun

Strengths:
- Owners and other senior managers personify culture
- Hiring process designed to help identify candidates who "fit in"

Limitations:
- Culture becoming attenuated as the firm grows
- Lack formal culture management system
- Need a culture that supports being both a private-label and branded olive company

MANAGEMENT SYSTEMS
- Plans are developed on a yearly basis for the company
- Structured for private label business

Strengths:
- Recognizes need to become more strategic

Limitations:
- Lack formal strategic planning system
- Lack formal management development system
- Control is more individual vs. system-based
- Structure needs to be redefined to support business

OPERATIONAL SYSTEMS
- Systems in place to manage private-label business
- Focus on becoming the low cost producer

Strengths:
- Strong focus on continuous improvement

Limitations:
- Systems stretched by growth
- May need to adapt existing or create new systems to support branded business
- Need to automate some systems.

RESOURCES
- Focus on getting the people, the equipment and the facilities needed to support growth

Strengths:
- Knowledgeable people
- Stable workforce
- Continuous focus on acquiring equipment needed to support low-cost production

Limitations:
- May need people with different skills to take organization into the future

PRODUCTS
- Private label black olives
- Good service

Strengths:
- Ability to acquire needed product from a variety of sources

Limitations:
- Focus on only private-label black olives may be limiting

MARKETS
- Focus on meeting private label customer needs

Strengths:
- Understands private label customer needs
- Dominates private label market
- Strong industry knowledge

Limitations:
- Servicing branded customers is less of a focus
- May not fully understand branded market

BUSINESS FOUNDATION
- Current Business Concept: Private-label black olive company

Figure 12-2. Results of Bell-Carter's Business Review (1994).

a number of strengths, it also needed to focus on some areas if it was going to successfully change its game.

Markets and Products. Bell-Carter basically "owned" the private-label black olive market (i.e., it had the dominant market share in the United States). It had been able to successfully develop products to meet private label customer needs. In the branded side of the firm's business (which now included the Lindsay as well as the Bell's brand), the direction that Bell-Carter wanted to take was less clear. Bell-Carter had to develop a better understanding of the national branded business and create products to meet the needs of branded customers (while at the same time not losing sight of its private-label market).

One of the greatest challenges Bell-Carter and other olive companies faced (and continue to face today) is acquiring enough raw product to meet anticipated market demand. Crop size varies dramatically from year to year and is difficult to predict. In some cases, early crop forecasts can be off by as much as 30%, thus resulting in some unique challenges when it comes to developing plans. Bell-Carter, through the efforts of Jud Carter and a team of field service specialists who work closely with growers, had historically been able to acquire the fruit needed to meet market demands. The company recognized that, during its transformation, it could not lose the focus it had on developing effective grower relationships. It also realized that it had to look outside California for additional raw product to minimize the impact on its business of a "short crop" in California. The firm began to develop relationships with growers in Mexico and obtain some of its total fruit each year from outside its traditional market. This gave and continues to give Bell-Carter an advantage.

Resources and Operational Systems. A key focus for Bell-Carter, beginning in the 1970s, had been on making its processing plant in Corning (California) the most efficient in the business. In 1992, new equipment was put in place that not only helped produce a superior product, but also helped reduce costs. The company's management knew, however, that this was an area it needed to continue to focus on. In addition, the company recognized that it had to continue focusing on ensuring that it was in compliance with key environmental standards set by the state of California. Meeting environmental standards (particularly regarding waste water) was becoming a significant challenge for all olive processors.

A major asset that Bell-Carter has had throughout its history has been its people. The company has been able to attract and retain employees who possess both a positive attitude and a willingness to learn. In addition, the firm's management early on recognized that to take the company into the future, an investment in skilled professionals in such areas as finance, plant management, and sales was necessary. When the Lindsay brand was acquired, for example, the firm hired a national sales manager who had experience in managing branded products. They also worked to acquire/develop very knowledgeable, experienced salespeople (although the skills possessed by the company's salespeople in 1994 were primarily in the area of how to effectively market/sell a private-label product).

Many of the operational systems at Bell-Carter's plant were functioning reasonably effectively in 1994 and there was a focus on continuously improving these processes. This represented a key strength. However, the company had not necessarily developed all the operational systems needed to support its new branded business. The Carters recognized that there was a need to review all operational systems to determine whether they needed to be changed and/or new systems created to effectively support the brand. It was also felt that the firm could benefit from automating certain processes to create the efficiencies for competing effectively in the future.

Management Systems.   Perhaps the most significant changes the firm needed to make were at this level in the pyramid of organizational success. Bell-Carter's management realized that it could no longer run its business "by the seat of its pants." To become the dominant player in its industry, management recognized the need for and began, in 1994, the process of developing and implementing formal strategic transformational planning and management development processes. The firm's management also recognized that changes in its structure and its performance management systems were required to support both a private-label and a branded business. In general, it was felt that people had to be held more accountable for performance against goals that would help the company achieve success in both the private-label and branded sides of its business.

Corporate Culture.   Bell-Carter's culture had been a source of competitive advantage throughout its history. The company's culture reflected the family-oriented and "fun" personalities of its owners. Employees genuinely liked being a part of the "Bell-Carter family." One of the key challenges the firm faced was to help transform its culture into one that would support being both a private-label and a branded company. Employees were struggling with what this was going to mean for them and their company. Another challenge was to help employees understand that the firm had now become a large company and that some of the old ways of doing things would no longer support the company's goals. In other words, the culture had to be supportive of the firm's transformation to professional management. How the firm worked to manage its culture is detailed later in this chapter.

Size.   The firm's rapid growth (in part brought on as a result of the Lindsay acquisition) had, at times, left management scrambling to keep up. Management realized that as the firm approached $100 million in revenues, new systems, structures, and processes would need to be put in place to take Bell-Carter into the future. In other words, the company's infrastructure needed to be designed/redesigned so that it was more in alignment with its size.

Key issues that emerged from this business review that needed to be resolved in the planning process included:
- What steps need to be taken to establish Bell-Carter as both a private-label and branded olive company?
- What changes need to be made in the organization's infrastructure in order to become an efficient and effective player in both the private label and branded olive markets?

Addressing Key Strategic Issues

During an off-site retreat held in the fall of 1994, Bell-Carter's senior management began the process of addressing key transformational planning issues. The management team utilized information gathered from the planning surveys as well as data from other sources, including industry and competitive studies. The output of analyzing and discussing key strategic issues is discussed further below.

What Business Should We Be in? Bell-Carter's senior management spent nearly a full day of the two-day retreat discussing and attempting to identify the firm's future business concept. After much discussion, it was agreed that the firm's future business concept would be: "To process, market, and sell ripe and green olive-based products to retail and food service customers." The intent of this business concept was to focus the firm on providing private label as well as branded ripe olives to its customers and to perhaps become *the* category manager in the olive business.

Where Do We Want to Play the Game? Bell-Carter's management team also spent some time during the retreat discussing which tiers of the market the company served and wanted to serve in the future. The strategic planning team agreed that customers for branded products were primarily in upper Tier II or Tier I.[2] True Tier I olive customers consisted of those who purchased highly priced gourmet olives produced by small, boutique companies. In the private-label business, the firm was competing primarily in lower Tier II and/or Tier III. This analysis suggested that the firm needed to focus greater attention on ensuring that the quality of its brand and the service provided to those who sold it (e.g., grocery stores, restaurants, etc.) would justify a higher cost. Research conducted by an independent firm in 1993 suggested that the Lindsay brand (with proper service) should be able to command a premium price.

What Are Our Differential Competitive Advantages? Bell-Carter's senior management team spent quite a bit of time during its first retreat and throughout the years that it has been continuing to refine and implement its transformational plan examining what it does better than its competition. One of the many things that differentiates Bell-Carter from its competition is its culture: employees like to work for Bell-Carter, are committed to its success, and are committed to helping ensure that the products produced are of the highest quality. This culture is communicated through the words and actions of its owners and senior management team. Other competitive advantages that the team identified included:

- The strong relationships the company has built with its customers (as a result of the service it provides and the quality of its product).
- The ability to acquire the fruit needed to support its growth (through the relationships it has built with its growers).
- The scale of its plant and the willingness of the Carters and Floyds (who are also owners and who sit on the firm's board) to continue to invest in making the plant state-of-the-art.
- The company's knowledge of the olive industry.

Throughout its transformational process, the company has tried to focus on maintaining and building on these competitive advantages. It has also focused on continuing to track its performance relative to its competition. While Tim Carter has suggested that at times it has been difficult to accurately determine Bell-Carter's strengths and limitations he believes that "getting the facts and knowing where you are relative to your competition is very important to a firm's success."

What Do We Want to Become? During the retreat, the firm's management established a three-year vision for what the company should become. This vision included developing into a $100-million company (from $85 million in 1993) and

> . . . becoming the leader in the ripe olive category (defined as the company that is able to set prices, have the best cost production, and move toward a dominant share in the branded business), and having a strong regional presence in green olives and olive-based food products.[3]

The company's management also determined that Bell-Carter was really in four separate, but related businesses:

1. Private label olives;
2. Branded olives (including the Bell's and Lindsay brands).
3. Food service (selling to companies like Sysco, Olive Garden, etc.).
4. Green olives.

The feeling was that each of these "divisions" needed to be focused on (and have its own vision statement) if the firm was to be successful over the long term.

The Building Blocks of Organizational Success

Bell-Carter's first strategic plan defined what changes had to occur in each level of the pyramid of organizational success to support its vision. That vision and what each of the building blocks needed to look like are shown in Figure 12–3. These changes are outlined below in the form of strategic objectives.

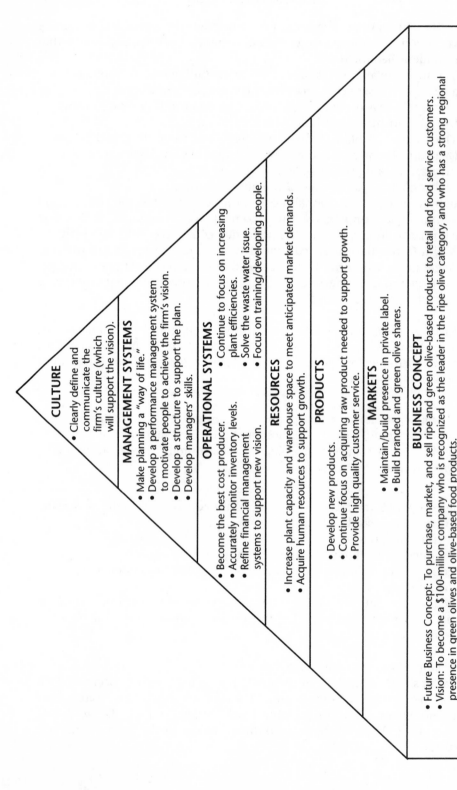

CULTURE
- Clearly define and communicate the firm's culture (which will support the vision).

MANAGEMENT SYSTEMS
- Make planning a "way of life."
- Develop a performance management system to motivate people to achieve the firm's vision.
- Develop a structure to support the plan.
- Develop managers' skills.

OPERATIONAL SYSTEMS
- Become the best cost producer.
- Accurately monitor inventory levels.
- Refine financial management systems to support new vision.
- Continue to focus on increasing plant efficiencies.
- Solve the waste water issue.
- Focus on training/developing people.

RESOURCES
- Increase plant capacity and warehouse space to meet anticipated market demands.
- Acquire human resources to support growth.

PRODUCTS
- Develop new products.
- Continue focus on acquiring raw product needed to support growth.
- Provide high quality customer service.

MARKETS
- Maintain/build presence in private label.
- Build branded and green olive shares.

BUSINESS CONCEPT
- Future Business Concept: To purchase, market, and sell ripe and green olive-based products to retail and food service customers.
- Vision: To become a $100-million company who is recognized as the leader in the ripe olive category, and who has a strong regional presence in green olives and olive-based food products.

Figure 12-3. Bell-Carter's Future Business Design.

Markets and Products: The firm's management recognized that it needed to focus on continuing to maintain and build its presence in the private-label business, while at the same time developing an understanding of and building a presence in the branded market. In addition, management wanted to focus on continuing to provide *all* customers with the products they needed when they needed them.

To help make the firm's vision a reality, the strategic planning team (including the Carters and their senior management team) established the following strategic objectives in the areas of markets and products:

- To increase the profitability of the private label business.
- To build branded ripe olive and green olive market shares.
- To acquire adequate raw product of the right quality and at the right price to meet anticipated customer needs.
- To develop new products.
- To provide high-quality customer service.
- To strategically manage the food service business (which provides olives to restaurants and industrial suppliers like Sysco) in order to meet Bell-Carter's and customers' needs.

Resources and Operational Systems: Although Bell-Carter had historically been fairly effective in these two areas, again the senior management team recognized that certain changes had to be made to support a company that was now in both the branded and private-label olive business. The company would need people with new and different skills in certain positions to support this transformation. In some cases, this might mean that some people would have to be replaced or placed in different positions.

In addition, the business review had revealed that certain operational systems might need to be modified or new systems created to more effectively support a company of Bell-Carter's current (and anticipated future) size. In particular, the planning team believed that the firm could benefit from greater automation in certain areas and needed to take almost immediate steps to "solve the waste water issue" before it could have a significant negative impact on production capabilities. In the plant, new and more efficient processes had to be implemented with respect to labeling, product inspection, and inventory control. Changes were also required in other areas, including development of a financial management system that would more effectively support a business that contained four operating divisions.

In the areas of resources and operational systems, Bell-Carter's planning team determined that the firm needed to focus on the following objectives to support the firm's vision:

- To solve the waste water issue.
- To increase plant capacity, while at the same time increasing plant efficiencies.
- To acquire and develop the human resources to support growth.
- To have sufficient warehouse space to meet anticipated needs.

- To accurately manage, monitor, and control inventory to meet requirements.
- To refine financial management systems to support the new vision.
- To become the "best cost" producer.

Management Systems and Corporate Culture: It was in the area of management systems that Bell-Carter felt it needed to devote the most attention. As stated earlier, many of the firm's management systems in 1994 were fairly informal. Although planning was being done, it tended to be more tactical than truly strategic and comprehensive in nature. The firm valued education, yet no systematic management development program existed. It was also clear that the firm's structure needed to be redefined to accommodate a focus on both the private label and branded businesses. Finally, the firm's management believed that it could improve its ability to hold people accountable for performance in relation to key strategic goals.

In terms of culture, the planning team felt that certain positive elements (like teamwork and a focus on quality) needed to be retained as the firm worked to make its vision a reality. At the same time, however, the culture also had to be managed in such a way that it helped people let go of the old ways of doing things that were interfering with Bell-Carter's ability to move forward with its plan of becoming a much larger (and more diversified) business.

To create the systems needed to support its new vision, the planning team established the following strategic objectives in the areas of management systems and corporate culture:
- To make planning a way of life.
- To develop a performance management system that motivates people to achieve the firm's vision.
- To develop an organizational structure to support the firm's transformational plan.
- To develop managers' skills so that they will be able to effectively/efficiently support the firm's vision.
- To clearly define and communicate the firm's desired culture (i.e., the culture needed to support the firm's vision).

Developing the Transformational Plan
Bell-Carter's first comprehensive transformational plan was developed in the fall of 1994 and incorporated much of the information outlined above, along with specific, measurable goals that would help the firm achieve its objectives. Every quarter since that time, the firm's senior management has met to discuss progress in achieving their plan, update their plan, and examine key strategic issues facing the firm. Each February during a two-day retreat, senior management also revisits the firm's long-term vision and discusses strategies for making this vision real.

Transforming the Organization's Structure

Like many entrepreneurial firms, Bell-Carter had traditionally operated with a fairly informal structure. Although there were some written job descriptions, they were not utilized as guides for the behavior of people within the firm. The first challenge the company faced was to formally define the roles and responsibilities of its players. During the course of a management development program (described in more depth later), senior and middle managers and first-line supervisors from throughout the company were trained in the technology of creating formal, written role descriptions that would help in better organizing the team to play the game laid out in the transformational plan. Each manager was asked to complete a job description for his or her position. Drafts of these role descriptions were then reviewed and approved by the head of the unit to which the position reported. Managers and eventually other employees were encouraged to utilize these job descriptions in helping to clarify what was expected of each person in his or her role. In addition, job descriptions became the basis, in many cases, for developing individual performance goals (a key component in the design and implementation of an effective performance management system).

With respect to its macro structure, the company also created unit heads for each of its major selling divisions—private-label, branded, and food service—who reported to the vice president of sales. This step was taken so that there would be a focus on each of the major aspects of the firm's business. This was especially important since the firm's new vision involved building a presence in the branded olive business. If only one person had been given responsibility for *all* of Bell-Carter's sales, there was a risk that the branded side of the business might not have received the attention required to help make the firm's vision a reality.

In 1995, the owners also decided that Jud Carter (who had been managing production, the growers, and industry relations) needed someone to manage the plant's day-to-day operations. It was determined that the firm hire a plant manager to free up Jud's time so that he could focus on increasing the number of growers the company had under contract, explore new avenues for securing crop (including Mexico), and continue working with Tim Carter on the strategic aspects of the business.

Another key component of the firm's macro structure put in place in 1995 was the creation of an Executive Committee—consisting of the Carter brothers, the CFO, and the vice president of sales. This Committee had responsibility for laying the foundation of the firm's strategy and for managing the entire firm on a day-to-day basis. Although this component of the structure helped the firm get its house in order, by 1997, the Executive Team had come to believe they were devoting too much time to day-to-day work and not enough to strategic issues. To solve this problem, it was decided that a COO would be appointed to focus on managing the firm on a day-to-day basis and that members of the Executive Committee would look for opportunities to delegate more day-to-day responsibilities to the next level of management.

This would allow this team to focus more on the firm's strategic development as the business continued to grow.

Transforming Behavior Through Management Development

In early 1994, Bell-Carter implemented a formal management development program that all senior and middle managers and first-line supervisors were expected to attend. This program (based on the concepts and ideas presented in Chapter 10) consisted of a series of courses (with each course building on the previous course) intended to provide participants with a set of tools they could use to improve their management effectiveness. The program was also intended to help managers throughout the company understand and develop strategies to manage the challenges that the firm was facing in planning for and implementing its transformation. In brief, this program focused on helping participants:

- Understand their roles as managers (from both a skills and mind-set perspective).
- Develop formal written role descriptions for their positions and be able to assist those who reported to them in doing the same.
- Learn how to manage their own and their direct reports' time more effectively to achieve the company's goals.
- Utilize tools and techniques of effective delegation to get the most out of their teams.
- Develop effective decision-making skills.
- Understand and develop the skills of effective leadership.
- Utilize effective interpersonal skills.
- Design and manage effective meetings.
- Understand the key elements of the transformational planning process and how to implement this process effectively.

As a part of the program, participants were given a series of four questionnaires that provided them with feedback on the extent to which they:

- Had, overall, made the successful transition to their roles as managers (in terms of behavior, skills, and mind-set).
- Were effectively managing their time.
- Were utilizing the tools and techniques of effective delegation.
- Were employing an appropriate leadership style and doing the things that effective leaders do.

Questionnaire results and discussions suggested that opportunities existed for managers at all levels to further refine their skills, develop a mind-set more appropriate to their current role, and learn how to behave in ways more consistent with being an effective manager.

The program, consisting of four full days of training (plus a special workshop on strategic planning) that occurred over the course of a year, was designed to provide participants with the opportunity to apply what they were learning and then come back and discuss it with their peers and the outside trainer. At the end of a year, the questionnaires were readministered to determine whether managers had improved their effectiveness. Both questionnaire results and anecdotal information (collected from and about participants) suggested that many participants had indeed improved their ability to effectively manage in the company's new environment. Some of the most significant improvements and/or changes included:

- Nearly all those in management positions (including first line supervisors) had developed a greater understanding of, and ability to effectively execute, their roles as *managers*.
- Many participants who had never before utilized a time management system began using one and found that they improved not only their own, but their team's productivity.
- Managers were setting aside time, on a regular basis, to focus on long-term issues and develop plans for addressing these issues, rather than spending all their time fighting fires.
- There was a higher degree of delegation throughout the company, which allowed managers to focus on planning and developing their teams.
- The quality of meetings was improving.
- Managers were devoting more attention to providing feedback to direct reports, a key ingredient in developing others' capabilities.

In addition to the group-based management development program, some of the more senior level managers also participated in one-on-one coaching sessions that were intended to provide them with an opportunity to discuss issues that were most relevant. Tim and Jud Carter were the first participants in these coaching sessions, which were conducted by outside consultants. During their sessions, the focus was primarily on helping them better define their current and future roles and on key organizational development issues (e.g., structure, culture, etc.). In 1996 and 1997, the CFO, vice president of sales, controller, head of customer service, COO, and the national sales managers of the branded and private-label businesses also participated in this program.

Since Bell-Carter views education as a continuous process, management development continued during 1995 and 1996. Workshops were designed to help participants from the 1994 program continue applying what they had learned. In addition, these participants were introduced to new topics like communication effectiveness, culture management, and performance management system design and management. Bell-Carter's management has also made a commitment to ensure that *all* new managers (whether they are promoted from within or hired from outside the company) attend a version of the original four-day program that was first implemented in 1994. The goal is to have all managers speak the same language concerning management effectiveness. This helps the firm more effectively identify and work to resolve problems with respect to the extent to which the behavior of managers is consistent with the firm's vision.

Transforming Behavior Through Corporate Culture

As mentioned earlier, Bell-Carter's culture had been one of the company's most significant strengths throughout its history. The company had been very family oriented and the low turnover of employees (particularly at its plant) seemed to be evidence that employees enjoyed working there. Both Jud and Tim Carter had helped to foster an environment of openness through spending time talking to employees at all levels of the company. This also helped to communicate their interest in, and appreciation of, their employees. Events—picnics, informational "wine meetings," birthday celebrations, and an annual off-site for all management personnel—helped promote the sense of teamwork that had been so important to the company's success. At the plant, Jud's birthday parties were significant annual events in which employees would do everything from writing and singing original songs about the owner to dressing up in costumes. A goal of these events (organized by the employees themselves) seemed to be to find something new each year to surprise Jud, but at the same time to make the event "fun" for everyone. Having fun was, in fact, a significant part of the firm's culture. More important, however, these events helped reinforce the belief among employees that Bell-Carter was a "good place to work."

Although many aspects of Bell-Carter's culture had had significant positive effects on performance and employee productivity, the company was not without problems. As it embarked on its transformation process, some employees felt that things were getting worse instead of better and "blamed" senior management for the "new set of problems." (This is a typical response to any organizational change process.) There were also problems with the extent to which people "bought into the new vision for the company." According to Tim, there was a "big underlying current of people that couldn't or wouldn't get on board." In some cases, senior management was able to convince people of the need for the changes taking place. In other cases, people left the firm because they could not or would not support the new game the firm needed to play. At the plant, certain problems arose that contributed to employees feeling that they might not be as valued as they once were, as Jud moved out of his role as plant manger. Both Tim and Jud Carter were extremely concerned (as were other senior managers) about ensuring that the positive aspects of the firm's culture remained as the firm grew (since they represented a competitive advantage). At the same time, however, they wanted to ensure that the culture was effectively changed to support the transformation.

In the summer of 1996, the firm embarked on a formal corporate culture study to better understand what its culture was and what it needed to be to support the transformation. A consultant worked with the company to design a program that consisted of:

- Workshops with senior and middle managers and first line supervisors during which participants were trained in the technology of culture management and during which the consultant began to collect information on the firm's real culture.

- Interviews with a select group of employees representing various areas of the company (with some interviews being conducted in Spanish, since about a quarter of the firm's workforce is Spanish speaking).
- The design of a culture survey that asked employees to comment on the extent to which they felt certain elements of the firm's culture were currently "real" and how much they felt these elements *should* be a part of the firm's culture in the future.
- The administration of the culture survey to *all* 350+ Bell-Carter employees.
- Analysis of survey and interview results that were then presented to members of the senior management team.
- Development of a culture management committee whose purpose was to focus on better understanding survey results and making recommendations to the senior management team about what might be done to help promote the desired culture.

Culture interview and survey results suggested that Bell-Carter employees live and breathe quality in the products and services they provide to internal and external customers. Results also revealed that people enjoy working for the firm and that there continues to be a strong sense of "family" among employees. Although these are very positive findings, results also suggested that there were opportunities to improve the extent to which the firm's culture effectively supported its new vision. In particular, results suggested that Bell-Carter's management needed to focus greater attention on recognizing people for performance against goals versus other factors (like seniority). They also suggested that Bell-Carter could benefit from better defining and more consistently holding people accountable for following policies and procedures. A key to helping make these values "real" for employees is to design and implement more effective performance management systems. This, in fact, was one area that the culture management task force recommended that management focus on.

Transforming Behavior Through Performance Management Systems

In early 1997, Bell-Carter began the process of re-examining its performance management systems and determining what changes (if any) needed to be made so that these systems would more effectively influence people to achieve the company's goals. At the same time, these systems needed to be designed to promote the firm's desired culture. At an individual level, the foundation of the performance management system had already been developed in the form of more formalized role descriptions (created as a part of the firm's management development program). The focus in 1997 would be on creating performance-based goals and/or standards of performance for each individual, given his or her position, and developing a process to track performance against these goals and/or standards of performance.

Results of the Transformation

Each year since 1994, Bell-Carter's management team has given itself a report card on its progress in completing its transformation. This is done through surveying the senior management team about what they view as the most significant positive changes that have taken place over the course of the year. In addition, the firm reviews the progress it is making in achieving its goals on a quarterly basis. Survey and plan review results for 1994 to 1997 suggested the following:

Business Vision
- Progress had been made in relaunching the Lindsay label and reestablishing Bell-Carter as a branded olive company.
- Bell-Carter had retained its position as the dominant player in the private label business.

Markets and Products
- The company now focused on managing not only the private label business, but also on managing and building its branded, green olive, and food service businesses.
- The number of acres of olives under contract to Bell-Carter continued to increase over the years, thus increasing the probability that the firm would have adequate product to meet customer needs.

Resources and Operational Systems
- Plant efficiencies had increased over the three years. The waste water problem had been resolved (within acceptable cost ranges and without adverse implications for the plant).
- The salesforce had continued to develop their skills (including the ability to now market and sell the brand).

Management Systems and Corporate Culture
- Managers had developed more sophisticated skills and were better able to execute their roles. According to Tim, managers are "far more strategic" with respect to how they approach and implement their roles.
- Systematic, written strategic planning had become a way of life at the company—with formal, written plans now being developed, implemented and monitored not only at the corporate level; but also within each major function (e.g., sales, production, etc.). According to Tim, the company is now "far more focused and employees have a clear sense of direction."
- The organization's structure had continued to evolve to help the firm more effectively and efficiently realize its vision.
- Corporate culture was still a significant strength, but one on which senior management now kept a close eye to ensure that it would continue to be an asset to the firm as it grew.

Conclusion and Final Thoughts

By 1997, Bell-Carter had basically completed its transformation from an entrepreneurship to a professionally managed firm. All the systems required to manage the $100-million firm that it had become were in place. The company, according to Tim, has changed "forever" to being pro-active versus reactive and the "results" have reached record heights. In 1996, the company had both record sales as well as record profits, in part, because of the infrastructure that it had built from 1994 through 1996. However, the company recognizes that the management of its infrastructure is a continuous process and that its transformation to a "private label company that is building a brand" is not yet complete. With this in mind, Bell-Carter's senior management continues to identify and work to resolve key strategic issues through its transformational planning process. The company keeps building its management capabilities to ensure that it will have the talent needed to manage the company that it will become in the next millennium. According to Tim: "We all know that this is only the beginning, but we are far more prepared for whatever the future brings" (including other transformations).

The example of Bell-Carter Olive Company has illustrated how the concepts, frameworks, and tools presented throughout this book can be applied successfully in managing organizational transformations. As we have seen, the process of changing the game at Bell-Carter required a sustained effort for a three-year period as well as the commitment of the firm's senior executives. It also involved the comprehensive application of the tools presented in this book.

Now that we have illustrated the overall value of the concepts, frameworks, and tools in *Changing the Game*, we will take a final look in Chapter 13 at the lessons we can distill from the many examples we have presented. Specifically, we will step back from the details and discuss a set of lessons for managing organizational transformations. We will also provide some additional guidance for management and boards of directors who are faced with the prospect of managing transformations of all three kinds.

13

CHANGING THE GAME

Lessons for Managers and Boards

This chapter steps back from the details of the various examples of transformations we have presented to revisit the big picture of key lessons for managing the transformation process. The chapter also focuses on the roles that senior executives, CEOs, boards of directors, and consultants play in managing the process of organizational transformations of the three kinds described throughout this book.

Ten Overall Lessons for Managing Transformations and Changing the Game

These lessons apply to all types of transformation faced by an organization and are summarized in Figure 13–1 and discussed in more detail below.

Lesson 1: The Name of the Game Is Transformation

One of the key lessons provided from the experience of the organizations examined in this book concerns the sustainability of success and the need for periodic transformations. Neither great empires nor great corporations last forever, especially if they do not adapt to changes in their environments, competition, trends, and even their own size.[1] Organizations must continuously adapt to change to remain successful and viable over the long term.

One company that understands this lesson and is currently in the process of transforming to a very different game over the long term is Toyota, the Japanese auto giant. According to David Holley, the company's senior executives have accepted the theory that industrial progress comes in roughly fifty-year waves.[2] These "waves of change" are reflected in the dominant industrial infrastructures of the time. This view is based on an economic the-

1. The name of the game is "transformation." Organizations must continually adapt to change or increase the risk of reduced success and even potential failure.

2. An organization's Business Design and Model must change over time.

3. The longer an organization has been successful, the more vulnerable it becomes.

4. Business Concepts are critical to provide true strategic focus for transformations.

5. Playing the game move by move does not work over the long term.

6. Organizations need to go where the game is going to be.

7. Successful transformations require time.

8. Transformations require a comprehensive perspective and a willingness to challenge all aspects of how a firm operates.

9. Transformations require different kinds of leadership at different stages.

10. The tempo of the business game being played needs to change.

Figure 13-1. Ten Overall Lessons for Managing Transformations and Changing the Game.

ory of "long industrial cycles" first developed by the Russian economist Kondratieff.[3] Figure 13–2 depicts four long waves of industrial cycles dating back to the 1800s including one that is currently in progress. The first wave involved the development of canals, the next involved the development of railroads, and the most recent involved the development of highways.

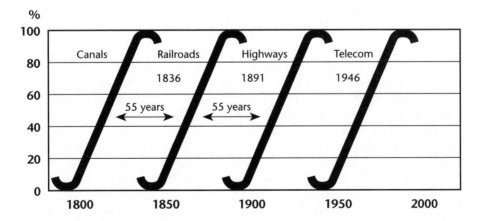

Figure 13-2. Toyota's View of Industrial Cycles.
   Source: Toyota Motor Corp., based on various academic studies, *Los Angeles Times* March 16, 1997.

According to Toyota executives, the next wave that is emerging is thought to be telecommunications. Although questions can be raised about the validity of this hypothesis, the most significant point is that Toyota is thinking and planning in terms of this view of industrial transformation.

Based on this long-run view, Toyota has begun a process of developing a telecommunications business. The company has, in fact, been gradually building experience in telecommunications since the mid-1980s.[4] It is expected that Toyota will focus on automobiles for the foreseeable future, but may make an ultimate shift in its core business in the very long run, perhaps many decades from now. This type of transformation at Toyota would not be unprecedented, as the company was founded more than sixty years ago as a textile firm and only moved into automobiles somewhat later. Toyota's President, Hiroshi Okuda, has stated that, by the year 2000, he wants 10% of the company's sales to come from outside the car and truck business.[5] According to Holley, Okuda has said that "the company's plan is driven by historical cycles dating to the 1700s suggesting that a single line of business rarely prospers for more than 60 years."[6] In addition, Okuda has also stated: "We are not arrogant enough to believe that the automotive business can prove to be profitable perpetually. We are now . . . entering non-automotive businesses as well . . . in order to prepare ourselves for the eventual conditions in the automotive industry."[7]

What Toyota is doing, under the leadership of Hiroshi Okuda, is essentially playing what can be termed a "big game" transformation. It is a Transformation of the Third Kind to the nth degree, based on a vision of what will happen in the very long term. It is very much in contrast to the move-by-move approach so many firms adopt. Toyota recognizes that, like biological organisms, organizations must transform and adapt to survive and be successful over the long term. As such, it can be admired for its sheer boldness.

Lesson 2: The Business Design Must Change Over Time

In addition to an organization's need to transform its overall game over time, as in the example of Toyota, it is also necessary to recognize the need to change the business design or business model periodically, even though the basic game remains the same. For example, IBM's long-term success was based on the business model or design it had developed to successfully dominate the mainframe computer business. Its strategy of emphasizing marketing and service was based on the assumption and existence of high gross margins. However, when technology shifted, and client servers became a credible alternative to many functions previously performed by mainframes, IBM resisted transforming its paradigm. Its first response to customers was: "You don't need these PC's. You can do anything you want with a mainframe and a terminal." IBM continued to think of itself in terms of its "mainframe-marketing-service-high-margin" paradigm, while a totally new class of competitors developed. Recognizing this lesson (i.e., that business design must change over time), companies such as Microsoft, Hewlett Packard, and Sun

Microsystems are all scrambling to transform themselves to embrace the Internet as a new technological platform and avoid what happened to IBM.

Although a business design or business model is intangible and even tenuous, it is real and has a profound impact on overall organizational behavior as well as ultimate success. Management must understand what its business design is in order to assess whether it continues to be appropriate or must be changed to better fit with its environment or its size.

Lesson 3: The Longer an Organization Has Been Successful, the More Vulnerable It Becomes

One somewhat surprising lesson concerns what may be termed "the paradox of long-term success." Ironically, the longer the period an organization has experienced success, the more likely it is to be vulnerable to future difficulties. This is not necessarily attributable to what statisticians refer to as "reversion to the mean," where a statistical series of numbers tend to approximate their long-term averages; rather, the paradox of success occurs because of psychological factors and the mind-set found in an organization.

After an extended period of success, which can be measured in years or even decades, there is a definite tendency for the expectation of continued success. As a result, there is also a tendency to avoid or ignore the warning signs that the organization is in need of making a transformation. This is more than confidence and self-esteem; it is a mentality that continued future success is inevitable, even an entitlement. For example, after IBM experienced decades of uninterrupted success, many people (both IBM employees and investors) came to believe in the inevitability of its future success. In fact, based on its past performance, IBM forecasted that it would be a $100-billion company by 1990 and a $200-billion company by the year 2000! These projections were the result of what can be termed "straight-line planning," which assumes that what happened in the past can be projected as a straight line to the future. "Straight-line planning" is not really planning but wishful thinking. Too many companies ignore changes in the environment and simply look at their sales growth and essentially draw a straight line from where they are into the indefinite future. IBM did this and ultimately learned, to its dismay, that it was unrealistic. This, in turn led them to finally change their game.

This phenomenon occurs not only in business enterprises, but in all organizations that play competitive games. It is based on the notion of a dynasty. For example, after UCLA won nine national championships under Coach John Wooden, it was expected that this would continue indefinitely, regardless of who was coaching. Indeed, after Wooden won his final championship in 1975 (his tenth at UCLA), one of the program's boosters said: "Well, John, you let us down last year, but you redeemed yourself this year." The prior year, UCLA had lost in the semifinal round of the NCAA Championship to North Carolina State, the eventual tournament winner. It seemed that nothing less than winning the national championship would be satisfactory to at least some Bruin fans. Similarly, fans of the New York Yankees had visions of continuing success, year after year.

One problem created by the expectation of continued success arises when it becomes detached from the effort that led to the success. As people come to believe that success is inevitable or entitled, they may begin to do less of the very things that created the success in the first place. At IBM, for example, the implicit cornerstone of the culture was: "You take care of IBM and IBM will take care of you." Unfortunately, too many people came to focus only on the last part of that notion. Ultimately, the IBM Corporation could no longer take care of its more than 400,000 employees and had to downsize through a series of (previously inconceivable) layoffs.

Another problem arises when people come to believe that "so long as we keep doing the same things in the same ways, we will be successful." When this belief is present, there is a reluctance to make the kinds of changes required for completing a successful transformation. Under these conditions, it may only be when the organization finds itself in a real crisis that management *will* begin taking steps to change the game. Unfortunately, for some organizations, these actions can come too late. The problem is compounded if senior management begins to believe in its own invincibility. The ancient Greeks had a word for this—they called it "hubris."

Lesson 4: Business Concepts Are Critical to Providing a Focus for Transformations

One of the lessons that cannot be overemphasized concerns the role that an organization's business concept plays in its ability to change its game. We have seen the difference in economic value that can be created by alternative business concepts, as in the examples of Coca-Cola and PepsiCo discussed in Chapter 1. In addition to the positive benefits of an effective business definition, it must also be noted that problems can arise when there is no true business focus. For example, Kodak tried to execute a revitalization transformation by focusing on its "core competencies," but did not have a true strategic business concept for its new game. This resulted in a series of problems for the organization that were discussed earlier.

Conversely, some organizations have a defined business concept that is too narrow, given the changes occurring in their environments. Railroads, for example, continued to focus on being in the "railroad business," even in the face of competitors who were offering new forms of transporting people and products. As a result, the railroad industry and the companies within it declined as these new forms of transportation—trucks, buses, cars, and planes—took away their traditional customers. Railroads did not die out, but their long-term success was negatively affected by their unwillingness or inability to expand their business concept.

The dilemma is to strike a delicate balance between a business concept that provides sufficient focus without being too narrow. There is limited strategic value in conceptualizing a business as a "telecommunications company" as AT&T did prior to its announced division into three separate companies because, quite simply, the concept is too broad and provides no real focus or direction. AT&T has now narrowed its focus to "telephony," and has divested itself of its computer operations (formerly NCR) and its equipment operations (formerly Western Electric), which now is known as Lucent Technologies, as described in Chapter 6. One might argue that telephony is still quite broad, but at least it is a narrower focus than under the "old" AT&T.

Another example of a transformational strategy involving the narrowing of a business concept is Navistar, which was described in Chapter 5. As you may recall, Navistar is the new name of the entity that was formerly International Harvester. International Harvester provided agricultural and construction equipment as well as trucks and diesel engines. By narrowing its focus to those markets in which it held the leading position (i.e., trucks, buses, and diesel engines), Navistar has given itself a chance for long-term viability.

Lesson 5: Playing the Game Move by Move Does Not Work Over the Longer Term

Another lesson derived from this book concerns the different "meta-strategies" that are either consciously or unconsciously adopted by organizations. Some organizations play the business game move by move. This means that their planning, which can be either strategic or tactical in nature, is focused on the moment. It tends to be deal-making planning rather than business planning. It is also oriented to solving current problems or "putting out fires" rather than building for the longer term (e.g., the type of planning we saw at Miller Brothers prior to their revitalization transformation, as described in Chapter 4).

There are a variety of reasons for this phenomenon. A very basic one is that many people are uncomfortable thinking conceptually and longterm about anything, let alone the management of their business. They are more comfortable dealing with concrete, immediate, tangible things. In addition, the future is inherently uncertain and complex, and people tend to feel overwhelmed by its possibilities. Many people desire to reduce complexity to very simple issues. It takes time, skill, and effort to analyze broad future trends and possibilities as well as distill meaningful insights. Further, the results of long-term planning will not be evident in the shortterm. Only after a period of time will people be able to say with conviction, "We have changed and we are better." Transformational planning and thinking, then, runs counter to some people's desire to deal with concrete issues and receive immediate feedback on the results of their efforts. Accordingly, long-range planning and strategy tend to be dismissed as impossible, irrelevant, and "academic." Unfortunately, staying in the comfort zone of focusing only on what is tangible and short term, potentially sets an organization up for significant problems in the long term.

Another reason for this type of thinking lies in the sometimes unconscious belief on the part of people and businesses that the trends of the past will continue into the future. This is because major "secular trends" (which are fundamental changes as opposed to changes in the level of business activity from stages of the business cycle) do tend to unfold over long periods. For example, during the period following World War II through the late 1960s, the supply of oil was plentiful and, in turn, its price was relatively low. The implicit assumption was that this condition would persist. "Cheap energy," in fact, was a cornerstone of many industrial business models and strategies, including that adopted by the airline industry, which purchased larger and larger planes. In 1971 to 1972, the oil embargo had a profound impact not only on businesses, but society as a whole. Cheap oil was no longer a reality and businesses had to adjust quickly to survive.

The early 1970s also brought the onset of inflation. Indeed, inflation was a major, if not *the* major, driving force in the economy for the period from 1971 through 1989. It can be recalled that there was an "inflation mentality" or paradigm for that period not only in business, but throughout the society as a whole. However, as early as 1982, steps were being taken by the U.S. Federal Reserve Bank (the Fed) to break the inflationary cycle. Nevertheless, the perception that "inflation was dead" or at least under control only began to emerge in the late 1980s and early 1990s. Throughout this period, many companies continued to base their strategies on conditions that had already changed. For example, many companies assumed that they could raise prices in response to rising costs. This became less and less feasible as inflation ebbed and a quasi-deflationary environment emerged. The key point is that "secular trends" do tend to persist for long periods, but they inevitably end. When they end, organizational transformations are required.

The problem and consequences of playing the game move by move are illustrated by what happened to U.S. automobile companies, including General Motors, Ford, and Chrysler, as discussed in Chapter 2. Specifically, U.S. automakers ignored the needs of customers who were looking for smaller, more fuel-efficient vehicles, and continued to produce model after model of virtually the same large "gas guzzlers" until foreign automakers had captured a significant market portion. Only when their market shares significantly eroded did U.S. firms begin to see that the game had changed.

Since secular trends do tend to persist for relatively long periods, people can be lulled into the spurious belief that "this is the way things are, and they will persist this way indefinitely." Unfortunately, when it becomes clear that business as usual is no longer appropriate, it is often difficult to adapt effectively. In contrast to the U.S. automakers in the 1970s, it is clear from what we described earlier in this chapter that Toyota is not playing the game move by move. They are preparing for the very long term by anticipating fundamental changes in the nature of industry in line with the Kondratieff notion of long waves of industrial cycles.

The bottom line is that playing the game move by move, rather than learning how to think strategically and transformationally about the environment and the business, can work for short or sometimes even long periods of time, but it can have a detrimental effect on an organization's ability to effectively change its game. Those firms (like Toyota) that understand and anticipate these types of changes dramatically increase their probability of long-term success when compared with those who must react quickly (and in a crisis mode) to major environmental shifts.

Lesson 6: Go Where the Game Is Going to Be

Wayne Gretsky has long been considered one of the best, if not *the* best, hockey player of all time. This is surprising if one looks at Gretsky as a physical specimen. He is not the biggest player, or the fastest, or the best shooter. He simply plays the game differently and better than most others. When Gretsky was once asked for the "secret" of his success, he replied, "Everybody else goes where the puck is. I go where the puck is going to be." This is a simple but profound difference in his strategy for playing the game and it is relevant to business. Howard Schultz of Starbucks Coffee Company decided to play his game differently. He saw coffee not only as it was, but as it was going to be. Accordingly, Schultz transformed Starbucks from a local roaster to a hybrid "specialty retailer/café." In the process, he redefined the nature of an industry and took what was essentially a commodity and created significant brand equity in the name Starbucks.

The ability to anticipate and plan for organizational transformations (i.e., to go where the game is going to be) involves learning to think long term about the business (as is being done at Toyota) and developing the ability to utilize the tools and techniques for managing transformations that were presented in Chapters 7 through 11. It also involves being willing to look "outside the box" and ask questions about "what might be."

Lesson 7: Successful Transformations Require Time

We have observed in the examples here that organizational transformations are complex and typically require extended periods of time. They are not susceptible to a quick fix or magic potion. The amount of time required for completing a transformation depends on a number of factors. One of the more significant factors, however, is size: the time it takes to complete a transformation is related to the size of the organization. Specifically, the larger the organization, the greater the amount of time typically required. Even in the smallest organization, any of the transformations described in this book will require one to two years. In some of the largest organizations, such as IBM, Chrysler, Bank of America, and the like, a transformation can require between five and ten years. People who have adopted a short-term, firefighting mentality and who want immediate results may find this unacceptable. However, changing the game is a complex process and sometimes little can be done to reduce the time required to *successfully* complete it. This information is important in terms of setting expectations. This is not to say that certain changes will not occur fairly rapidly. There may be dramatic changes taking place that, when completed will result in the transformation of the company. Although the changes will be noted and will help push the organization to its new game, only when they all come together and are working effectively will the transformation be complete.

We must note that every rule has an exception. In this case, as we have seen in the example of Compaq, revitalization was accomplished in a relatively short time. This is truly an exceptional example.

Lesson 8: Transformation Requires a Comprehensive Perspective in Which All Aspects of the Organization Are Subject to Review

The many examples presented in this book have shown that successful transformations require that management take a comprehensive approach to both planning for and implementing the firm's new game. This requires, in turn, that management be open to changing any and all aspects of the firm's operations. No aspect can be viewed as a "sacred cow" if the transformation is going to be successful. Successful transformations depend on management's willingness and ability to:

• Critically evaluate nearly every aspect of how their firm operates.
• Analyze the extent to which all the pieces of the firm's business design (including the business concept and building blocks of organizational success) fit together and are in alignment with the organization's size and environment.
• Change certain aspects of the firm's infrastructure so that it is more in alignment with the firm's environment and/or size.

When we examined some of the examples of companies such as Kodak, in which there was a lack of an overriding vision or a comprehensive perspective, we found that the transformation was less likely to be successful. When transformations were approached from a comprehensive perspective, such as in the case of American Century Investors, MediPro Industries, Navistar, Miller Brothers Inc., and Bell-Carter Olive Company, the transformations were all more likely to succeed.

Lesson 9: Transformations Require Different Leadership at Different Stages

Another lesson is that successful transformations can require different kinds of leadership at different stages of the process. We have seen several examples where the leadership of the transformation process shifted at various stages, including Chrysler, Miller Brothers, and Compaq.

Ultimately, if organizational transformations are to be successful, they need to be sponsored, championed, or at least blessed, by the senior managers of an organization, including the CEO and COO (as at Bell-Carter Olive Company). It is doubtful that many transformations can be successfully completed without the buy-in and support of the top people within an organization.

In this regard, the board of directors needs to make sure that there is commitment on the part of the most senior officers of the company to a transformation. Although this may seem clear, it does not always occur in all organizations. For example, in the case of Miller Brothers, there was not an acknowledgment at first that the organization needed a transformation, at least at the top of the organization. In fact, the need for the transformation was first seen by the president of a strategic business unit within the company who realized that unless the overall corporation was dramatically changed, it would not continue to be successful, and, in turn, his business unit would fail along with the overall company. It took more than two years to convince the CEO and COO of the company of the need for transformation.

Even when there is support for the transformation by the CEO, this may still not be sufficient to ensure a successful transformation. Buy-in by a critical core of people throughout a business can be required, as illustrated by the example of UAL presented in Chapter 10.

Lesson 10: The Tempo of the Game Being Played Needs to Change

It is well recognized that sports are often used as a metaphor for business. What is not as well perceived is how the specific sport used as a metaphor for business has changed over time. In the late 1800s and early 1900s, baseball was perceived as *the* American pastime. Not only was it the American pastime, but it was also symbolic of how both society, in general, and the businesses within it operated. The pace was relatively slow, the game was fairly controlled, and the field was open. The game itself was simple (hit the ball, catch the ball, run the bases, score runs) and it required only a limited amount of equipment so that nearly everyone could play it. American business at the time was like baseball: while the pace of the game was not necessarily slow (as the Industrial Revolution rolled through America bringing with it changes in technology), the playing field was relatively open. Businesses were not required to react very quickly to changes in their environments because their only competition came from known teams who occupied "space" within the United States. Companies were structured and most approached the game with a top-down approach in which employees were basically told what to do and how to do it.

Beginning in the 1960s, football began to emerge as the great American game. In football, unlike baseball, teams marched up the field and "conquered" their opponents (sometimes causing actual physical injuries). The goal in football was to gain yards at the expense of the competition and develop plays that would catch the opposing team off guard. The equipment needed to play the game was much more extensive because players had to be "protected" from their opponents. The field was still open, but now the game was won through battling over a few yards. In American business, the game had also changed. Competition had intensified and, in many cases, market share gains could only be achieved at the expense of another company. Equipment and technology increased in sophistication and employees required a higher degree of education to move into certain positions within the organization.

In the 1980s, basketball seemed to be the metaphor for American business, as well as society as a whole. As in basketball, the game of business was now much more fast paced and ever changing. It also required fewer players to effectively achieve results. Competition became more intense, unpredictable, and constantly changing. The 1980s brought with them a focus on globalization (this also occurred in basketball, which has been "exported" to Europe as well as Asia) and on developing new strategies to play a much faster-paced game with sometimes fewer players. In addition, companies were faced with developing strategies to motivate and retain their best players as competitors tried to attract them to their own organizations.

We believe that the best metaphor for the next phase of business evolution will be "speed" (or "lightning") chess. This is chess played with a time clock and a very small amount of time available for consideration of moves. This metaphor will best suit business in the future because the dynamics of the game are quite different today from what they were even a few years ago. Specifically, the tempo of the game has changed. It is a much faster tempo that is more similar to hockey or speed chess than even to basketball. In addition, however, there is a more cerebral quality to the game that includes the need to instantly process information, formulate strategy, and execute decisions with almost lightning speed.

What this means is that as the nature of the overall "business game" changes, the kinds of managerial capabilities required will need to change as well. Managers must develop the capabilities of anticipating and planning for transformations *before* their firms are in crisis. To do this effectively, managers will need to master the concepts and tools presented throughout this book. In brief, to be successful in the emerging environment, managers and their organizations must be able to anticipate and rapidly execute the steps needed to successfully change the game.

Lessons for Specific Types of Transformations

In addition to the overall lessons cited above, there are lessons specific to the three major types of transformations. We have examined these previously in Chapters 3 through 6, but we highlight them below to reinforce them as well as integrate them.

Lessons for Managing Entrepreneurial Transformations

From our examination of the examples of MediPro Industries, American Century Investors, and Compaq Computers, we have seen that an organization's own success is the ultimate cause of the need to make a Transformation of the First Kind from a "pure" entrepreneurship to an entrepreneurially oriented, professionally managed firm. As an organization grows, there is a need to change its infrastructure to better support the larger enterprise that it has become. This includes making changes in the top four building blocks of successful organizations: resources, operational systems, management systems, and culture.

One of the lessons to be learned about managing Type I Transformations is that when organizational growing pains are experienced, the company requires more than an "organizational tune-up." It needs to develop and implement a comprehensive program for "overhauling" or transforming the company. Management must "let go" of the old ways of doing things, even though they have been successful in the past, and make the transformation to a "different" kind of organization. Management must learn how to play the game of professional management; this involves knowing how to develop and implement more sophisticated systems, processes, and structures. No longer can the firm and its management team afford to operate in an informal manner. The sheer size of the company requires that it develop more formalized operational and management systems, and that the firm create a system for communicating and managing its corporate culture.

Although some have argued that the kinds of changes required by entrepreneurial transformations to professional management can only be accomplished by replacing the company's founder and existing management team, we have shown that it *is* possible for the entrepreneur and his or her team to successfully make a Transformation of the First Kind. For example, this was accomplished at American Century Investors, Miller Brothers, MediPro Industries, and Bell-Carter Olive Company. The key to success in these firms was senior management's willingness to change and support the changes that needed to be made within their organizations.

Lessons for Managing Revitalization Transformations

From our examination of the examples of Miller Brothers, Compaq, and Chrysler, we have also derived some specific lessons concerning Transformations of the Second Kind. One lesson is that the need for a revitalization transformation may not be apparent for some time as a company continues to grow. Management may ignore the classic symptoms of the need for revitalization (presented in Chapter 2) until a "crisis" occurs. This is exactly what happened at Miller Brothers, Compaq, and Chrysler, as described in Chapter 4.

We have also seen that once the need for a revitalization transformation does become evident, it is not typically feasible to do a "quick fix." The revitalization at Miller Brothers and Chrysler took three and five years, respectively, while at Compaq, where the process was exceptionally fast, it still took two years.

The final lesson that firms facing a revitalization need to learn is that changes can be quite extensive. Revitalizations typically require that many aspects of the firm's operations be changed for the firm to survive. Some of these changes—particularly those that require downsizing the workforce or reassigning employees to new roles—can be quite painful. Consequently, managers need to understand and manage their own emotions and mindsets as they embark on these transformations. They must carefully analyze what must be done and then, no matter how painful, they must make the changes required. When emotion gets in the way of sound judgment, the likelihood that a revitalization transformation will be successful is decreased. This is not to say that managers need to behave like tyrants. In contrast, they must remain sensitive to the feelings of their employees, while at the same time make some tough decisions. This can be accomplished through how the management team defines and communicates elements of the firm's culture during the transformation process, as described in Chapter 11. This includes managing the messages that are sent to employees regarding the extent to which the firm values them.

Lessons from Business Vision Transformations

From our examination of the examples of Starbucks, Disney, Navistar, Edison International, Hughes Electronics, and Nike, we have learned that a business vision transformation can be the result of either actual environmental changes or simply "seeing" the environment differently (as in the example of Starbucks). The most fundamental lesson from these examples is that business vision transformations require the creation of a "new" business. Although some companies have tried to superimpose a business vision on an existing organization (e.g., Sears and Kodak), the correct way of accomplishing a successful business vision transformation is to identify the new business concept as a foundation and then design the six key building blocks comprising the pyramid of organizational success, as described in Chapter 7, to support the new vision.

Another lesson for business vision transformations concerns the nature of the "new vision." Although some people assume that the "vision" must involve a profound idea, it may in fact be quite simple, as was Howard Schultz's idea for Starbucks cafés, Noah Alper's idea (Noah's Bagels) to employ nostalgia as an ingredient in selling bagels, or Phillip Knight's vision of "better" athletic shoes.

We have also seen that an "outsider" with a different perspective can be critical to the development of a new vision. It will be recalled that Howard Schultz was not the original founder of Starbucks, and Michael Eisner was certainly an outsider at Disney. They saw possibilities that were not obvious to corporate insiders. The ability of an organization to accept an outsider depends, in turn, on its culture.

Another lesson concerns the possibility of narrowing rather than broadening the vision for an enterprise. Although there is a tendency to think of new business visions as being broader, we have seen that several organizations have all narrowed their business concept to achieve a greater focus. For example, Navistar, Kodak (under the leadership of first Kay Whitmore and then George M.C. Fischer), Sears, and, more recently, AT&T have all narrowed their vision.

Implications for Management, the Board, and Consultants

The previous sections have presented some overall lessons concerning the management of transformations. In this next section, we examine more specific implications for the senior management of an enterprise, its board, and organizational advisors such as consultants.

Lessons for Senior Management

One of the major lessons for senior management concerns the role they play not only in managing current operations, but also helping their businesses adapt to present and anticipated future changes in the environment and in their size. Although this may seem clear, most managers and therefore most companies simply do *not* operate this way. People are more comfortable in focusing on tangible things, and dealing with the future is not comfortable. For many people it is too abstract, and, especially if the company is publicly held, the pressures of meeting quarterly earnings-per-share expectations make it seem foolish to worry much about the longer term. In this type of environment, the long term is next year. As we have seen throughout, this type of mind-set can lead to serious problems. Management is simply not performing its stewardship function unless a sufficient amount of effort is involved in attempting to anticipate and plan for organizational transformations of the three kinds. Stated differently, a business model or design is vulnerable to obsolescence and must be changed if an organization is to thrive over the long run. Changes in products, systems, and technology are not sufficient to ensure survival. There must be a good fit among the four key determinants of organizational success: the business concept, the six key building blocks of organizational success, the organizational size, and the environment, as explained in Chapter 2.

A related lesson for management is that, regardless of good intentions, the environment will inevitably change and this may lead to a reversal of fortune for an organization. Although management may prefer certainty, change and transformations, are the name of the game over the longer term. Management must learn to let go of what it knows and does well and adjust to living in the discomfort zone of change and transformation. Although this may seem clear, we have observed situations where it simply does not occur. For example, Rod Canion, one of the founders of Compaq who had done a brilliant job in both its inception as well as its transformation to professional management, was unable to "let go" of the old strategy when the market changed, even when it was clearly no longer successful. His replacement, Eckhard Pfeiffer, was not wedded to the old strategy and ultimately led Compaq's revitalization process.

This means that management must learn how to manage organizational transformations. It also means, in turn, that management must learn how to analyze the business design of their own and competing companies. They must develop the ability to successfully change their business model (when appropriate), while at the same time devote sufficient attention to managing day-to-day operations. We are not saying that this is easy, but it is a necessary prerequisite for long-term organizational survival and prosperity. Learning this type of thinking and cascading it throughout the organization is probably the biggest challenge management has. Unfortunately, the larger the organization, the more complex this process is. It is, however, the ultimate challenge to any organization that would position itself as a "learning organization."[8]

Lessons for Middle Management

When the need for a transformation is not first perceived by the top management of an organization, but is seen by others in that organization such as middle managers, what can be done? The strategy to help initiate a transformation in this case is one of "managing upward." At first glance, this term may seem like a contradiction. How can someone manage upward? In fact, if we understand "management" to mean the process of influencing the behavior of others to achieve organizational goals, then management can occur in any direction: downward, sideways, and even upward. The process of managing upward requires an indirect effort to influence the way people think in an organization and facilitate their recognition of the need for transformation.

Sometimes it is necessary for middle management or even lower senior management to "manage" or influence the behavior of those above them. This need occurs when middle management "sees" situations and implications that are either not clear to senior management or when there is a political stalemate. Over the years when managers have discussed this with us as advisors, we have counseled them to manage upward carefully. The process of managing upward involves helping to define the "agenda" of issues facing the organization. If something is not perceived as an issue, there is no discussion and no resolution. A variety of tactics can assist an individual or team in putting an issue such as the need for organizational transformation on the table. These range from direct approaches such as preparing a memo articulating the issues to more indirect approaches such as providing articles or books to be read, discussing the experiences of other companies, suggesting seminars to be attended, or bringing in outside speakers in a "leadership development" or "mind-stretching" forum. In one situation, the president of a strategic business unit of a larger company was concerned about the viability of the parent organization. His strategy was to introduce new ideas and a transformational planning process to *his* unit and hope that his results would lead to a recognition of the benefits of the same process at the corporate level. It took slightly more than two years, but it had the desired effect. In addition, he was selected to lead the broader corporate transformational effort.

There is no one best strategy for managing upward. However, middle management and the heads of SBUs need to recognize that they are not powerless to change things at the corporate level, although there is risk and it is not necessarily a simple task.

Lessons for the Board

There are lessons for the board of directors as well. Ultimately, the board has an oversight responsibility to ensure that management fulfills its long term stewardship function. Any experienced board member will appreciate the pressures management is under and the temptation to focus on the present rather than deal with the complex transformational issues facing virtually any organization in the current era. The Board's role is to ensure that management fulfills its longer term role as well as its immediate need to operate the organization profitably. Optimizing long-term shareholder value requires that management has thought through transformational issues. Unfortunately, the problems facing an organization will be compounded if the board does not appreciate the need for this type of activity. In that case, the board will not have performed *its* fiduciary responsibility. This suggests the need for the board to develop its capacity to think "transformationally." To achieve this, the board can use the concepts and framework presented throughout this book, especially the tools presented in Chapter 7.

The Role of Consultants

Not all people possess the same skills and abilities. This is why a team is necessary for a successful transformation. Having stated that it is desirable or even necessary for management and the board to learn to think in transformational terms, we need to be realistic about peoples' capabilities. A CEO may be a very effective or even a great leader, but simply not a transformational thinker. Similarly, the board may have valuable advice but still not be first-rate at transformational thinking. This suggests a clear role for consultants as advisors to management and the board. Consultants can add a great deal of value to this process, if they are truly experts in understanding and managing transformations. One function of consultants is to train management and the board in transformational thinking. Another is to serve as coaches and/or facilitators of the transformational planning process.

At their best, consultants bring objectivity and independence from the political system of the firm. They can bring knowledge of the management process and the lessons of other organizations that have encountered similar kinds of transformational issues. Consultants were used in several of the examples presented throughout this book, including MediPro Industries, American Century Investors, Miller Brothers, Navistar International, and Bell-Carter Olive Company. In other examples, consultants were employed in some phases of the transformation process and not in others. Some companies have executed transformations on their own without the aid of outside consultants, or with minimal use of them, including Edison International and Compaq. However, consultants can play a valuable role in both planning and executing of the transformation process.

What should consultants do and not do? Consultants should never be used as decision-makers or in lieu of decision-makers. A company's executives have the responsibility for the management of their company and for making decisions about its future. Consultants need to serve as advisors and facilitators. They can help raise questions, analyze data, challenge assumptions and arguments, provide examples, and facilitate processes. At their best, they are a catalyst to an effective and successful transformation process. However, consultants are not equipped to substitute for a management that "lives" in an organization 24 hours a day, 365 days a year.

Although some consultants position themselves as decision-makers, we believe that this is an inappropriate use of consulting resources. In addition, although internal facilitators of the transformation process can be very useful as part of an overall team responsible for changing the game, they are not good substitutes for consultants who typically are not dependent for their livelihood on a single organization. Accordingly, consultants are in the position of challenging management to a greater extent than insiders. Unfortunately, consulting is like any other professional process; not all consultants are equally skilled at this type of thinking and facilitation. The key is getting someone who is experienced with this process.

One issue involved in selecting consultants concerns their experience in the particular industry in which a company operates. Sometimes management wants consultants who have worked with similar companies. This is not necessarily an advantage and at times can even be a disadvantage. Often knowing how others do it or what "cannot be done" inhibits creative thinking, or thinking "out of the box." Management must be the industry expert, not consultants. The consultants' role is to help guide the transformation process, and they should be selected based on their ability to do that (rather than on their specific industry knowledge/experience).

To select consultants effectively, management has to focus on their experience in dealing with transformations. As in other professional situations, it can be useful to talk with their clients. These discussions ought to be for the purpose of determining how satisfied the clients were with the services provided and the role that the consultant played in helping them manage their organization's transformation process.

The Game Without an End

Unlike chess and the NCAA basketball tournament, business is a game without an end. There is no national championship tournament for business. The game goes on and on. In a sense, a basketball program is like a business. A given team may win a championship one year, but there is always the next year and the next and the next, just as in business. As soon as one profitable year is completed, the next emerges. There is, however, one constant in the business game year after year: the need to understand the process of managing organizational transformations. Accordingly, the final lesson is: adapt and increase the probability of future success; or remain "fixed in the existing paradigm" and risk failure. The game is there for the taking.

NOTES

Chapter 1

1. *Webster's New Collegiate Dictionary* (Springfield, MA: G&C Merriam Co., 1979).
2. Eric Flamholtz, *Growing Pains: How to Make the Transition from Entrepreneurship to a Professionally Managed Firm* (San Francisco: Jossey-Bass Publishers, 1990).

Chapter 2

1. For additional information and research findings, see: Yvonne Randle, "Toward an Ecological Life Cycle Model of Organizational Success and Failure." *Doctoral Dissertation* (Anderson School of Management, UCLA, 1990); Eric Flamholtz, "Managing Organizational Transitions: Implications for Corporate and Human Resource Management," *European Management Journal* (1995): Vol. 13, No. 1, pp. 39–51; Eric G. Flamholtz, *Growing Pains* (San Francisco: Jossey-Bass Publishers, 1990).
2. When an organization has been successful in carving out a significant niche, it is also sometimes referred to as having developed a "franchise."
3. Alfred P. Sloan, *My Years With General Motors* (New York: McFadden-Bartell, 1964).
4. Ibid.
5. It is clearly true that there are barriers to entry in many markets. For example, there are huge costs in creating ship-building, airplane-manufacturing, or locomotive-manufacturing enterprises. However, the key point is that most products can be copied by someone who has the resources required. In an era of world-class competition, an enterprise cannot assume that its products and markets will remain theirs indefinitely, as the U.S. automobile manufacturers of the 1960s and 1970s believed.
6. *AT&T Shareowner's Report* (for quarter ending September 30, 1995).
7. Empirical research has supported the notion that criteria for organizational effectiveness, as well as the means for achieving it, shift from stage to stage of the organizational life cycle. See: R. E. Quinn and K. Cameron, "Organizational Life Cycle and Shifting Criteria for Effectiveness: Some Preliminary Evidence," *Management Science*, 29 (1), 1983, pp. 33–51.
8. Empirical research has supported the stages identified as well as the approximate size (measured in revenues) shown in Figure 2–3. See: Y. Randle, op. cit.

Chapter 3

1. MediPro Industries is a pseudonym for an actual organization. The names of all individuals have been changed to preserve anonymity. Some facts have been changed.
2. For a detailed discussion of this syndrome, see Eric Flamholtz and Yvonne Randle, *The Inner Game of Management* (New York: AMACOM, 1987).
3. James E. Stowes, Jr., *Yes You can . . . Achieve Financial Independence* (Kansas City: Deer Publishing, Inc., 1992).
4. This discussion of the transformation of American Century Investors to professional management focuses on the aspects that are most relevant to the themes of this book.

5. Barry Henderson, "Good Deal?," *BARRON'S* (August 4, 1997), pp. 36–37.

6. M. L. Tushman, E. Virany, and E. Romanelli, "Executive Succession, Strategic Reorientation, and Organizational Evolution: The Mini-Computer Industry as a Case in Point," *Technology in Society* (1985), Vol. 7, pp. 297–313, and "Executive Team Succession: A Longitudinal Analysis," Columbia University Graduate School of Business Working Papers (1987).

Chapter 4

1. This example was prepared by *ManagementSystems* Consulting Corporation. It is based on actual work over a four-year period. Names and certain other descriptive information have been changed to maintain the organization's confidentiality.

Chapter 5

1. The material in this example is based on an interview with Howard Schultz, Santa Monica, California, April 26, 1995. All direct quotations are from this interview.

2. *Starbucks Corporation 1995 Annual Report* (Seattle, WA, 1995, p. 9).

3. C. Borucki and C. K. Barnett, "Restructuring for Self-Renewal: Navistar International Corporation," *The Executive* (1990), Vol. 4, No. 1, pp. 36–49.

4. "Navistar: Managing Change," Harvard Business School Case 9-490-003 (1989).

5. Gary Slutsker, "Let's Make a Deal," *Forbes* (April 26, 1993).

6. "Navistar Incorporated Team Approach and Consistent Planning Process in All of Its Businesses." *Inside Navistar* (November/December, 1991), p. 9.

7. *Mission Energy Company 1987 Corporate Annual Report* (Irvine, CA, p. 9).

8. *Southern California Edison Company 1986 Annual Report* (Rosemead, CA).

9. *Mission Energy Company 1985 Annual Report* (Irvine, CA p. 5.

10. Donald Kantz, "Triumph of the Swoosh," *Sports Illustrated* (August 16, 1993), p. 61.

11. Ibid., p. 56.

12. Ibid., p. 63.

Chapter 6

1. Adam Osborne and John Dvorak, *Hypergrowth: The Rise and Fall of Osborne Computer* (Berkeley, CA: Idthekkethan, 1984), p. 120.

2. Robert A. Mamis, "Face to Face with Adam Osborne" *Inc.* (November 1983), p. 21.

3. Osborne and Dvorak, *op. cit.*, p. 88.

4. Steve Coll, "The Rise and Fall of Adam Osborne," *Inc.* (November 1983), p. 92.

5. Simon Caulkin, "Compaq's Fortunes," *Management Today* (May 1985), p. 92.

6. Mamis, *op. cit.*, p. 21.

7. For a description of the "market share-growth" matrix, see Michael E. Porter, "Competitive Strategy: Techniques for Analyzing Industries and Competitors," (New York: The Free Press, 1980), pp. 361–367.

8. Kay R. Whitmore, *Management Comments* (*Eastman Kodak Company 1990 Annual Report*), p. 2.

9. Kay R. Whitmore, *Management Overview* (*Eastman Kodak Company 1991 Annual Report*), p. 2.

10. Kay R. Whitmore, *Management Comments* (*Eastman Kodak Company 1992 Annual Report*), p. 2.

11. Robert E. Hoskisson and Michael A. Hitt, *Downscoping: How to Tame the Diversified Firm* (New York: Oxford University Press, 1994), p. 4.

12. *Sears, Roebuck and Co. 1984 Annual Report*, p. 2.

13. George M C. Fisher, *Management Comments* (*Eastman Kodak Company 1994 Annual Report*), pp. 2–3.

14. Sweet Treats Inc. is a real company whose product line and other information have been disguised in order to maintain the anonymity of the firm.

Chapter 7

1. Richard Rainwater, "Change is Good," *Worth* (March 1987), p. 67.
2. Ibid.
3. Ibid.

Chapter 8

1. Alfred P. Sloan, *My Years at General Motors* (New York: Currency/Doubleday, 1963).
2. Ibid., p. 46.
3. Eric Flamholtz, *Human Resource Accounting* (San Francisco: Jossey-Bass Publishers, 1985).
4. See, for example, J. Child, "Predicting and Understanding Organizational Structure," *Administrative Science Quarterly*, 18, 2 (June 1973), pp. 168–187; P. M. Blau and R. A. Schoenherr, *The Structure of Organizations* (New York: Basic Books, 1971); S. J. Chapman and T. S. Ashton, "The Sizes of Businesses, Mainly in the Textile Industry," *Journal of the Royal Statistical Society* (1914), pp. 510–522; and L. R. Pondy, "Effects of Size, Complexity, and Ownership on Administrative Intensity," *Administrative Science Quarterly* (1969), pp. 47–61.
5. E. F. Schumacher, *Small Is Beautiful* (New York: Harper & Row, 1973).
6. L. Donaldson, P. H. Grinyer, and J. Child, "Divisionalization and Size: A Theoretical and Empirical Critique," *Organization Studies*, 3, 4, (1982), pp. 321–353; and Andrea Bonaccorsi, "On the Relationship between Firm Size and Export Intensity," *Journal of International Studies of Management & Organization*, 7, 2 (Summer 1977), pp. 110–126.
7. *General Electric Company 1995 Annual Report*, p. 4.
8. For further discussion of issues involved in designing organizations, see David Nadler and Michael Tushman, *Competing by Design* (New York: Oxford University Press, forthcoming).

Chapter 9

1. This example is based on a real company, although certain aspects of their structural design process have been genericized to protect the firm's anonymity.
2. For further discussion of the role of structural design in organizational competition and performance, see David Nadler and Michael Tushman, *Competing by Design* (New York: Oxford University Press, forthcoming).

Chapter 10

1. *Allegis Corporation 1987 Annual Report*.
2. *UAL, Inc. 1986 Annual Report*, p. 1.
3. Eric G. Flamholtz and Yvonne Randle, *The Inner Game of Management* (New York: AMA-COM, 1987; Los Angeles: *ManagementSystems* Consulting Corporation, 1996).
4. *Ibid.*

Chapter 11

1. For further discussion of performance management and organizational control systems, see Eric G. Flamholtz, *Effective Management Control: Theory and Practice* (Boston/London/Dordrecht: Kluwer Academic Publishers, 1996).
2. S. S. Stevens, "On the Theory of scales of Measurement," *Science*, 103, No. 2684 (June 9, 1946), p. 677.
3. See K. A. Kovach, "What Motivates Employees? Workers and Supervisors Give Different Answers," *Business Horizons* (September/October 1987).
4. For further discussion of corporate culture and how to manage it, see Edgar Schein, *Organizational Culture and Leadership* (San Francisco: Jossey-Bass Publishers, 1985) and Joanne Martin, *Cultures in Organizations* (New York: Oxford University Press, 1992).

Chapter 12

1. The authors wish to gratefully acknowledge the contribution made by Tim Carter, CEO, and Jud Carter, President of Bell-Carter Olive Company in allowing us to tell the story of their firm's transformation. We also want to acknowledge their assistance in providing input feedback on this chapter's content.

2. For a discussion of the concept of "market tiers," see Chapter 7.

3. 1994 Bell-Carter Olive Company Strategic Plan (unpublished document).

Chapter 13

1. Paul Kennedy, *The Rise and Fall of the Great Powers: Economic Change and Military Conflict from 1500 to 2000* (New York: Random House, 1987).

2. David Holley, "Toyota Heads Down a New Road," *Los Angeles Times* (March 16, 1997), Section D, p. 1.

3. Vincent J. Tarascio, "Kondratieff's Theory of Long Cycles," *Atlantic Economic Journal* (December 1988), V. 16, n. 4.

4. Holley, *op. cit.,* p. 12.

5. Ibid., p. 12.

6. Ibid., p. 1.

7. Ibid., p. 12.

8. For a discussion of "learning organizations," see Peter M. Senge, *The Fifth Discipline: The Art and Practice of the Learning Organization* (New York: Doubleday Currency, 1990).

INDEX